THE LSAT DECONSTRUCTED SERIES

VOLUME 62:
THE DECEMBER 2010 LSAT

POWERSCORE
TEST PREPARATION

Published by
PowerScore Publishing, a division of PowerScore Incorporated
57 Hasell Street
Charleston, SC 29401

Authors: David M. Killoran
Steven G. Stein
Nicolay I. Siclunov

Printed in Canada, May 2011

ISBN: 978-0-9826618-7-1

PowerScore Publications

PowerScore LSAT Logic Games Bible

The ultimate guide for attacking the analytical reasoning section of the LSAT. *The LSAT Logic Games Bible* features a detailed methodology for attacking the games section, extensive drills, and 30 real LSAT logic games with detailed analyses.

Available on the PowerScore website for $51.99.
Website: www.powerscore.com/pubs.htm

PowerScore LSAT Logic Games Bible Workbook

The PowerScore LSAT Logic Games Bible Workbook™ is the ideal companion to the *PowerScore Logic Games Bible*™, providing the opportunity to apply the concepts and approaches presented in the renowned *Games Bible. The Logic Games Workbook* contains thirty logic games, reproduced in their entirety from actual released past LSATs, and multiple drills created to reinforce the skills you need to effectively attack the Logic Games section. Each game's answer key presents an ideal setup for the game, with every rule and important logical inference discussed and diagrammed, and all of the questions answered and explained.

Available on the PowerScore website for $29.99.
Website: www.powerscore.com/pubs.htm

PowerScore LSAT Logic Games Setups Encyclopedia

The PowerScore LSAT Logic Games Setups Encyclopedia Volume I provides extensive discussions of each and every game from LSAT PrepTests 1 – 20, including complete game setups and detailed analyses of the rules and inferences for each game. Every single question is clearly explained by the author of the renowned *PowerScore LSAT Logic Games Bible*, using PowerScore's patented techniques, strategies, and overall approach to the Logic Games section. With expansive discussions of 20 full game sections, and 80 logic games, the 340-page *Setups Encyclopedia* provides the most complete and effective solutions available.

Available on the PowerScore website for $29.99.
Website: www.powerscore.com/pubs.htm

PowerScore LSAT Game Type Training

LSAT Game Type Training provides you with the complete text of every LSAT Logic Game from LSAT PrepTests 1 through 20, sorted according to the games classification system created by PowerScore and used in the *PowerScore LSAT Logic Games Bible.*

Containing 80 different games, including hard-to-find games from the early PrepTests, this book is an ideal training tool to increase your LSAT Logic Games score.

Available on the PowerScore website for $29.99.
Website: www.powerscore.com/pubs.htm

PowerScore LSAT Game Type Training II

LSAT Game Type Training II provides you with the complete text of every LSAT Logic Game from LSAT PrepTests 21 through 40, sorted according to the games classification system created by PowerScore and used in the *PowerScore LSAT Logic Games Bible.* Containing 80 different games, this book is an ideal training tool to increase your LSAT Logic Games score.

Available on the PowerScore website for $44.99.
Website: www.powerscore.com/pubs.htm

Available at www.PowerScore.com

PowerScore LSAT Logical Reasoning Bible

One of the most highly anticipated publications in LSAT history, the *PowerScore LSAT Logical Reasoning Bible™* is a comprehensive how-to manual for solving every type of Logical Reasoning question. Featuring over 100 real Logical Reasoning questions with detailed explanations, the Bible is the ultimate resource for improving your LSAT Logical Reasoning score.

Available on the PowerScore website for $49.99.
Website: www.powerscore.com/pubs.htm

PowerScore LSAT Logical Reasoning Bible Workbook

The PowerScore LSAT Logical Reasoning Bible Workbook™ is an ideal companion to the renowned *PowerScore Logical Reasoning Bible™*, designed specifically to test and reinforce *Logical Reasoning Bible™* concepts and strategies. The Workbook features a full chapter of reasoning drills, as well as six LSAT Logical Reasoning sections presented in their entirety (over 150 LSAC-released Logical Reasoning questions in all), followed by complete explanations of every stimulus, question, and answer choice.

Available on the PowerScore website for $34.99.
Website: www.powerscore.com/pubs.htm

PowerScore LSAT Logical Reasoning: Question Type Training

LSAT Logical Reasoning: Question Type Training provides you with the complete text of every LSAT Logical Reasoning question from LSAT PrepTests 1 through 20, sorted according to the questions classification system created by PowerScore and used in the *PowerScore LSAT Logical Reasoning Bible.*

Containing 997 different questions, including hard-to-find questions from the early PrepTests, this book is an ideal training tool to increase your LSAT Logical Reasoning score.

Available on the PowerScore website for $54.99.
Website: www.powerscore.com/pubs.htm

PowerScore LSAT Reading Comprehension Bible

The Reading Comprehension Bible provides the complete guide to reading difficult passages, increasing comprehension, understanding argumentation, and effectively attacking different question types. It includes complete explanations of passages and questions drawn from actual LSATs, guides to passage diagramming, and multiple practice drills.

Available on the PowerScore website for $47.99.
Website: www.powerscore.com/pubs.htm

PowerScore LSAT Reading Comprehension: Passage Type Training

LSAT Reading Comprehension: Passage Type Training provides you with the complete text of every LSAT Reading Comprehension section from LSAT PrepTests 1 through 20, sorted according to the passage classification system created by PowerScore and used in the *PowerScore LSAT Reading Comprehension Bible.*

Containing 80 different passages, including hard-to-find passages from the early PrepTests, this book is an ideal training tool to increase your LSAT Reading Comprehension score.

Available on the PowerScore website for $34.99.
Website: www.powerscore.com/pubs.htm

PowerScore Flashcards

PowerScore Logic Games Bible Flashcards

The Logic Games Bible Flashcards relay and test foundational concepts such as games terminology, game-type recognition, and rule language, as well as advanced conceptual approaches including conditional reasoning, formal logic, and numerical distribution. Mini-challenges allow test takers to develop the skills necessary to create effective diagrams and draw sound logical inferences. Each set includes 140 cards that test the concepts and approaches to logic games taught in the *PowerScore LSAT Logic Games Bible* and in PowerScore LSAT courses.

Available on the PowerScore website for $24.99.
Website: www.powerscore.com/pubs.htm

PowerScore Logical Reasoning Bible Flashcards

The Logical Reasoning Bible Flashcards introduce and test concepts taught in our courses and in PowerScore's LSAT Logical Reasoning Bible. The flashcards cover everything from foundational definitions and question type recognition to more advanced Logical Reasoning skills, including causal reasoning, conditional reasoning, and understanding formal logic. *The Logical Reasoning Bible Flashcards* can be used as a stand-alone study aid, or as an ideal complement to the renowned *Logical Reasoning Bible*.

Available on the PowerScore website for $29.99.
Website: www.powerscore.com/pubs.htm

Tutoring and Admissions Counseling

PowerScore LSAT Private, Virtual, and Telephone Tutoring

PowerScore Private Tutoring gives students the opportunity to work one-on-one with a PowerScore Tutor for the most customized approach to LSAT preparation. Whether you need personalized lesson plans or just want to review a few concepts, PowerScore can create a tutoring plan that suits your specific needs.

Our tutors have all scored in the 99th percentile on an actual LSAT. Aside from having mastered the test themselves, every PowerScore tutor can clearly explain the underlying principles of the LSAT and the most effective approaches to the test.

PowerScore offers hourly tutoring as well as tutoring packages. Please visit www.powerscore.com, or call 1-800-545-1750 for more information.

PowerScore Law School Admissions Counseling

While your LSAT score and GPA will undeniably be major factors during your admissions cycle, to truly separate yourself from the rest of the applicant pool you must assemble the most powerful application folder possible. To do this you must have an outstanding personal statement, top-notch letters of recommendation, and flawless overall presentation.

PowerScore has gathered a team of admissions experts—including former law school admissions board members, top lawyers, and students from top-twenty law schools—to address your admissions counseling and personal statement needs and help you get to where you want to be.

Please visit www.powerscore.com, or call 1-800-545-1750 for more information.

Contents

Chapter One: Introduction

Chapter Two: The December 2010 LSAT

Chapter Three: The December 2010 Reading Comprehension Section Deconstructed

Chapter Four: The December 2010 Logical Reasoning Section Deconstructed

Chapter Five: The December 2010 Logic Games Section Deconstructed

Chapter Six: The December 2010 Logical Reasoning Section Deconstructed

Chapter Seven: Glossary

More Information

About PowerScore

PowerScore is one of the nation's fastest growing test preparation companies. Founded in 1997, PowerScore offers LSAT, GMAT, GRE, and SAT preparation classes in over 150 locations in the U.S. and abroad. Offerings include Full-length courses, Weekend courses, Virtual courses, and private tutoring. For more information, please visit our website at www.powerscore.com or call us at (800) 545-1750.

About the Authors

David M. Killoran is an expert in test preparation with over 20 years of teaching experience and a 99th percentile score on a Law Services-administered LSAT. In addition to having written the renowned *PowerScore LSAT Logic Games Bible*, the *PowerScore LSAT Logical Reasoning Bible*, and many other popular publications, Dave has overseen the preparation of countless students and founded two national LSAT preparation companies.

Steven G. Stein is a test expert who has scored in the 99th percentile on an officially administered LSAT, GMAT, and GRE, and has co-authored many books on test preparation, including *PowerScore's LSAT Reading Comprehension Bible*, *LSAT Logical Reasoning Bible Workbook*, and several volumes of *PowerScore's LSATs Deconstructed Series*. Steve earned his J.D. from the University of Virginia School of Law, and his MBA from the Fuqua School of Business at Duke University.

Nicolay I. Siclunov is a senior LSAT Instructor with a 99th percentile score on an officially administered LSAT. Having worked with thousands of students in Boston, Philadelphia, Montreal, and New York since 2005, Nikki is currently the managing director of PowerScore's operations in New York City. Originally from Bulgaria, Nikki earned his A.B. magna cum laude at Harvard College and his M.A. from Yale University.

CHAPTER ONE: INTRODUCTION

Introduction

Welcome to *The LSAT Deconstructed Series, Volume 62* by PowerScore. The purpose of this book is to help you better understand the methods and procedures of the test makers by deconstructing every question in an actual Law School Admission Test (LSAT). We strongly believe that by studying the logic behind each question you will increase your ability to perform well on the LSAT.

The use of real questions while preparing is essential to your success on the LSAT, and no question in this book has been modified from its original form.

How to Use this Book

We strongly suggest that you take the test in this book as a timed practice test. After you complete the test, we suggest that you carefully read the explanation of each problem, including the explanation of the correct answer choice as well as those of the incorrect answer choices. Closely examine each problem and determine which elements led to the correct answer, and then study the analyses provided in the book and check them against your own work. By doing so you will greatly increase your chances of recognizing the patterns present within the LSAT.

The remainder of this chapter provides a brief overview of the sections of the LSAT, how the LSAT is scored, the uses of the LSAT in law school admissions, and how to approach each section of the test. The next chapter contains the LSAT followed by complete explanations. The final chapter provides a glossary of terms used in this book and a brief overview of the concepts that appear on the LSAT.

If you are looking to further improve your LSAT score, we recommend that you pick up a copy of the renowned *PowerScore LSAT Logic Games Bible, PowerScore LSAT Logical Reasoning Bible,* and *PowerScore LSAT Reading Comprehension Bible*. The *Logic Games Bible* contains our system for attacking the Analytical Reasoning section of the LSAT. The *Logical Reasoning Bible* details the PowerScore approach to understanding and solving the various question types that appear in the Logical Reasoning sections of the LSAT. The *Reading Comprehension Bible* provides an understandable approach to reading and diagramming LSAT passages, noting varied perspectives and attacking passage questions. When combined, the three bibles provide a formidable methodology for attacking the test. The *LSAT Bibles* are available through our website at www.powerscore.com and at fine retailers everywhere.

Because access to accurate and up-to-date information is critical, we have devoted a section of our website to *Deconstructed Series* students. This free online resource area offers supplements to the book material, answers questions posed by students, and provides updates as needed. There is also an official book evaluation form that we strongly encourage you to use. The exclusive *Deconstructed Series* online area can be accessed at:

www.powerscore.com/deconseries

If we can assist you in your LSAT preparation in any way, or if you have any questions or comments, please do not hesitate to contact us via email at lsat@powerscore.com. Additional contact information is provided at the end of this book. We look forward to hearing from you!

A Brief Overview of the LSAT

The Law School Admission Test is administered four times a year: in February, June, September/October, and December. This standardized test is required for admission to any American Bar Association-approved law school. According to Law Services, the producers of the test, the LSAT is designed "to measure skills that are considered essential for success in law school: the reading and comprehension of complete texts with accuracy and insight; the organization and management of information and the ability to draw reasonable inferences from it; the ability to reason critically; and the analysis and evaluation of the reasoning and argument of others." The LSAT consists of the following five sections:

- 2 Sections of Logical Reasoning (short arguments, 24-26 total questions)
- 1 Section of Reading Comprehension (3 long reading passages, 2 short comparative reading passages, 26-28 total questions)
- 1 Section of Analytical Reasoning (4 logic games, 22-24 total questions)
- 1 Experimental Section of one of the above three section types.

You are given 35 minutes to complete each section. The experimental section is unscored and is not returned to the test taker. A break of 10 to 15 minutes is given between the 3rd and 4th sections.

The five-section test is followed by a 35 minute writing sample.

The Logical Reasoning Section

Each Logical Reasoning Section is composed of approximately 24 to 26 short arguments. Every short argument is followed by a question such as: "Which one of the following weakens the argument?" "Which one of the following parallels the argument?" or "Which one of the following must be true according to the argument?" The key to this section is time management and an understanding of the reasoning types and question types that frequently appear.

At the conclusion of the LSAT, and for five business days after the LSAT, you have the option to cancel your score. Unfortunately, there is no way to determine exactly what your score would be before cancelling.

Since there are two scored sections of Logical Reasoning on every LSAT, this section accounts for approximately 50% of your score.

The Analytical Reasoning Section

This section, also known as Logic Games, is probably the most difficult for students taking the LSAT for the first time. The section consists of four games or puzzles, each followed by a series of five to eight questions. The questions are designed to test your ability to evaluate a set of relationships and to make inferences about those relationships. To perform well on this section you must understand the major types of games that frequently appear and develop the ability to properly diagram the rules and make inferences.

The Reading Comprehension Section

This section is composed of three long reading passages, each approximately 450 words in length, and two shorter comparative reading passages. The passage topics are drawn from a variety of subjects, and each passage is followed by a series of five to eight questions that ask you to determine viewpoints in the passage, analyze organizational traits, evaluate specific sections of the passage, or compare facets of two different passages. The key to this section is to read quickly with understanding and to carefully analyze the passage structure.

The Experimental Section

Each LSAT contains one experimental section, which does not count towards your score. The experimental can be any of the three section types described above, and the purpose of the section is to test and evaluate questions that will be used on *future* LSATs. By pretesting questions before their use in a scored section, the experimental helps the makers of the test determine the test scale. To learn more about the experimental section, we suggest you visit the PowerScore website, where you can find an extensive discussion of the experimental section, including how to identify the section and how to approach the section.

The Writing Sample

A 35-minute Writing Sample is given at the conclusion of the LSAT. The Writing Sample is not scored, but a copy is sent to each of the law schools to which you apply.

The format of the Writing Sample is called the Decision Prompt: you are asked to consider two possible courses of action, decide which one is superior, and then write a short essay supporting your choice. Each course of action is described in a short paragraph and you are given two primary criteria to consider in making your decision. Typically the two courses of action each have different strengths and weaknesses, and there is no clearly correct decision.

You must attempt the Writing Sample! If you do not, Law Services reserves the right not to score your test.

Do not agonize over the Writing Sample; in law school admissions, the Writing Sample is usually not a determining element for three reasons: the admissions committee is aware that the essay is given after a grueling three hour test and is about a subject you have no personal interest in; they already have a better sample of your writing ability in the personal statement; and the committee has a limited amount of time to evaluate applications.

The LSAT Scoring Scale

Each administered LSAT contains approximately 101 questions, and your LSAT score is based on the total number of questions you answer correctly, a total known as the raw score. After the raw score is determined, a unique Score Conversion Chart is used for each LSAT to convert the raw score into a scaled LSAT score. Since June 1991, the LSAT has utilized a 120 to 180 scoring scale, with 120 being the lowest possible score and 180 being the highest possible score. Notably, this 120 to 180 scale is just a renumbered version of the 200 to 800 scale most test takers are familiar with from such tests as the SAT and GMAT. Just drop the "1" and add a "0" to the 120 and 180.

Since the LSAT has 61 possible scores, why didn't the test makers change the scale to 0 to 60? Probably for merciful reasons. How would you tell your friends that you scored a 3 on the LSAT? 123 sounds so much better.

Although the number of questions per test has remained relatively constant over the last eight years, the overall logical difficulty of each test has varied. This is not surprising since the test is made by humans and there is no precise way to completely predetermine logical difficulty. To account for these variances in test "toughness," the test makers adjust the Scoring Conversion Chart for each LSAT in order to make similar LSAT scores from different tests mean the same thing. For example, the LSAT given in June may be logically more difficult than the LSAT given in December, but by making the June LSAT scale "looser" than the December scale, a 160 on each test would represent the same level of performance. This scale adjustment, known as equating, is extremely important to law school admissions offices around the country. Imagine the difficulties that would be posed by unequated tests: admissions officers would have to not only examine individual LSAT scores, but also take into account which LSAT each score came from. This would present an information nightmare.

The LSAT Percentile Table

It is important not to lose sight of what LSAT scaled scores actually represent. The 120 to 180 test scale contains 61 different possible scores. Each score places a student in a certain relative position compared to other test takers. These relative positions are represented through a percentile that correlates to each score. The percentile indicates where the test taker ranks in the overall pool of test takers. For example, a score of 165 represents the 93rd percentile, meaning a student with a score of 165 scored better than 93 percent of the people who have taken the test in the last three years. The percentile is critical since it is a true indicator of your positioning relative to other test takers, and thus law school applicants.

There is no penalty for answering incorrectly on the LSAT. Therefore, you should guess on any questions you cannot complete.

Charting out the entire percentage table yields a rough "bell curve." The number of test takers in the 120s and 170s is very low (only 1.9% of all test takers receive a score in the 170s), and most test takers are bunched in the middle, comprising the "top" of the bell. In fact, approximately 40% of all test takers score between 145 and 155 inclusive, and about 70% of all test takers score between 140 and 160 inclusive.

The median score on the LSAT scale is approximately 151. The median, or middle, score is the score at which approximately 50% of test takers have a lower score and 50% of test takers have a higher score. Typically, to achieve a score of 151, you must answer between 56 and 61 questions correctly from a total of 101 questions. In other words, to achieve a score that is perfectly average, you can miss between 40 and 45 questions. Thus, it is important to remember that you do not have to answer every question correctly in order to receive an excellent LSAT score. There is room for error, and accordingly you should never let any single question occupy an inordinate amount of your time.

The Use of the LSAT

The use of the LSAT in law school admissions is not without controversy. Experts agree that your LSAT score is one of the most important determinants of the type of school you can attend. At many law schools an admissions index consisting of your LSAT score and your undergraduate grade point average is used to help determine the relative standing of applicants, and at some schools a sufficiently high admissions index guarantees your admission.

For all the importance of the LSAT, the exam is not without flaws. As a standardized test currently given in the paper-and-pencil format, there are a number of skills that the LSAT cannot measure, including listening skills, note-taking ability, perseverance, etc. Law Services is aware of these limitations and on an annual basis they warn all law school admission offices about overemphasizing LSAT results. Still, because the test ultimately returns a number for each student, the tendency to rank applicants is strong. Fortunately, once you get to law school the LSAT is forgotten. For the time being, consider the test a temporary hurdle you must leap in order to reach the ultimate goal.

For more information on the LSAT or to register for the test, contact Law Services at (215) 968-1001 or at their website at www.lsac.org.

Basic Approaches for Each Section of the LSAT

The Logic Games Section

There are three parts to every Logic Game: the scenario, the rules, and the questions. The scenario describes the game—what players are involved in the game and what situation those players are involved in; the rules provide the parameters those players must act under. Always read the scenario and rules before you begin diagramming.

After reading the scenario and the rules, make a main diagram at the bottom of the page. Your diagram should include the following:

- A list of the variables and their exact total number
- An identification of any variable that is random (that is, a variable that does not appear in any of the rules)
- A diagram of the variable sets
- A diagram of each rule
- A listing of each inference

Logic Games Question Types

Games questions are either Global or Local. Global questions ask about information derived only from the initial rules, such as "Who can finish first?" or "Which one of the following must be true?" Use your main diagram to answer global questions. Local questions occur when the question imposes a new condition in addition to the initial rules, such as "If Laura sits in the third chair, which one of the following must be true?" The additional conditions imposed by local questions apply to that question only and do not apply to any of the other questions. It is essential that you focus on the implications of the new conditions. Ask yourself how this condition affects the variables and the existing rules. For local questions, do your work next to the question; do not use your main diagram except as a reference.

Local questions almost always require you to produce a "mini-setup" next to the question.

Within the global/local designation, all questions ultimately ask for one of four things: what must be true, what is not necessarily true, what could be true, and what cannot be true. All questions are a variation of one of these four basic ideas. At all times, you must be aware of the exact nature of the question you are being asked, especially when "except" questions appear. If you find that you are missing questions because you miss words such as "false" or "except" when reading, then take a moment at the beginning of the game to circle the key words in each question, words such as "must," "could," etc.

If you frequently misread games questions, circle the key part of each question before you begin the game. You will not forget about a word like "except" if you have it underlined!

Logic Games General Notes

The key to optimal performance on Logic Games is to be focused and organized. This involves a number of factors:

1. Play to your strengths and away from your weaknesses

You are not required to do the games in the order presented on the test, and you should not expect that the test makers will present the games in the best order for you. Students who expect to have difficulty on the games section should attack the games in order of their personal preferences and strengths and weaknesses.

2. Create a strong setup for the game

The key to powerful games performance is often to create a good setup. At least 80% of the games on the LSAT are "setup games" wherein the quality of your setup dictates whether or not you are successful in answering the questions.

3. Look to make inferences

There are always inferences in a game, and the test makers expect you to make at least a few of them. Always check the rules and your setup with an eye towards finding inferences, and then always look to use your inferences when answering questions.

4. Be smart during the game

If necessary, skip over time consuming questions and return to them later. Remember that it is sometimes advisable to do the questions out of order. For example, if the first question in a game asks you for a complete and accurate list of the positions "C" could occupy, because of time considerations it would be advisable to skip that question and complete the remaining questions. Then you could return to the first question and use the knowledge you gained from the other questions to quickly and easily answer the first question.

5. Do not be intimidated by size

A lengthy game scenario and a large number of initial rules do not necessarily equal greater difficulty. Some of the longest games are easy because they contain so many restrictions and limitations.

PowerScore offers a selection of silent timers on our website, powerscore.com.

6. Keep an awareness of time

With four games and 35 minutes to complete the section, you have approximately eight minutes and forty-five seconds to complete each game and bubble in your answers. Use an analog watch during the LSAT so you always know how much time remains, and avoid spending too much time on any one game or question.

If you do only three games, you have 11 minutes and 40 seconds to complete each game. If you do just two games, you have 17 minutes and 30 seconds to complete each game.

7. Maintain a positive attitude and concentrate

Above all, you must attack each game with a positive and energetic attitude. The games themselves are often challenging yet fun, and students who actively involve themselves in the games generally perform better overall.

The Logical Reasoning Section

As outlined in the *Logical Reasoning Bible*, to attack Logical Reasoning questions we use a general approach that systematically breaks down the stimulus and the answer choices. This approach is organized in steps called the Primary Objectives™:

Primary Objective #1: Determine whether the stimulus contains an argument or if it is only a set of factual statements.

Primary Objective #2: If the stimulus contains an argument, identify the conclusion of the argument. If the stimulus contains a fact set, examine each fact.

Primary Objective #3: If the stimulus contains an argument, determine if the argument is strong or weak.

Primary Objective #4: Read closely and know precisely what the author said. Do not generalize!

Primary Objective #5: Carefully read and identify the question stem. Do not assume that certain words are automatically associated with certain question types.

Primary Objective #6: Prephrase: after reading the question stem, take a moment to mentally formulate your answer to the question stem.

Primary Objective #7: Always read each of the five answer choices.

Primary Objective #8: Separate the answer choices into Contenders and Losers. After you complete this process, review the Contenders and decide which answer is the correct one.

Primary Objective #9: If all five answer choices appear to be Losers, return to the stimulus and re-evaluate the argument.

By consistently applying the points above, you give yourself the best opportunity to succeed on each question.

The Thirteen Logical Reasoning Question Types

Each question stem that appears in the Logical Reasoning section of the LSAT can be classified into one of thirteen different types:

1. Must Be True/Most Supported
2. Main Point
3. Point at Issue
4. Assumption
5. Justify the Conclusion
6. Strengthen/Support
7. Resolve the Paradox
8. Weaken
9. Method of Reasoning
10. Flaw in the Reasoning
11. Parallel Reasoning
12. Evaluate the Argument
13. Cannot Be True

Occasionally, students ask if we refer to the question types by number or by name. We always refer to the questions by name as that is an easier and more efficient approach. Numerical question type classification systems force you to add two unnecessary levels of abstraction to your thinking process. For example, consider a question that asks you to "weaken" the argument. In a numerical question classification system, you must first recognize that the question asks you to weaken the argument, then you must classify that question into a numerical category (say, Type 10), and then you must translate Type 10 to mean "Weaken." Literally, numerical classification systems force you to perform an abstract, circular translation of the meaning of the question, and the translation process is both time-consuming and valueless.

In the following pages we will discuss each question type in brief. Later we will examine the various question types as they appear on the test.

1. <u>Must Be True/Most Supported</u>

    This category is simply known as "Must Be True." Must Be True questions ask you to identify the answer choice that is best proven by the information in the stimulus. Question stem examples:

    "If the statements above are true, which one of the following must also be true?"

    "Which one of the following can be properly inferred from the passage?"

2. Main Point

Main Point questions are a variant of Must Be True questions. As you might expect, a Main Point question asks you to find the primary conclusion made by the author. Question stem example:

"The main point of the argument is that"

3. Point at Issue

Point at Issue questions require you to identify a point of contention between two speakers, and thus these questions appear almost exclusively with two-speaker stimuli. Question stem example:

"Larew and Mendota disagree about whether"

4. Assumption

These questions ask you to identify an assumption of the author's argument. Question stem example:

"Which one of the following is an assumption required by the argument above?"

5. Justify the Conclusion

Justify the Conclusion questions ask you to supply a piece of information that, when added to the premises, proves the conclusion. Question stem example:

"Which one of the following, if assumed, allows the conclusion above to be properly drawn?"

6. Strengthen/Support

These questions ask you to select the answer choice that provides support for the author's argument or strengthens it in some way. Question stem examples:

"Which one of the following, if true, most strengthens the argument?"

"Which one of the following, if true, most strongly supports the statement above?"

7. Resolve the Paradox

   Every Resolve the Paradox stimulus contains a discrepancy or seeming contradiction. You must find the answer choice that best resolves the situation. Question stem example:

   "Which one of the following, if true, would most effectively resolve the apparent paradox above?"

8. Weaken

   Weaken questions ask you to attack or undermine the author's argument. Question stem example:

   "Which one of the following, if true, most seriously weakens the argument?"

9. Method of Reasoning

   Method of Reasoning questions ask you to describe, in abstract terms, the way in which the author made his or her argument. Question stem example:

   "Which one of the following describes the technique of reasoning used above?"

10. Flaw in the Reasoning

    Flaw in the Reasoning questions ask you to describe, in abstract terms, the error of reasoning committed by the author. Question stem example:

    "The reasoning in the astronomer's argument is flawed because this argument"

11. Parallel Reasoning

    Parallel Reasoning questions ask you to identify the answer choice that contains reasoning most similar in structure to the reasoning presented in the stimulus. Question stem example:

    "Which one of the following arguments is most similar in its pattern of reasoning to the argument above?"

12. Evaluate the Argument

With Evaluate the Argument questions you must decide which answer choice will allow you to determine the logical validity of the argument. Question stem example:

"The answer to which one of the following questions would contribute most to an evaluation of the argument?"

13. Cannot Be True

Cannot Be True questions ask you to identify the answer choice that cannot be true or is most weakened based on the information in the stimulus. Question stem example:

"If the statements above are true, which one of the following CANNOT be true?"

As you attack each problem, remember that each question stem falls into one of four Families that governs the flow of information within the problem:

- The First Family uses the stimulus to prove that one of the answer choices must be true. No information outside the sphere of the stimulus is allowed in the correct answer choice. Example question types include Must Be True, Main Point, Point at Issue, Method of Reasoning, Flaw in the Reasoning, and Parallel Reasoning.

- The Second Family takes the answer choices as true and uses them to help the stimulus. Information outside the sphere of the stimulus is allowed in the correct answer choice. Example question types include Strengthen, Justify the Conclusion, Assumption, and Resolve the Paradox.

- The Third Family takes the answer choices as true and uses them to hurt the stimulus. Information outside the sphere of the stimulus is allowed in the correct answer choice. The primary question type is Weaken.

- The Fourth Family uses the stimulus to prove that one of the answer choices cannot occur. No information outside the sphere of the stimulus is allowed in the answer choices. The primary question type is Cannot Be True.

Within the stimulus, there are different types of reasoning used, such as Conditional Reasoning and Causal Reasoning, and we will address these as they appear in each question.

The Reading Comprehension Section

As you begin the Reading Comprehension section, search for passages with interesting or appealing subject matter, and those written in the most straightforward and accessible style. If all else is equal, choose the passage with the greatest number of questions. Also keep in mind that on a number of occasions the last passage has been the easiest passage.

Be sure to read each passage at the high end of your normal reading speed. Reading too slowly will prevent you from having adequate time to answer all of the questions. Reading too quickly, however, will cause you to miss much of the detailed information presented in the passage and will force you to reread most of the passage, something that will also prevent you from answering all the questions. Do not skim the paragraphs. The test makers are familiar with this tactic, so generally skimming will not effectively prepare you to answer all the questions.

Your primary goal while reading is to find the main point of the passage. Although in the majority of passages the main point is stated in the first paragraph, it is not always the case that the main point appears in the first or second sentence. The main point of many passages has appeared in the final sentence of the first paragraph or in the first sentence of the second paragraph. On average, about 30% of the questions deal directly with the main idea.

As you read, attempt to identify the underlying logical structure of the passage. This will help you quickly find information once you begin to answer the questions. For example, many passages open by stating the background of a thesis that will be challenged later in the passage. In the following paragraphs the author will present an alternative viewpoint to the thesis and perhaps specific counterexamples which provide support for the alternative view. Awareness of this general structure will allow you to reduce the time you spend searching for information when you need to refer back to the passage.

Keep in mind that it is neither possible nor necessary for you to know every detail of a passage. For many questions you should return to the passage to confirm what you remember from your first reading of the passage.

Once you have finished reading the passage, take a moment to focus on the main point and the arguments that support the main point. Many students get so caught up in absorbing the information presented in a passage that they fail to take the time to mentally organize that information. If you are having difficulty remembering the main point of the passage, take a moment after reading the passage to write down the main point in a short, simple sentence.

Refrain from heavily underlining or marking up the passage. This will waste entirely too much time. Limit what you write to noting where the author makes a major point or changes the course of his or her argument.

Pay attention to the language the author uses in the passage. The following words can point to the direction the author is taking with his or her argument:

Continuing the same idea
furthermore
moreover
additionally
similarly
in fact
indeed
for example

Introducing a new idea
however
but
still
yet
although
in contrast
nevertheless

Your state of mind when approaching these passages is extremely important. Make sure that you take a positive, energetic attitude to the passages. Many passages in the Reading Comprehension section discuss conflicts between different viewpoints and this makes the reading inherently more interesting. Getting involved in the argument will make the passage more enjoyable for you and will also allow you to focus more clearly on the material.

Always remember what the author is trying to achieve. In almost every case, he or she is discussing a body of information and trying to draw new points about that information. Rarely will the writer simply restate known situations without bringing in a new view of the situation. As is the case with any person trying to sound perceptive, the author will often use intellectual and complex language. Don't be intimidated by this—although the terminology may be difficult, the main point seldom is.

Reading Comprehension Question Types

Over 70% of the questions in the Reading Comprehension section are exactly the same as Must Be True Logical Reasoning questions. Whether the question asks for the main point or for details from the passage, the answer must be true according to what you have read. The following question types appear within the Must Be True designation:

- Main Point/Primary Purpose (MP)

  As in the Logical Reasoning section, main point questions ask you to select the statement which best sums up the author's core ideas. Primary purpose questions ask you to describe why the author wrote the passage.

- Passage Organization (PO)

  These questions ask you to describe a characteristic of the overall structure of the passage.

For example, "The second paragraph serves primarily to...," and "Which one of the following best describes the organization of the passage." These questions are similar to the Method of Reasoning questions in the Logical Reasoning section, but they are generally broader.

- Author's Perspective and Tone (AP)

  Author's perspective questions ask you to select the answer choice that best reflects the author's views, such as "The author of the passage would most likely agree with which one of the following statements?" Tone questions ask you to identify the author's attitude toward a subject.

- Function (F)

  Function questions ask why the author referred to a particular word, phrase, or idea. This is essentially an extended Method of Reasoning question, requiring you to go beyond simply identifying the argument structure, and asking you the reasons behind the author's use of words or ideas.

- Specific Reference (SR)

  These questions provide you with a specific line reference or a reference to an easily found word or phrase within the passage. To attack these questions, refer to the reference in the question and then begin reading about 5 lines above the reference.

The following question types appear outside of the Must Be True designation:

- Strengthen and Weaken Questions

  These questions are the same in both the Logical Reasoning section and Reading Comprehension section.

- Parallel Reasoning Questions

  In Reading Comprehension, Parallel Reasoning questions are usually broader in scope, asking you to find the scenario most analogous to an action in the passage. There is less of a focus on identifying premises and conclusions than in the Logical Reasoning section

As always, if you have difficulty answering one of the questions in a passage, continue on and complete the other questions in the passage first. Many students have a tendency to stop when confronted with a difficult question and reread the answer choices over and over. If you cannot choose an answer within a reasonable amount of time, go on and return to the question later.

Reading Comprehension Passage Features

Reading Comprehension passages tend to possess many of the same general characteristics. The most common are:

- **Strong purpose or main point:** Always remember that your primary goal while reading is to find the main point. There will almost always be at least one question on this idea.

- **Difficult words, phrases, or concepts:** The test makers use these words and ideas to distract you. Try to look past the word or phrase; instead, focus on the underlying meaning in order to understand the big picture.

- **Enumerations/Lists:** If a decision was made in the passage and several reasons are given to explain that decision, expect to be questioned on your knowledge of those reasons. This is a very common question indicator!

- **Authoritative references:** When authorities are cited by the text, be prepared to be asked about the function and application of the citation. Sometimes different groups will be associated with conflicting ideas—be sure that you are careful not to confuse the groups being referenced.

- **Dates and Numbers:** These are useful because they help mark the chronology of the passage. If there are many dates, they can also be confusing, so make sure you are careful to match the dates given to the correct event.

- **Mixed References:** If a phrase or topic is mentioned in one area of the passage and then again in an entirely different area, be prepared for a specific reference question which will refer to only one of the two citings. Although you will be referred to a specific line in the passage, the relevant information for answering the question is usually found elsewhere in the passage where that same topic or phrase was discussed.

- **Competing perspectives:** If several alternative viewpoints are offered on a particular subject, make certain you know the details of each view as well as who is supporting each view. Several of the questions will probably test your knowledge of the different viewpoints.

  Further, when explaining arguments, many authors bring up counterpoints or drawbacks to that argument in an effort to show their awareness of other viewpoints. These counterpoints are often introduced by terms such as "however," "although," and "yet," and test takers are sometimes questioned on their understanding of these counterpoints, however brief they might have been.

- **Definitions:** If a definition is given during the course of a passage, make a notation and expect to be questioned on your understanding of that definition.

- **Initial Information:** Many questions are asked about information that is presented in the first five lines of a passage. The test makers have found that students often forget what was initially stated in the passage and instead concentrate on the information presented in the main body of the passage, so these questions could be hard to answer if you were not reading carefully from the very beginning.

As you read through each passage, you must keep track of each of these elements as they appear, as you are likely to be tested on each idea if it is present.

Comparative Reading Passages

In addition to the three single passages, the LSAT also contains one pair of dual passages, for total of four question sets. Dual passages are quite similar to the single passages, but rather than just one selection from a single author, two passages are given on a similar or related subject (by two separate authors, generally with different points of view). Comparative reading passages are followed by five to eight questions, and, like the single passage sets, these questions should be answered only on the basis of the information provided in their accompanying passages.

As you read the passages for their respective main points, remember that the passages will relate to each other in various ways. As the test makers recently stated, "In some cases, the authors of the passages will be in general agreement with each other, while in others their views will be directly opposed. Passage pairs may also exhibit more complex types of relationships: for example, one passage might articulate a set of principles, while the other passage applies those or similar principles to a particular situation."

The primary goal for comparative reading is clearly to identify the main point of each passage and then to relate those ideas to each other, focusing on the passages' similarities and differences. Questions in comparative reading tend to focus less on the detailed common question indicators observed in single passages—specific examples, new terms or phrases, lists—and more on broader, holistic ideas—main point, author's tone and opinion, and function. Many students find it useful to pause briefly after reading Passage A to organize their thoughts about what they have just read. Once you have taken a moment to ensure that you are comfortable with the information from the first passage, move on to Passage B and read with the intention of establishing the relationship between the approach and attitude of both authors.

Finally, as with all Reading Comprehension, remember that maintaining a positive attitude is critical. Do not be intimidated by the dual format; you should find the comparative reading to be extremely similar to (and possibly easier than) the other three passages in your Reading Comprehension section.

CHAPTER TWO: THE DECEMBER 2010 LSAT

Taking the December 2010 LSAT

This chapter contains the complete text of the December 2010 LSAT, including an answer key and scoring scale. For the closest possible re-creation of the conditions of the LSAT, take this exam as a timed exercise. The exam will take just less than three hours, and there is an answer sheet included so that you can record your answers. Per Law Services protocol, here are the directions for taking the test under timed conditions:

> Section 1 = allow yourself exactly 35 minutes
> Section 2 = allow yourself exactly 35 minutes
> Section 3 = allow yourself exactly 35 minutes
> Section 4 = allow yourself exactly 35 minutes
>
> Writing Sample = allow yourself exactly 35 minutes

The rules for the test are as follows:

> During the test you are allowed to work only on the section being timed. You cannot go back or forward to work on any other section of the test.
>
> Do not take a break between any of the sections (on the actual LSAT, an unscored experimental section will be included, and a 10-15 minute break will be given after section 3; because this test has no experimental section, you should not take a break between any of the sections).
>
> You may not use any scratch paper while working on the test; only the test pages themselves are available for your use.

After completing the test, refer to the answer key and the "Computing Your Score" section at the end of the test to find your LSAT score.

Complete explanations are in the following chapters, and a score sheet is provided at the end of this book.

SECTION I
Time—35 minutes
27 Questions

Directions: Each set of questions in this section is based on a single passage or a pair of passages. The questions are to be answered on the basis of what is stated or implied in the passage or pair of passages. For some of the questions, more than one of the choices could conceivably answer the question. However, you are to choose the best answer; that is, the response that most accurately and completely answers the question, and blacken the corresponding space on your answer sheet.

To study centuries-old earthquakes and the geologic faults that caused them, seismologists usually dig trenches along visible fault lines, looking for sediments that show evidence of having shifted. Using radiocarbon dating, they measure the quantity of the radioactive isotope carbon 14 present in wood or other organic material trapped in the sediments when they shifted. Since carbon 14 occurs naturally in organic materials and decays at a constant rate, the age of organic materials can be reconstructed from the amount of the isotope remaining in them. These data can show the location and frequency of past earthquakes and provide hints about the likelihood and location of future earthquakes.

Geologists William Bull and Mark Brandon have recently developed a new method, called lichenometry, for detecting and dating past earthquakes. Bull and Brandon developed the method based on the fact that large earthquakes generate numerous simultaneous rockfalls in mountain ranges that are sensitive to seismic shaking. Instead of dating fault-line sediments, lichenometry involves measuring the size of lichens growing on the rocks exposed by these rockfalls. Lichens—symbiotic organisms consisting of a fungus and an alga—quickly colonize newly exposed rock surfaces in the wake of rockfalls, and once established they grow radially, flat against the rocks, at a slow but constant rate for as long as 1,000 years if left undisturbed. One species of North American lichen, for example, spreads outward by about 9.5 millimeters each century. Hence, the diameter of the largest lichen on a boulder provides direct evidence of when the boulder was dislodged and repositioned. If many rockfalls over a large geographic area occurred simultaneously, that pattern would imply that there had been a strong earthquake. The location of the earthquake's epicenter can then be determined by mapping these rockfalls, since they decrease in abundance as the distance from the epicenter increases.

Lichenometry has distinct advantages over radiocarbon dating. Radiocarbon dating is accurate only to within plus or minus 40 years, because the amount of the carbon 14 isotope varies naturally in the environment depending on the intensity of the radiation striking Earth's upper atmosphere. Additionally, this intensity has fluctuated greatly during the past 300 years, causing many radiocarbon datings of events during this period to be of little value. Lichenometry, Bull and Brandon claim, can accurately date an earthquake to within ten years. They note, however, that using lichenometry requires careful site selection and accurate calibration of lichen growth rates, adding that the method is best used for earthquakes that occurred within the last 500 years. Sites must be selected to minimize the influence of snow avalanches and other disturbances that would affect normal lichen growth, and conditions like shade and wind that promote faster lichen growth must be factored in.

1. Which one of the following most accurately expresses the main idea of the passage?

(A) Lichenometry is a new method for dating past earthquakes that has advantages over radiocarbon dating.
(B) Despite its limitations, lichenometry has been proven to be more accurate than any other method of discerning the dates of past earthquakes.
(C) Most seismologists today have rejected radiocarbon dating and are embracing lichenometry as the most reliable method for studying past earthquakes.
(D) Two geologists have revolutionized the study of past earthquakes by developing lichenometry, an easily applied method of earthquake detection and dating.
(E) Radiocarbon dating, an unreliable test used in dating past earthquakes, can finally be abandoned now that lichenometry has been developed.

2. The passage provides information that most helps to answer which one of the following questions?

(A) How do scientists measure lichen growth rates under the varying conditions that lichens may encounter?
(B) How do scientists determine the intensity of the radiation striking Earth's upper atmosphere?
(C) What are some of the conditions that encourage lichens to grow at a more rapid rate than usual?
(D) What is the approximate date of the earliest earthquake that lichenometry has been used to identify?
(E) What are some applications of the techniques involved in radiocarbon dating other than their use in studying past earthquakes?

GO ON TO THE NEXT PAGE.

3. What is the author's primary purpose in referring to the rate of growth of a North American lichen species (lines 29–31)?

(A) to emphasize the rapidity with which lichen colonies can establish themselves on newly exposed rock surfaces
(B) to offer an example of a lichen species with one of the slowest known rates of growth
(C) to present additional evidence supporting the claim that environmental conditions can alter lichens' rate of growth
(D) to explain why lichenometry works best for dating earthquakes that occurred in the last 500 years
(E) to provide a sense of the sort of timescale on which lichen growth occurs

4. Which one of the following statements is most strongly supported by the passage?

(A) Lichenometry is less accurate than radiocarbon dating in predicting the likelihood and location of future earthquakes.
(B) Radiocarbon dating is unlikely to be helpful in dating past earthquakes that have no identifiable fault lines associated with them.
(C) Radiocarbon dating and lichenometry are currently the only viable methods of detecting and dating past earthquakes.
(D) Radiocarbon dating is more accurate than lichenometry in dating earthquakes that occurred approximately 400 years ago.
(E) The usefulness of lichenometry for dating earthquakes is limited to geographic regions where factors that disturb or accelerate lichen growth generally do not occur.

5. The primary purpose of the first paragraph in relation to the rest of the passage is to describe

(A) a well-known procedure that will then be examined on a step-by-step basis
(B) an established procedure to which a new procedure will then be compared
(C) an outdated procedure that will then be shown to be nonetheless useful in some situations
(D) a traditional procedure that will then be contrasted with other traditional procedures
(E) a popular procedure that will then be shown to have resulted in erroneous conclusions about a phenomenon

6. It can be inferred that the statements made by Bull and Brandon and reported in lines 52–60 rely on which one of the following assumptions?

(A) While lichenometry is less accurate when it is used to date earthquakes that occurred more than 500 years ago, it is still more accurate than other methods for dating such earthquakes.
(B) There is no reliable method for determining the intensity of the radiation now hitting Earth's upper atmosphere.
(C) Lichens are able to grow only on the types of rocks that are common in mountainous regions.
(D) The mountain ranges that produce the kinds of rockfalls studied in lichenometry are also subject to more frequent snowfalls and avalanches than other mountain ranges are.
(E) The extent to which conditions like shade and wind have affected the growth of existing lichen colonies can be determined.

7. The passage indicates that using radiocarbon dating to date past earthquakes may be unreliable due to

(A) the multiplicity of the types of organic matter that require analysis
(B) the variable amount of organic materials caught in shifted sediments
(C) the fact that fault lines related to past earthquakes are not always visible
(D) the fluctuations in the amount of the carbon 14 isotope in the environment over time
(E) the possibility that radiation has not always struck the upper atmosphere

8. Given the information in the passage, to which one of the following would lichenometry likely be most applicable?

(A) identifying the number of times a particular river has flooded in the past 1,000 years
(B) identifying the age of a fossilized skeleton of a mammal that lived many thousands of years ago
(C) identifying the age of an ancient beach now underwater approximately 30 kilometers off the present shore
(D) identifying the rate, in kilometers per century, at which a glacier has been receding up a mountain valley
(E) identifying local trends in annual rainfall rates in a particular valley over the past five centuries

GO ON TO THE NEXT PAGE.

While courts have long allowed custom-made medical illustrations depicting personal injury to be presented as evidence in legal cases, the issue of whether they have a legitimate place in the courtroom is surrounded by ongoing debate and misinformation. Some opponents of their general use argue that while illustrations are sometimes invaluable in presenting the physical details of a personal injury, in all cases except those involving the most unusual injuries, illustrations from medical textbooks can be adequate. Most injuries, such as fractures and whiplash, they say, are rather generic in nature—certain commonly encountered forces act on particular areas of the body in standard ways—so they can be represented by generic illustrations.

Another line of complaint stems from the belief that custom-made illustrations often misrepresent the facts in order to comply with the partisan interests of litigants. Even some lawyers appear to share a version of this view, believing that such illustrations can be used to bolster a weak case. Illustrators are sometimes approached by lawyers who, unable to find medical experts to support their clients' claims, think that they can replace expert testimony with such deceptive professional illustrations. But this is mistaken. Even if an unscrupulous illustrator could be found, such illustrations would be inadmissible as evidence in the courtroom unless a medical expert were present to testify to their accuracy.

It has also been maintained that custom-made illustrations may subtly distort the issues through the use of emphasis, coloration, and other means, even if they are technically accurate. But professional medical illustrators strive for objective accuracy and avoid devices that have inflammatory potential, sometimes even eschewing the use of color. Unlike illustrations in medical textbooks, which are designed to include the extensive detail required by medical students, custom-made medical illustrations are designed to include only the information that is relevant for those deciding a case. The end user is typically a jury or a judge, for whose benefit the depiction is reduced to the details that are crucial to determining the legally relevant facts. The more complex details often found in textbooks can be deleted so as not to confuse the issue. For example, illustrations of such things as veins and arteries would only get in the way when an illustration is supposed to be used to explain the nature of a bone fracture.

Custom-made medical illustrations, which are based on a plaintiff's X rays, computerized tomography scans, and medical records and reports, are especially valuable in that they provide visual representations of data whose verbal description would be very complex. Expert testimony by medical professionals often relies heavily on the use of technical terminology, which those who are not specially trained in the field find difficult to translate mentally into visual imagery. Since, for most people, adequate understanding of physical data depends on thinking at least partly in visual terms, the clearly presented visual stimulation provided by custom-made illustrations can be quite instructive.

9. Which one of the following is most analogous to the role that, according to the author, custom-made medical illustrations play in personal injury cases?

(A) schematic drawings accompanying an engineer's oral presentation
(B) road maps used by people unfamiliar with an area so that they will not have to get verbal instructions from strangers
(C) children's drawings that psychologists use to detect wishes and anxieties not apparent in the children's behavior
(D) a reproduction of a famous painting in an art history textbook
(E) an artist's preliminary sketches for a painting

10. Based on the passage, which one of the following is the author most likely to believe about illustrations in medical textbooks?

(A) They tend to rely less on the use of color than do custom-made medical illustrations.
(B) They are inadmissible in a courtroom unless a medical expert is present to testify to their accuracy.
(C) They are in many cases drawn by the same individuals who draw custom-made medical illustrations for courtroom use.
(D) They are believed by most lawyers to be less prone than custom-made medical illustrations to misrepresent the nature of a personal injury.
(E) In many cases they are more apt to confuse jurors than are custom-made medical illustrations.

11. The passage states that a role of medical experts in relation to custom-made medical illustrations in the courtroom is to

(A) decide which custom-made medical illustrations should be admissible
(B) temper the impact of the illustrations on judges and jurors who are not medical professionals
(C) make medical illustrations understandable to judges and jurors
(D) provide opinions to attorneys as to which illustrations, if any, would be useful
(E) provide their opinions as to the accuracy of the illustrations

GO ON TO THE NEXT PAGE.

12. According to the passage, one of the ways that medical textbook illustrations differ from custom-made medical illustrations is that

(A) custom-made medical illustrations accurately represent human anatomy, whereas medical textbook illustrations do not
(B) medical textbook illustrations employ color freely, whereas custom-made medical illustrations must avoid color
(C) medical textbook illustrations are objective, while custom-made medical illustrations are subjective
(D) medical textbook illustrations are very detailed, whereas custom-made medical illustrations include only details that are relevant to the case
(E) medical textbook illustrations are readily comprehended by nonmedical audiences, whereas custom-made medical illustrations are not

13. The author's attitude toward the testimony of medical experts in personal injury cases is most accurately described as

(A) appreciation of the difficulty involved in explaining medical data to judges and jurors together with skepticism concerning the effectiveness of such testimony
(B) admiration for the experts' technical knowledge coupled with disdain for the communications skills of medical professionals
(C) acceptance of the accuracy of such testimony accompanied with awareness of the limitations of a presentation that is entirely verbal
(D) respect for the medical profession tempered by apprehension concerning the tendency of medical professionals to try to overwhelm judges and jurors with technical details
(E) respect for expert witnesses combined with intolerance of the use of technical terminology

14. The author's primary purpose in the third paragraph is to

(A) argue for a greater use of custom-made medical illustrations in court cases involving personal injury
(B) reply to a variant of the objection to custom-made medical illustrations raised in the second paragraph
(C) argue against the position that illustrations from medical textbooks are well suited for use in the courtroom
(D) discuss in greater detail why custom-made medical illustrations are controversial
(E) describe the differences between custom-made medical illustrations and illustrations from medical textbooks

GO ON TO THE NEXT PAGE.

Passage A

Because dental caries (decay) is strongly linked to consumption of the sticky, carbohydrate-rich staples of agricultural diets, prehistoric human teeth can provide clues about when a population made the transition from a hunter-gatherer diet to an agricultural one. Caries formation is influenced by several factors, including tooth structure, bacteria in the mouth, and diet. In particular, caries formation is affected by carbohydrates' texture and composition, since carbohydrates more readily stick to teeth.

Many researchers have demonstrated the link between carbohydrate consumption and caries. In North America, Leigh studied caries in archaeologically derived teeth, noting that caries rates differed between indigenous populations that primarily consumed meat (a Sioux sample showed almost no caries) and those heavily dependent on cultivated maize (a Zuni sample had 75 percent carious teeth). Leigh's findings have been frequently confirmed by other researchers, who have shown that, in general, the greater a population's dependence on agriculture is, the higher its rate of caries formation will be.

Under some circumstances, however, nonagricultural populations may exhibit relatively high caries rates. For example, early nonagricultural populations in western North America who consumed large amounts of highly processed stone-ground flour made from gathered acorns show relatively high caries frequencies. And wild plants collected by the Hopi included several species with high cariogenic potential, notably pinyon nuts and wild tubers.

Passage B

Archaeologists recovered human skeletal remains interred over a 2,000-year period in prehistoric Ban Chiang, Thailand. The site's early inhabitants appear to have had a hunter-gatherer-cultivator economy. Evidence indicates that, over time, the population became increasingly dependent on agriculture.

Research suggests that agricultural intensification results in declining human health, including dental health. Studies show that dental caries is uncommon in pre-agricultural populations. Increased caries frequency may result from increased consumption of starchy-sticky foodstuffs or from alterations in tooth wear. The wearing down of tooth crown surfaces reduces caries formation by removing fissures that can trap food particles. A reduction of fiber or grit in a diet may diminish tooth wear, thus increasing caries frequency. However, severe wear that exposes a tooth's pulp cavity may also result in caries.

The diet of Ban Chiang's inhabitants included some cultivated rice and yams from the beginning of the period represented by the recovered remains. These were part of a varied diet that also included wild plant and animal foods. Since both rice and yams are carbohydrates, increased reliance on either or both should theoretically result in increased caries frequency.

Yet comparisons of caries frequency in the Early and Late Ban Chiang Groups indicate that overall caries frequency is slightly greater in the Early Group. Tooth wear patterns do not indicate tooth wear changes between Early and Late Groups that would explain this unexpected finding. It is more likely that, although dependence on agriculture increased, the diet in the Late period remained varied enough that no single food dominated. Furthermore, there may have been a shift from sweeter carbohydrates (yams) toward rice, a less cariogenic carbohydrate.

15. Both passages are primarily concerned with examining which one of the following topics?

    (A) evidence of the development of agriculture in the archaeological record
    (B) the impact of agriculture on the overall health of human populations
    (C) the effects of carbohydrate-rich foods on caries formation in strictly agricultural societies
    (D) the archaeological evidence regarding when the first agricultural society arose
    (E) the extent to which pre-agricultural populations were able to obtain carbohydrate-rich foods

16. Which one of the following distinguishes the Ban Chiang populations discussed in passage B from the populations discussed in the last paragraph of passage A?

    (A) While the Ban Chiang populations consumed several highly cariogenic foods, the populations discussed in the last paragraph of passage A did not.
    (B) While the Ban Chiang populations ate cultivated foods, the populations discussed in the last paragraph of passage A did not.
    (C) While the Ban Chiang populations consumed a diet consisting primarily of carbohydrates, the populations discussed in the last paragraph of passage A did not.
    (D) While the Ban Chiang populations exhibited very high levels of tooth wear, the populations discussed in the last paragraph of passage A did not.
    (E) While the Ban Chiang populations ate certain highly processed foods, the populations discussed in the last paragraph of passage A did not.

GO ON TO THE NEXT PAGE.

17. Passage B most strongly supports which one of the following statements about fiber and grit in a diet?

(A) They can either limit or promote caries formation, depending on their prevalence in the diet.
(B) They are typically consumed in greater quantities as a population adopts agriculture.
(C) They have a negative effect on overall health since they have no nutritional value.
(D) They contribute to the formation of fissures in tooth surfaces.
(E) They increase the stickiness of carbohydrate-rich foods.

18. Which one of the following is mentioned in both passages as evidence tending to support the prevailing view regarding the relationship between dental caries and carbohydrate consumption?

(A) the effect of consuming highly processed foods on caries formation
(B) the relatively low incidence of caries among nonagricultural people
(C) the effect of fiber and grit in the diet on caries formation
(D) the effect of the consumption of wild foods on tooth wear
(E) the effect of agricultural intensification on overall human health

19. It is most likely that both authors would agree with which one of the following statements about dental caries?

(A) The incidence of dental caries increases predictably in populations over time.
(B) Dental caries is often difficult to detect in teeth recovered from archaeological sites.
(C) Dental caries tends to be more prevalent in populations with a hunter-gatherer diet than in populations with an agricultural diet.
(D) The frequency of dental caries in a population does not necessarily correspond directly to the population's degree of dependence on agriculture.
(E) The formation of dental caries tends to be more strongly linked to tooth wear than to the consumption of a particular kind of food.

20. Each passage suggests which one of the following about carbohydrate-rich foods?

(A) Varieties that are cultivated have a greater tendency to cause caries than varieties that grow wild.
(B) Those that require substantial processing do not play a role in hunter-gatherer diets.
(C) Some of them naturally have a greater tendency than others to cause caries.
(D) Some of them reduce caries formation because their relatively high fiber content increases tooth wear.
(E) The cariogenic potential of a given variety increases if it is cultivated rather than gathered in the wild.

21. The evidence from Ban Chiang discussed in passage B relates to the generalization reported in the second paragraph of passage A (lines 21–23) in which one of the following ways?

(A) The evidence confirms the generalization.
(B) The evidence tends to support the generalization.
(C) The evidence is irrelevant to the generalization.
(D) The evidence does not conform to the generalization.
(E) The evidence disproves the generalization.

GO ON TO THE NEXT PAGE.

Recent criticism has sought to align Sarah Orne Jewett, a notable writer of regional fiction in the nineteenth-century United States, with the domestic novelists of the previous generation. Her work does resemble the domestic novels of the 1850s in its focus on women, their domestic occupations, and their social interactions, with men relegated to the periphery. But it also differs markedly from these antecedents. The world depicted in the latter revolves around children. Young children play prominent roles in the domestic novels and the work of child rearing—the struggle to instill a mother's values in a child's character—is their chief source of drama. By contrast, children and child rearing are almost entirely absent from the world of Jewett's fiction. Even more strikingly, while the literary world of the earlier domestic novelists is insistently religious, grounded in the structures of Protestant religious belief, to turn from these writers to Jewett is to encounter an almost wholly secular world.

To the extent that these differences do not merely reflect the personal preferences of the authors, we might attribute them to such historical transformations as the migration of the rural young to cities or the increasing secularization of society. But while such factors may help to explain the differences, it can be argued that these differences ultimately reflect different conceptions of the nature and purpose of fiction. The domestic novel of the mid-nineteenth century is based on a conception of fiction as part of a continuum that also included writings devoted to piety and domestic instruction, bound together by a common goal of promoting domestic morality and religious belief. It was not uncommon for the same multipurpose book to be indistinguishably a novel, a child-rearing manual, and a tract on Christian duty. The more didactic aims are absent from Jewett's writing, which rather embodies the late nineteenth-century "high-cultural" conception of fiction as an autonomous sphere with value in and of itself.

This high-cultural aesthetic was one among several conceptions of fiction operative in the United States in the 1850s and 1860s, but it became the dominant one later in the nineteenth century and remained so for most of the twentieth. On this conception, fiction came to be seen as pure art: a work was to be viewed in isolation and valued for the formal arrangement of its elements rather than for its larger social connections or the promotion of extraliterary goods. Thus, unlike the domestic novelists, Jewett intended her works not as a means to an end but as an end in themselves. This fundamental difference should be given more weight in assessing their affinities than any superficial similarity in subject matter.

22. The passage most helps to answer which one of the following questions?

(A) Did any men write domestic novels in the 1850s?
(B) Were any widely read domestic novels written after the 1860s?
(C) How did migration to urban areas affect the development of domestic fiction in the 1850s?
(D) What is an effect that Jewett's conception of literary art had on her fiction?
(E) With what region of the United States were at least some of Jewett's writings concerned?

23. It can be inferred from the passage that the author would be most likely to view the "recent criticism" mentioned in line 1 as

(A) advocating a position that is essentially correct even though some powerful arguments can be made against it
(B) making a true claim about Jewett, but for the wrong reasons
(C) making a claim that is based on some reasonable evidence and is initially plausible but ultimately mistaken
(D) questionable, because it relies on a currently dominant literary aesthetic that takes too narrow a view of the proper goals of fiction
(E) based on speculation for which there is no reasonable support, and therefore worthy of dismissal

24. In saying that domestic fiction was based on a conception of fiction as part of a "continuum" (line 31), the author most likely means which one of the following?

(A) Domestic fiction was part of an ongoing tradition stretching back into the past.
(B) Fiction was not treated as clearly distinct from other categories of writing.
(C) Domestic fiction was often published in serial form.
(D) Fiction is constantly evolving.
(E) Domestic fiction promoted the cohesiveness and hence the continuity of society.

GO ON TO THE NEXT PAGE.

25. Which one of the following most accurately states the primary function of the passage?

(A) It proposes and defends a radical redefinition of several historical categories of literary style.
(B) It proposes an evaluation of a particular style of writing, of which one writer's work is cited as a paradigmatic case.
(C) It argues for a reappraisal of a set of long-held assumptions about the historical connections among a group of writers.
(D) It weighs the merits of two opposing conceptions of the nature of fiction.
(E) It rejects a way of classifying a particular writer's work and defends an alternative view.

26. Which one of the following most accurately represents the structure of the second paragraph?

(A) The author considers and rejects a number of possible explanations for a phenomenon, concluding that any attempt at explanation does violence to the unity of the phenomenon.
(B) The author shows that two explanatory hypotheses are incompatible with each other and gives reasons for preferring one of them.
(C) The author describes several explanatory hypotheses and argues that they are not really distinct from one another.
(D) The author proposes two versions of a classificatory hypothesis, indicates the need for some such hypothesis, and then sets out a counterargument in preparation for rejecting that counterargument in the following paragraph.
(E) The author mentions a number of explanatory hypotheses, gives a mildly favorable comment on them, and then advocates and elaborates another explanation that the author considers to be more fundamental.

27. The differing conceptions of fiction held by Jewett and the domestic novelists can most reasonably be taken as providing an answer to which one of the following questions?

(A) Why was Jewett unwilling to feature children and religious themes as prominently in her works as the domestic novelists featured them in theirs?
(B) Why did both Jewett and the domestic novelists focus primarily on rural as opposed to urban concerns?
(C) Why was Jewett not constrained to feature children and religion as prominently in her works as domestic novelists were?
(D) Why did both Jewett and the domestic novelists focus predominantly on women and their concerns?
(E) Why was Jewett unable to feature children or religion as prominently in her works as the domestic novelists featured them in theirs?

S T O P

IF YOU FINISH BEFORE TIME IS CALLED, YOU MAY CHECK YOUR WORK ON THIS SECTION ONLY.
DO NOT WORK ON ANY OTHER SECTION IN THE TEST.

SECTION II
Time—35 minutes
26 Questions

Directions: The questions in this section are based on the reasoning contained in brief statements or passages. For some questions, more than one of the choices could conceivably answer the question. However, you are to choose the best answer; that is, the response that most accurately and completely answers the question. You should not make assumptions that are by commonsense standards implausible, superfluous, or incompatible with the passage. After you have chosen the best answer, blacken the corresponding space on your answer sheet.

1. In a recent study, a group of young children were taught the word "stairs" while walking up and down a flight of stairs. Later that day, when the children were shown a video of a person climbing a ladder, they all called the ladder stairs.

Which one of the following principles is best illustrated by the study described above?

(A) When young children repeatedly hear a word without seeing the object denoted by the word, they sometimes apply the word to objects not denoted by the word.
(B) Young children best learn words when they are shown how the object denoted by the word is used.
(C) The earlier in life a child encounters and uses an object, the easier it is for that child to learn how not to misuse the word denoting that object.
(D) Young children who learn a word by observing how the object denoted by that word is used sometimes apply that word to a different object that is similarly used.
(E) Young children best learn the names of objects when the objects are present at the time the children learn the words and when no other objects are simultaneously present.

2. Among people who live to the age of 100 or more, a large proportion have led "unhealthy" lives: smoking, consuming alcohol, eating fatty foods, and getting little exercise. Since such behavior often leads to shortened life spans, it is likely that exceptionally long-lived people are genetically disposed to having long lives.

Which one of the following, if true, most strengthens the argument?

(A) There is some evidence that consuming a moderate amount of alcohol can counteract the effects of eating fatty foods.
(B) Some of the exceptionally long-lived people who do not smoke or drink do eat fatty foods and get little exercise.
(C) Some of the exceptionally long-lived people who exercise regularly and avoid fatty foods do smoke or consume alcohol.
(D) Some people who do not live to the age of 100 also lead unhealthy lives.
(E) Nearly all people who live to 100 or more have siblings who are also long-lived.

3. Medications with an unpleasant taste are generally produced only in tablet, capsule, or soft-gel form. The active ingredient in medication M is a waxy substance that cannot tolerate the heat used to manufacture tablets because it has a low melting point. So, since the company developing M does not have soft-gel manufacturing technology and manufactures all its medications itself, M will most likely be produced in capsule form.

The conclusion is most strongly supported by the reasoning in the argument if which one of the following is assumed?

(A) Medication M can be produced in liquid form.
(B) Medication M has an unpleasant taste.
(C) No medication is produced in both capsule and soft-gel form.
(D) Most medications with a low melting point are produced in soft-gel form.
(E) Medications in capsule form taste less unpleasant than those in tablet or soft-gel form.

GO ON TO THE NEXT PAGE.

4. Carol Morris wants to own a majority of the shares of the city's largest newspaper, *The Daily.* The only obstacle to Morris's amassing a majority of these shares is that Azedcorp, which currently owns a majority, has steadfastly refused to sell. Industry analysts nevertheless predict that Morris will soon be the majority owner of *The Daily.*

Which one of the following, if true, provides the most support for the industry analysts' prediction?

(A) Azedcorp does not own shares of any newspaper other than *The Daily.*
(B) Morris has recently offered Azedcorp much more for its shares of *The Daily* than Azedcorp paid for them.
(C) No one other than Morris has expressed any interest in purchasing a majority of *The Daily*'s shares.
(D) Morris already owns more shares of *The Daily* than anyone except Azedcorp.
(E) Azedcorp is financially so weak that bankruptcy will probably soon force the sale of its newspaper holdings.

5. Area resident: Childhood lead poisoning has declined steadily since the 1970s, when leaded gasoline was phased out and lead paint was banned. But recent statistics indicate that 25 percent of this area's homes still contain lead paint that poses significant health hazards. Therefore, if we eliminate the lead paint in those homes, childhood lead poisoning in the area will finally be eradicated.

The area resident's argument is flawed in that it

(A) relies on statistical claims that are likely to be unreliable
(B) relies on an assumption that is tantamount to assuming that the conclusion is true
(C) fails to consider that there may be other significant sources of lead in the area's environment
(D) takes for granted that lead paint in homes can be eliminated economically
(E) takes for granted that children reside in all of the homes in the area that contain lead paint

6. Although some nutritional facts about soft drinks are listed on their labels, exact caffeine content is not. Listing exact caffeine content would make it easier to limit, but not eliminate, one's caffeine intake. If it became easier for people to limit, but not eliminate, their caffeine intake, many people would do so, which would improve their health.

If all the statements above are true, which one of the following must be true?

(A) The health of at least some people would improve if exact caffeine content were listed on soft-drink labels.
(B) Many people will be unable to limit their caffeine intake if exact caffeine content is not listed on soft-drink labels.
(C) Many people will find it difficult to eliminate their caffeine intake if they have to guess exactly how much caffeine is in their soft drinks.
(D) People who wish to eliminate, rather than simply limit, their caffeine intake would benefit if exact caffeine content were listed on soft-drink labels.
(E) The health of at least some people would worsen if everyone knew exactly how much caffeine was in their soft drinks.

7. When the famous art collector Vidmar died, a public auction of her collection, the largest privately owned, was held. "I can't possibly afford any of those works because hers is among the most valuable collections ever assembled by a single person," declared art lover MacNeil.

The flawed pattern of reasoning in which one of the following is most closely parallel to that in MacNeil's argument?

(A) Each word in the book is in French. So the whole book is in French.
(B) The city council voted unanimously to adopt the plan. So councilperson Martinez voted to adopt the plan.
(C) This paragraph is long. So the sentences that comprise it are long.
(D) The members of the company are old. So the company itself is old.
(E) The atoms comprising this molecule are elements. So the molecule itself is an element.

GO ON TO THE NEXT PAGE.

8. A leading critic of space exploration contends that it would be wrong, given current technology, to send a group of explorers to Mars, since the explorers would be unlikely to survive the trip. But that exaggerates the risk. There would be a well-engineered backup system at every stage of the long and complicated journey. A fatal catastrophe is quite unlikely at any given stage if such a backup system is in place.

The reasoning in the argument is flawed in that the argument

(A) infers that something is true of a whole merely from the fact that it is true of each of the parts
(B) infers that something cannot occur merely from the fact that it is unlikely to occur
(C) draws a conclusion about what must be the case based on evidence about what is probably the case
(D) infers that something will work merely because it could work
(E) rejects a view merely on the grounds that an inadequate argument has been made for it

9. A retrospective study is a scientific study that tries to determine the causes of subjects' present characteristics by looking for significant connections between the present characteristics of subjects and what happened to those subjects in the past, before the study began. Because retrospective studies of human subjects must use the subjects' reports about their own pasts, however, such studies cannot reliably determine the causes of human subjects' present characteristics.

Which one of the following, if assumed, enables the argument's conclusion to be properly drawn?

(A) Whether or not a study of human subjects can reliably determine the causes of those subjects' present characteristics may depend at least in part on the extent to which that study uses inaccurate reports about the subjects' pasts.
(B) A retrospective study cannot reliably determine the causes of human subjects' present characteristics unless there exist correlations between the present characteristics of the subjects and what happened to those subjects in the past.
(C) In studies of human subjects that attempt to find connections between subjects' present characteristics and what happened to those subjects in the past, the subjects' reports about their own pasts are highly susceptible to inaccuracy.
(D) If a study of human subjects uses only accurate reports about the subjects' pasts, then that study can reliably determine the causes of those subjects' present characteristics.
(E) Every scientific study in which researchers look for significant connections between the present characteristics of subjects and what happened to those subjects in the past must use the subjects' reports about their own pasts.

GO ON TO THE NEXT PAGE.

10. Gigantic passenger planes currently being developed will have enough space to hold shops and lounges in addition to passenger seating. However, the additional space will more likely be used for more passenger seating. The number of passengers flying the air-traffic system is expected to triple within 20 years, and it will be impossible for airports to accommodate enough normal-sized jet planes to carry that many passengers.

Which one of the following most accurately states the conclusion drawn in the argument?

(A) Gigantic planes currently being developed will have enough space in them to hold shops and lounges as well as passenger seating.
(B) The additional space in the gigantic planes currently being developed is more likely to be filled with passenger seating than with shops and lounges.
(C) The number of passengers flying the air-traffic system is expected to triple within 20 years.
(D) In 20 years, it will be impossible for airports to accommodate enough normal-sized planes to carry the number of passengers that are expected to be flying then.
(E) In 20 years, most airline passengers will be flying in gigantic passenger planes.

11. Scientist: To study the comparative effectiveness of two experimental medications for athlete's foot, a representative sample of people with athlete's foot were randomly assigned to one of two groups. One group received only medication M, and the other received only medication N. The only people whose athlete's foot was cured had been given medication M.

Reporter: This means, then, that if anyone in the study had athlete's foot that was not cured, that person did not receive medication M.

Which one of the following most accurately describes the reporter's error in reasoning?

(A) The reporter concludes from evidence showing only that M can cure athlete's foot that M always cures athlete's foot.
(B) The reporter illicitly draws a conclusion about the population as a whole on the basis of a study conducted only on a sample of the population.
(C) The reporter presumes, without providing justification, that medications M and N are available to people who have athlete's foot but did not participate in the study.
(D) The reporter fails to allow for the possibility that athlete's foot may be cured even if neither of the two medications studied is taken.
(E) The reporter presumes, without providing justification, that there is no sizeable subgroup of people whose athlete's foot will be cured only if they do not take medication M.

12. Paleontologist: Plesiosauromorphs were gigantic, long-necked marine reptiles that ruled the oceans during the age of the dinosaurs. Most experts believe that plesiosauromorphs lurked and quickly ambushed their prey. However, plesiosauromorphs probably hunted by chasing their prey over long distances. Plesiosauromorph fins were quite long and thin, like the wings of birds specialized for long-distance flight.

Which one of the following is an assumption on which the paleontologist's argument depends?

(A) Birds and reptiles share many physical features because they descend from common evolutionary ancestors.
(B) During the age of dinosaurs, plesiosauromorphs were the only marine reptiles that had long, thin fins.
(C) A gigantic marine animal would not be able to find enough food to meet the caloric requirements dictated by its body size if it did not hunt by chasing prey over long distances.
(D) Most marine animals that chase prey over long distances are specialized for long-distance swimming.
(E) The shape of a marine animal's fin affects the way the animal swims in the same way as the shape of a bird's wing affects the way the bird flies.

13. Buying elaborate screensavers—programs that put moving images on a computer monitor to prevent damage—can cost a company far more in employee time than it saves in electricity and monitor protection. Employees cannot resist spending time playing with screensavers that flash interesting graphics across their screens.

Which one of the following most closely conforms to the principle illustrated above?

(A) A school that chooses textbooks based on student preference may not get the most economical package.
(B) An energy-efficient insulation system may cost more up front but will ultimately save money over the life of the house.
(C) The time that it takes to have a pizza delivered may be longer than it takes to cook a complete dinner.
(D) A complicated hotel security system may cost more in customer goodwill than it saves in losses by theft.
(E) An electronic keyboard may be cheaper to buy than a piano but more expensive to repair.

GO ON TO THE NEXT PAGE.

14. Music professor: Because rap musicians can work alone in a recording studio, they need not accommodate supporting musicians' wishes. Further, learning to rap is not as formal a process as learning an instrument. Thus, rap is an extremely individualistic and nontraditional musical form.

Music critic: But rap appeals to tradition by using bits of older songs. Besides, the themes and styles of rap have developed into a tradition. And successful rap musicians do not perform purely idiosyncratically but conform their work to the preferences of the public.

The music critic's response to the music professor's argument

(A) challenges it by offering evidence against one of the stated premises on which its conclusion concerning rap music is based
(B) challenges its conclusion concerning rap music by offering certain additional observations that the music professor does not take into account in his argument
(C) challenges the grounds on which the music professor generalizes from the particular context of rap music to the broader context of musical tradition and individuality
(D) challenges it by offering an alternative explanation of phenomena that the music professor cites as evidence for his thesis about rap music
(E) challenges each of a group of claims about tradition and individuality in music that the music professor gives as evidence in his argument

15. Speaker: Like many contemporary critics, Smith argues that the true meaning of an author's statements can be understood only through insight into the author's social circumstances. But this same line of analysis can be applied to Smith's own words. Thus, if she is right we should be able, at least in part, to discern from Smith's social circumstances the "true meaning" of Smith's statements. This, in turn, suggests that Smith herself is not aware of the true meaning of her own words.

The speaker's main conclusion logically follows if which one of the following is assumed?

(A) Insight into the intended meaning of an author's work is not as important as insight into its true meaning.
(B) Smith lacks insight into her own social circumstances.
(C) There is just one meaning that Smith intends her work to have.
(D) Smith's theory about the relation of social circumstances to the understanding of meaning lacks insight.
(E) The intended meaning of an author's work is not always good evidence of its true meaning.

16. Tissue biopsies taken on patients who have undergone throat surgery show that those who snored frequently were significantly more likely to have serious abnormalities in their throat muscles than those who snored rarely or not at all. This shows that snoring can damage the throat of the snorer.

Which one of the following, if true, most strengthens the argument?

(A) The study relied on the subjects' self-reporting to determine whether or not they snored frequently.
(B) The patients' throat surgery was not undertaken to treat abnormalities in their throat muscles.
(C) All of the test subjects were of similar age and weight and in similar states of health.
(D) People who have undergone throat surgery are no more likely to snore than people who have not undergone throat surgery.
(E) The abnormalities in the throat muscles discovered in the study do not cause snoring.

GO ON TO THE NEXT PAGE.

17. One should never sacrifice one's health in order to acquire money, for without health, happiness is not obtainable.

The conclusion of the argument follows logically if which one of the following is assumed?

(A) Money should be acquired only if its acquisition will not make happiness unobtainable.
(B) In order to be happy one must have either money or health.
(C) Health should be valued only as a precondition for happiness.
(D) Being wealthy is, under certain conditions, conducive to unhappiness.
(E) Health is more conducive to happiness than wealth is.

18. Vanessa: All computer code must be written by a pair of programmers working at a single workstation. This is needed to prevent programmers from writing idiosyncratic code that can be understood only by the original programmer.

Jo: Most programming projects are kept afloat by the best programmers on the team, who are typically at least 100 times more productive than the worst. Since they generally work best when they work alone, the most productive programmers must be allowed to work by themselves.

Each of the following assignments of computer programmers is consistent both with the principle expressed by Vanessa and with the principle expressed by Jo EXCEPT:

(A) Olga and Kensuke are both programmers of roughly average productivity who feel that they are more productive when working alone. They have been assigned to work together at a single workstation.
(B) John is experienced but is not among the most productive programmers on the team. He has been assigned to mentor Tyrone, a new programmer who is not yet very productive. They are to work together at a single workstation.
(C) Although not among the most productive programmers on the team, Chris is more productive than Jennifer. They have been assigned to work together at a single workstation.
(D) Yolanda is the most productive programmer on the team. She has been assigned to work with Mike, who is also very productive. They are to work together at the same workstation.
(E) Kevin and Amy both have a reputation for writing idiosyncratic code; neither is unusually productive. They have been assigned to work together at the same workstation.

19. In West Calverton, most pet stores sell exotic birds, and most of those that sell exotic birds also sell tropical fish. However, any pet store there that sells tropical fish but not exotic birds does sell gerbils; and no independently owned pet stores in West Calverton sell gerbils.

If the statements above are true, which one of the following must be true?

(A) Most pet stores in West Calverton that are not independently owned do not sell exotic birds.
(B) No pet stores in West Calverton that sell tropical fish and exotic birds sell gerbils.
(C) Some pet stores in West Calverton that sell gerbils also sell exotic birds.
(D) No independently owned pet store in West Calverton sells tropical fish but not exotic birds.
(E) Any independently owned pet store in West Calverton that does not sell tropical fish sells exotic birds.

20. Astronomer: Earlier estimates of the distances of certain stars from Earth would mean that these stars are about 1 billion years older than the universe itself, an impossible scenario. My estimates of the distances indicate that these stars are much farther away than previously thought. And the farther away the stars are, the greater their intrinsic brightness must be, given their appearance to us on Earth. So the new estimates of these stars' distances from Earth help resolve the earlier conflict between the ages of these stars and the age of the universe.

Which one of the following, if true, most helps to explain why the astronomer's estimates of the stars' distances from Earth help resolve the earlier conflict between the ages of these stars and the age of the universe?

(A) The stars are the oldest objects yet discovered in the universe.
(B) The younger the universe is, the more bright stars it is likely to have.
(C) The brighter a star is, the younger it is.
(D) How bright celestial objects appear to be depends on how far away from the observer they are.
(E) New telescopes allow astronomers to see a greater number of distant stars.

GO ON TO THE NEXT PAGE.

21. Most large nurseries sell raspberry plants primarily to commercial raspberry growers and sell only plants that are guaranteed to be disease-free. However, the shipment of raspberry plants that Johnson received from Wally's Plants carried a virus that commonly afflicts raspberries.

Which one of the following is most strongly supported by the information above?

(A) If Johnson is a commercial raspberry grower and Wally's Plants is not a large nursery, then the shipment of raspberry plants that Johnson received was probably guaranteed to be disease-free.
(B) Johnson is probably not a commercial raspberry grower if the shipment of raspberry plants that Johnson received from Wally's Plants was not entirely as it was guaranteed to be.
(C) If Johnson is not a commercial raspberry grower, then Wally's Plants is probably not a large nursery.
(D) Wally's Plants is probably not a large, well-run nursery if it sells its raspberry plants primarily to commercial raspberry growers.
(E) If Wally's Plants is a large nursery, then the raspberry plants that Johnson received in the shipment were probably not entirely as they were guaranteed to be.

22. Drug company manager: Our newest product is just not selling. One way to save it would be a new marketing campaign. This would not guarantee success, but it is one chance to save the product, so we should try it.

Which one of the following, if true, most seriously weakens the manager's argument?

(A) The drug company has invested heavily in its newest product, and losses due to this product would be harmful to the company's profits.
(B) Many new products fail whether or not they are supported by marketing campaigns.
(C) The drug company should not undertake a new marketing campaign for its newest product if the campaign has no chance to succeed.
(D) Undertaking a new marketing campaign would endanger the drug company's overall position by necessitating cutbacks in existing marketing campaigns.
(E) Consumer demand for the drug company's other products has been strong in the time since the company's newest product was introduced.

23. Consumer advocate: TMD, a pesticide used on peaches, shows no effects on human health when it is ingested in the amount present in the per capita peach consumption in this country. But while 80 percent of the population eat no peaches, others, including small children, consume much more than the national average, and thus ingest disproportionately large amounts of TMD. So even though the use of TMD on peaches poses minimal risk to most of the population, it has not been shown to be an acceptable practice.

Which one of the following principles, if valid, most helps to justify the consumer advocate's argumentation?

(A) The possibility that more data about a pesticide's health effects might reveal previously unknown risks at low doses warrants caution in assessing that pesticide's overall risks.
(B) The consequences of using a pesticide are unlikely to be acceptable when a majority of the population is likely to ingest it.
(C) Use of a pesticide is acceptable only if it is used for its intended purpose and the pesticide has been shown not to harm any portion of the population.
(D) Society has a special obligation to protect small children from pesticides unless average doses received by the population are low and have not been shown to be harmful to children's health.
(E) Measures taken to protect the population from a harm sometimes turn out to be the cause of a more serious harm to certain segments of the population.

24. Legal commentator: The goal of a recently enacted law that bans smoking in workplaces is to protect employees from secondhand smoke. But the law is written in such a way that it cannot be interpreted as ever prohibiting people from smoking in their own homes.

The statements above, if true, provide a basis for rejecting which one of the following claims?

(A) The law will be interpreted in a way that is inconsistent with the intentions of the legislators who supported it.
(B) Supporters of the law believe that it will have a significant impact on the health of many workers.
(C) The law offers no protection from secondhand smoke for people outside of their workplaces.
(D) Most people believe that smokers have a fundamental right to smoke in their own homes.
(E) The law will protect domestic workers such as housecleaners from secondhand smoke in their workplaces.

GO ON TO THE NEXT PAGE.

25. University president: Our pool of applicants has been shrinking over the past few years. One possible explanation of this unwelcome phenomenon is that we charge too little for tuition and fees. Prospective students and their parents conclude that the quality of education they would receive at this institution is not as high as that offered by institutions with higher tuition. So, if we want to increase the size of our applicant pool, we need to raise our tuition and fees.

The university president's argument requires the assumption that

(A) the proposed explanation for the decline in applications applies in this case
(B) the quality of a university education is dependent on the amount of tuition charged by the university
(C) an increase in tuition and fees at the university would guarantee a larger applicant pool
(D) there is no additional explanation for the university's shrinking applicant pool
(E) the amount charged by the university for tuition has not increased in recent years

26. Editorial: It has been suggested that private, for-profit companies should be hired to supply clean drinking water to areas of the world where it is unavailable now. But water should not be supplied by private companies. After all, clean water is essential for human health, and the purpose of a private company is to produce profit, not to promote health.

Which one of the following principles, if valid, would most help to justify the reasoning in the editorial?

(A) A private company should not be allowed to supply a commodity that is essential to human health unless that commodity is also supplied by a government agency.
(B) If something is essential for human health and private companies are unwilling or unable to supply it, then it should be supplied by a government agency.
(C) Drinking water should never be supplied by an organization that is not able to consistently supply clean, safe water.
(D) The mere fact that something actually promotes human health is not sufficient to show that its purpose is to promote health.
(E) If something is necessary for human health, then it should be provided by an organization whose primary purpose is the promotion of health.

S T O P

IF YOU FINISH BEFORE TIME IS CALLED, YOU MAY CHECK YOUR WORK ON THIS SECTION ONLY.
DO NOT WORK ON ANY OTHER SECTION IN THE TEST.

SECTION III
Time—35 minutes
23 Questions

Directions: Each group of questions in this section is based on a set of conditions. In answering some of the questions, it may be useful to draw a rough diagram. Choose the response that most accurately and completely answers each question and blacken the corresponding space on your answer sheet.

Questions 1-6

A motel operator is scheduling appointments to start up services at a new motel. Appointments for six services—gas, landscaping, power, satellite, telephone, and water—will be scheduled, one appointment per day for the next six days. The schedule for the appointments is subject to the following conditions:

The water appointment must be scheduled for an earlier day than the landscaping appointment.
The power appointment must be scheduled for an earlier day than both the gas and satellite appointments.
The appointments scheduled for the second and third days cannot be for either gas, satellite, or telephone.
The telephone appointment cannot be scheduled for the sixth day.

1. Which one of the following is an acceptable schedule of appointments, listed in order from earliest to latest?

(A) gas, water, power, telephone, landscaping, satellite
(B) power, water, landscaping, gas, satellite, telephone
(C) telephone, power, landscaping, gas, water, satellite
(D) telephone, water, power, landscaping, gas, satellite
(E) water, telephone, power, gas, satellite, landscaping

2. If neither the gas nor the satellite nor the telephone appointment is scheduled for the fourth day, which one of the following must be true?

(A) The gas appointment is scheduled for the fifth day.
(B) The power appointment is scheduled for the third day.
(C) The satellite appointment is scheduled for the sixth day.
(D) The telephone appointment is scheduled for the first day.
(E) The water appointment is scheduled for the second day.

3. Which one of the following must be true?

(A) The landscaping appointment is scheduled for an earlier day than the telephone appointment.
(B) The power appointment is scheduled for an earlier day than the landscaping appointment.
(C) The telephone appointment is scheduled for an earlier day than the gas appointment.
(D) The telephone appointment is scheduled for an earlier day than the water appointment.
(E) The water appointment is scheduled for an earlier day than the gas appointment.

4. Which one of the following CANNOT be the appointments scheduled for the fourth, fifth, and sixth days, listed in that order?

(A) gas, satellite, landscaping
(B) landscaping, satellite, gas
(C) power, satellite, gas
(D) telephone, satellite, gas
(E) water, gas, landscaping

5. If neither the gas appointment nor the satellite appointment is scheduled for the sixth day, which one of the following must be true?

(A) The gas appointment is scheduled for the fifth day.
(B) The landscaping appointment is scheduled for the sixth day.
(C) The power appointment is scheduled for the third day.
(D) The telephone appointment is scheduled for the fourth day.
(E) The water appointment is scheduled for the second day.

6. Which one of the following, if substituted for the condition that the telephone appointment cannot be scheduled for the sixth day, would have the same effect in determining the order of the appointments?

(A) The telephone appointment must be scheduled for an earlier day than the gas appointment or the satellite appointment, or both.
(B) The telephone appointment must be scheduled for the day immediately before either the gas appointment or the satellite appointment.
(C) The telephone appointment must be scheduled for an earlier day than the landscaping appointment.
(D) If the telephone appointment is not scheduled for the first day, it must be scheduled for the day immediately before the gas appointment.
(E) Either the gas appointment or the satellite appointment must be scheduled for the sixth day.

GO ON TO THE NEXT PAGE.

LOGIC GAMES

Questions 7-13

An artisan has been hired to create three stained glass windows. The artisan will use exactly five colors of glass: green, orange, purple, rose, and yellow. Each color of glass will be used at least once, and each window will contain at least two different colors of glass. The windows must also conform to the following conditions:

Exactly one of the windows contains both green glass and purple glass.
Exactly two of the windows contain rose glass.
If a window contains yellow glass, then that window contains neither green glass nor orange glass.
If a window does not contain purple glass, then that window contains orange glass.

7. Which one of the following could be the color combinations of the glass in the three windows?

(A) window 1: green, purple, rose, and orange
window 2: rose and yellow
window 3: green and orange
(B) window 1: green, purple, and rose
window 2: green, rose, and orange
window 3: purple and yellow
(C) window 1: green, purple, and rose
window 2: green, purple, and orange
window 3: purple, rose, and yellow
(D) window 1: green, purple, and orange
window 2: rose, orange, and yellow
window 3: purple and rose
(E) window 1: green, purple, and orange
window 2: purple, rose, and yellow
window 3: purple and orange

8. Which one of the following CANNOT be the complete color combination of the glass in one of the windows?

(A) green and orange
(B) green and purple
(C) green and rose
(D) purple and orange
(E) rose and orange

9. If two of the windows are made with exactly two colors of glass each, then the complete color combination of the glass in one of those windows could be

(A) rose and yellow
(B) orange and rose
(C) orange and purple
(D) green and rose
(E) green and orange

10. If the complete color combination of the glass in one of the windows is purple, rose, and orange, then the complete color combination of the glass in one of the other windows could be

(A) green, orange, and rose
(B) green, orange, and purple
(C) orange and rose
(D) orange and purple
(E) green and orange

11. If orange glass is used in more of the windows than green glass, then the complete color combination of the glass in one of the windows could be

(A) orange and purple
(B) green, purple, and rose
(C) green and purple
(D) green and orange
(E) green, orange, and rose

12. Which one of the following could be used in all three windows?

(A) green glass
(B) orange glass
(C) purple glass
(D) rose glass
(E) yellow glass

13. If none of the windows contains both rose glass and orange glass, then the complete color combination of the glass in one of the windows must be

(A) green and purple
(B) green, purple, and orange
(C) green and orange
(D) purple and orange
(E) purple, rose, and yellow

GO ON TO THE NEXT PAGE.

Questions 14-18

A conference on management skills consists of exactly five talks, which are held successively in the following order: Feedback, Goal Sharing, Handling People, Information Overload, and Leadership. Exactly four employees of SoftCorp—Quigley, Rivera, Spivey, and Tran—each attend exactly two of the talks. No talk is attended by more than two of the employees, who attend the talks in accordance with the following conditions:

Quigley attends neither Feedback nor Handling People.
Rivera attends neither Goal Sharing nor Handling People.
Spivey does not attend either of the talks that Tran attends.
Quigley attends the first talk Tran attends.
Spivey attends the first talk Rivera attends.

14. Which one of the following could be a complete and accurate matching of the talks to the SoftCorp employees who attend them?

(A) Feedback: Rivera, Spivey
Goal Sharing: Quigley, Tran
Handling People: None
Information Overload: Quigley, Rivera
Leadership: Spivey, Tran

(B) Feedback: Rivera, Spivey
Goal Sharing: Quigley, Tran
Handling People: Rivera, Tran
Information Overload: Quigley
Leadership: Spivey

(C) Feedback: Rivera, Spivey
Goal Sharing: Quigley, Tran
Handling People: Tran
Information Overload: Quigley, Rivera
Leadership: Spivey

(D) Feedback: Rivera, Spivey
Goal Sharing: Tran
Handling People: Tran
Information Overload: Quigley, Rivera
Leadership: Quigley, Spivey

(E) Feedback: Spivey
Goal Sharing: Quigley, Tran
Handling People: Spivey
Information Overload: Quigley, Rivera
Leadership: Rivera, Tran

15. If none of the SoftCorp employees attends Handling People, then which one of the following must be true?

(A) Rivera attends Feedback.
(B) Rivera attends Leadership.
(C) Spivey attends Information Overload.
(D) Tran attends Goal Sharing.
(E) Tran attends Information Overload.

16. Which one of the following is a complete and accurate list of the talks any one of which Rivera and Spivey could attend together?

(A) Feedback, Information Overload, Leadership
(B) Feedback, Goal Sharing, Information Overload
(C) Information Overload, Leadership
(D) Feedback, Leadership
(E) Feedback, Information Overload

17. If Quigley is the only SoftCorp employee to attend Leadership, then which one of the following could be false?

(A) Rivera attends Feedback.
(B) Rivera attends Information Overload.
(C) Spivey attends Feedback.
(D) Spivey attends Handling People.
(E) Tran attends Goal Sharing.

18. If Rivera is the only SoftCorp employee to attend Information Overload, then which one of the following could be false?

(A) Quigley attends Leadership.
(B) Rivera attends Feedback.
(C) Spivey attends Feedback.
(D) Tran attends Goal Sharing.
(E) Tran attends Handling People.

GO ON TO THE NEXT PAGE.

Questions 19-23

Exactly six witnesses will testify in a trial: Mangione, Ramirez, Sanderson, Tannenbaum, Ujemori, and Wong. The witnesses will testify one by one, and each only once. The order in which the witnesses testify is subject to the following constraints:

Sanderson must testify immediately before either Tannenbaum or Ujemori.
Ujemori must testify earlier than both Ramirez and Wong.
Either Tannenbaum or Wong must testify immediately before Mangione.

19. Which one of the following lists the witnesses in an order in which they could testify?

(A) Ramirez, Sanderson, Tannenbaum, Mangione, Ujemori, Wong
(B) Sanderson, Tannenbaum, Ujemori, Ramirez, Wong, Mangione
(C) Sanderson, Ujemori, Tannenbaum, Wong, Ramirez, Mangione
(D) Tannenbaum, Mangione, Ujemori, Sanderson, Ramirez, Wong
(E) Wong, Ramirez, Sanderson, Tannenbaum, Mangione, Ujemori

20. If Tannenbaum testifies first, then which one of the following could be true?

(A) Ramirez testifies second.
(B) Wong testifies third.
(C) Sanderson testifies fourth.
(D) Ujemori testifies fifth.
(E) Mangione testifies sixth.

21. If Sanderson testifies fifth, then Ujemori must testify

(A) first
(B) second
(C) third
(D) fourth
(E) sixth

22. Which one of the following pairs of witnesses CANNOT testify third and fourth, respectively?

(A) Mangione, Tannenbaum
(B) Ramirez, Sanderson
(C) Sanderson, Ujemori
(D) Tannenbaum, Ramirez
(E) Ujemori, Wong

23. Which one of the following pairs of witnesses CANNOT testify first and second, respectively?

(A) Sanderson, Ujemori
(B) Tannenbaum, Mangione
(C) Tannenbaum, Sanderson
(D) Ujemori, Tannenbaum
(E) Ujemori, Wong

S T O P

IF YOU FINISH BEFORE TIME IS CALLED, YOU MAY CHECK YOUR WORK ON THIS SECTION ONLY.
DO NOT WORK ON ANY OTHER SECTION IN THE TEST.

SECTION IV
Time—35 minutes
25 Questions

Directions: The questions in this section are based on the reasoning contained in brief statements or passages. For some questions, more than one of the choices could conceivably answer the question. However, you are to choose the best answer; that is, the response that most accurately and completely answers the question. You should not make assumptions that are by commonsense standards implausible, superfluous, or incompatible with the passage. After you have chosen the best answer, blacken the corresponding space on your answer sheet.

1. Marine biologist: Scientists have long wondered why the fish that live around coral reefs exhibit such brilliant colors. One suggestion is that coral reefs are colorful and, therefore, that colorful fish are camouflaged by them. Many animal species, after all, use camouflage to avoid predators. However, as regards the populations around reefs, this suggestion is mistaken. A reef stripped of its fish is quite monochromatic. Most corals, it turns out, are relatively dull browns and greens.

Which one of the following most accurately expresses the main conclusion drawn in the marine biologist's argument?

(A) One hypothesis about why fish living near coral reefs exhibit such bright colors is that the fish are camouflaged by their bright colors.
(B) The fact that many species use camouflage to avoid predators is one reason to believe that brightly colored fish living near reefs do too.
(C) The suggestion that the fish living around coral reefs exhibit bright colors because they are camouflaged by the reefs is mistaken.
(D) A reef stripped of its fish is relatively monochromatic.
(E) It turns out that the corals in a coral reef are mostly dull hues of brown and green.

2. To discover what percentage of teenagers believe in telekinesis—the psychic ability to move objects without physically touching them—a recent survey asked a representative sample of teenagers whether they agreed with the following statement: "A person's thoughts can influence the movement of physical objects." But because this statement is particularly ambiguous and is amenable to a naturalistic, uncontroversial interpretation, the survey's responses are also ambiguous.

The reasoning above conforms most closely to which one of the following general propositions?

(A) Uncontroversial statements are useless in surveys.
(B) Every statement is amenable to several interpretations.
(C) Responses to surveys are always unambiguous if the survey's questions are well phrased.
(D) Responses people give to poorly phrased questions are likely to be ambiguous.
(E) Statements about psychic phenomena can always be given naturalistic interpretations.

GO ON TO THE NEXT PAGE.

3. A recent study of perfect pitch—the ability to identify the pitch of an isolated musical note—found that a high percentage of people who have perfect pitch are related to someone else who has it. Among those without perfect pitch, the percentage was much lower. This shows that having perfect pitch is a consequence of genetic factors.

Which one of the following, if true, most strengthens the argument?

(A) People who have relatives with perfect pitch generally receive no more musical training than do others.
(B) All of the researchers conducting the study had perfect pitch.
(C) People with perfect pitch are more likely than others to choose music as a career.
(D) People with perfect pitch are more likely than others to make sure that their children receive musical training.
(E) People who have some training in music are more likely to have perfect pitch than those with no such training.

4. Paleontologists recently excavated two corresponding sets of dinosaur tracks, one left by a large grazing dinosaur and the other by a smaller predatory dinosaur. The two sets of tracks make abrupt turns repeatedly in tandem, suggesting that the predator was following the grazing dinosaur and had matched its stride. Modern predatory mammals, such as lions, usually match the stride of prey they are chasing immediately before they strike those prey. This suggests that the predatory dinosaur was chasing the grazing dinosaur and attacked immediately afterwards.

Which one of the following most accurately describes the role played in the argument by the statement that the predatory dinosaur was following the grazing dinosaur and had matched its stride?

(A) It helps establish the scientific importance of the argument's overall conclusion, but is not offered as evidence for that conclusion.
(B) It is a hypothesis that is rejected in favor of the hypothesis stated in the argument's overall conclusion.
(C) It provides the basis for an analogy used in support of the argument's overall conclusion.
(D) It is presented to counteract a possible objection to the argument's overall conclusion.
(E) It is the overall conclusion of the argument.

5. Researchers announced recently that over the past 25 years the incidence of skin cancer caused by exposure to harmful rays from the sun has continued to grow in spite of the increasingly widespread use of sunscreens. This shows that using sunscreen is unlikely to reduce a person's risk of developing such skin cancer.

Which one of the following, if true, most weakens the argument?

(A) Most people who purchase a sunscreen product will not purchase the most expensive brand available.
(B) Skin cancer generally develops among the very old as a result of sunburns experienced when very young.
(C) The development of sunscreens by pharmaceutical companies was based upon research conducted by dermatologists.
(D) People who know that they are especially susceptible to skin cancer are generally disinclined to spend a large amount of time in the sun.
(E) Those who use sunscreens most regularly are people who believe themselves to be most susceptible to skin cancer.

6. University administrator: Any proposal for a new department will not be funded if there are fewer than 50 people per year available for hire in that field and the proposed department would duplicate more than 25 percent of the material covered in one of our existing departments. The proposed Area Studies Department will duplicate more than 25 percent of the material covered in our existing Anthropology Department. However, we will fund the new department.

Which one of the following statements follows logically from the university administrator's statements?

(A) The field of Area Studies has at least 50 people per year available for hire.
(B) The proposed Area Studies Department would not duplicate more than 25 percent of the material covered in any existing department other than Anthropology.
(C) If the proposed Area Studies Department did not duplicate more than 25 percent of the material covered in Anthropology, then the new department would not be funded.
(D) The Anthropology Department duplicates more than 25 percent of the material covered in the proposed Area Studies Department.
(E) The field of Area Studies has fewer than 50 people per year available for hire.

GO ON TO THE NEXT PAGE.

7. Researcher: Over the course of three decades, we kept records of the average beak size of two populations of the same species of bird, one wild population, the other captive. During this period, the average beak size of the captive birds did not change, while the average beak size of the wild birds decreased significantly.

Which one of the following, if true, most helps to explain the researcher's findings?

(A) The small-beaked wild birds were easier to capture and measure than the large-beaked wild birds.
(B) The large-beaked wild birds were easier to capture and measure than the small-beaked wild birds.
(C) Changes in the wild birds' food supply during the study period favored the survival of small-beaked birds over large-beaked birds.
(D) The average body size of the captive birds remained the same over the study period.
(E) The researcher measured the beaks of some of the wild birds on more than one occasion.

8. Storytelling appears to be a universal aspect of both past and present cultures. Comparative study of traditional narratives from widely separated epochs and diverse cultures reveals common themes such as creation, tribal origin, mystical beings and quasi-historical figures, and common story types such as fables and tales in which animals assume human personalities.

The evidence cited above from the study of traditional narratives most supports which one of the following statements?

(A) Storytellers routinely borrow themes from other cultures.
(B) Storytellers have long understood that the narrative is a universal aspect of human culture.
(C) Certain human concerns and interests arise in all of the world's cultures.
(D) Storytelling was no less important in ancient cultures than it is in modern cultures.
(E) The best way to understand a culture is to understand what motivates its storytellers.

9. If a mother's first child is born before its due date, it is likely that her second child will be also. Jackie's second child was not born before its due date, so it is likely that Jackie's first child was not born before its due date either.

The questionable reasoning in the argument above is most similar in its reasoning to which one of the following?

(A) Artisans who finish their projects before the craft fair will probably go to the craft fair. Ben will not finish his project before the fair. So he probably will not go to the craft fair.
(B) All responsible pet owners are likely to be good with children. So anyone who is good with children is probably a responsible pet owner.
(C) If a movie is a box-office hit, it is likely that its sequel will be also. *Hawkman II*, the sequel to *Hawkman I*, was not a box-office hit, so *Hawkman I* was probably not a box-office hit.
(D) If a business is likely to fail, people will not invest in it. Pallid Starr is likely to fail, therefore no one is likely to invest in it.
(E) Tai will go sailing only if the weather is nice. The weather will be nice, thus Tai will probably go sailing.

10. Science journalist: Europa, a moon of Jupiter, is covered with ice. Data recently transmitted by a spacecraft strongly suggest that there are oceans of liquid water deep under the ice. Life as we know it could evolve only in the presence of liquid water. Hence, it is likely that at least primitive life has evolved on Europa.

The science journalist's argument is most vulnerable to criticism on the grounds that it

(A) takes for granted that if a condition would be necessary for the evolution of life as we know it, then such life could not have evolved anywhere that this condition does not hold
(B) fails to address adequately the possibility that there are conditions necessary for the evolution of life in addition to the presence of liquid water
(C) takes for granted that life is likely to be present on Europa if, but only if, life evolved on Europa
(D) overlooks the possibility that there could be unfamiliar forms of life that have evolved without the presence of liquid water
(E) takes for granted that no conditions on Europa other than the supposed presence of liquid water could have accounted for the data transmitted by the spacecraft

GO ON TO THE NEXT PAGE.

11. A bacterial species will inevitably develop greater resistance within a few years to any antibiotics used against it, unless those antibiotics eliminate that species completely. However, no single antibiotic now on the market is powerful enough to eliminate bacterial species X completely.

Which one of the following is most strongly supported by the statements above?

(A) It is unlikely that any antibiotic can be developed that will completely eliminate bacterial species X.
(B) If any antibiotic now on the market is used against bacterial species X, that species will develop greater resistance to it within a few years.
(C) The only way of completely eliminating bacterial species X is by a combination of two or more antibiotics now on the market.
(D) Bacterial species X will inevitably become more virulent in the course of time.
(E) Bacterial species X is more resistant to at least some antibiotics that have been used against it than it was before those antibiotics were used against it.

12. Political scientist: It is not uncommon for a politician to criticize his or her political opponents by claiming that their exposition of their ideas is muddled and incomprehensible. Such criticism, however, is never sincere. Political agendas promoted in a manner that cannot be understood by large numbers of people will not be realized for, as every politician knows, political mobilization requires commonality of purpose.

Which one of the following is the most accurate rendering of the political scientist's main conclusion?

(A) People who promote political agendas in an incomprehensible manner should be regarded as insincere.
(B) Sincere critics of the proponents of a political agenda should not focus their criticisms on the manner in which that agenda is promoted.
(C) The ineffectiveness of a confusingly promoted political agenda is a reason for refraining from, rather than engaging in, criticism of those who are promoting it.
(D) A politician criticizing his or her political opponents for presenting their political agendas in an incomprehensible manner is being insincere.
(E) To mobilize large numbers of people in support of a political agenda, that political agenda must be presented in such a way that it cannot be misunderstood.

13. Many symptoms of mental illnesses are affected by organic factors such as a deficiency in a compound in the brain. What is surprising, however, is the tremendous variation among different countries in the incidence of these symptoms in people with mental illnesses. This variation establishes that the organic factors that affect symptoms of mental illnesses are not distributed evenly around the globe.

The reasoning above is most vulnerable to criticism on the grounds that it

(A) does not say how many different mental illnesses are being discussed
(B) neglects the possibility that nutritional factors that contribute to deficiencies in compounds in the brain vary from culture to culture
(C) fails to consider the possibility that cultural factors significantly affect how mental illnesses manifest themselves in symptoms
(D) presumes, without providing justification, that any change in brain chemistry manifests itself as a change in mental condition
(E) presumes, without providing justification, that mental phenomena are only manifestations of physical phenomena

14. Politician: It has been proposed that the national parks in our country be managed by private companies rather than the government. A similar privatization of the telecommunications industry has benefited consumers by allowing competition among a variety of telephone companies to improve service and force down prices. Therefore, the privatization of the national parks would probably benefit park visitors as well.

Which one of the following, if true, most weakens the politician's argument?

(A) It would not be politically expedient to privatize the national parks even if doing so would, in the long run, improve service and reduce the fees charged to visitors.
(B) The privatization of the telecommunications industry has been problematic in that it has led to significantly increased unemployment and economic instability in that industry.
(C) The vast majority of people visiting the national parks are unaware of proposals to privatize the management of those parks.
(D) Privatizing the national parks would benefit a much smaller number of consumers to a much smaller extent than did the privatization of the telecommunications industry.
(E) The privatization of the national parks would produce much less competition between different companies than did the privatization of the telecommunications industry.

GO ON TO THE NEXT PAGE.

15. Jewel collectors, fearing that their eyes will be deceived by a counterfeit, will not buy a diamond unless the dealer guarantees that it is genuine. But why should a counterfeit give any less aesthetic pleasure when the naked eye cannot distinguish it from a real diamond? Both jewels should be deemed of equal value.

Which one of the following principles, if valid, most helps to justify the reasoning in the argument above?

(A) Jewel collectors should collect only those jewels that provide the most aesthetic pleasure.
(B) The value of a jewel should depend at least partly on market demand.
(C) It should not be assumed that everyone who likes diamonds receives the same degree of aesthetic pleasure from them.
(D) The value of a jewel should derive solely from the aesthetic pleasure it provides.
(E) Jewel collectors should not buy counterfeit jewels unless they are unable to distinguish counterfeit jewels from real ones.

16. All etching tools are either pin-tipped or bladed. While some bladed etching tools are used for engraving, some are not. On the other hand, all pin-tipped etching tools are used for engraving. Thus, there are more etching tools that are used for engraving than there are etching tools that are not used for engraving.

The conclusion of the argument follows logically if which one of the following is assumed?

(A) All tools used for engraving are etching tools as well.
(B) There are as many pin-tipped etching tools as there are bladed etching tools.
(C) No etching tool is both pin-tipped and bladed.
(D) The majority of bladed etching tools are not used for engraving.
(E) All etching tools that are not used for engraving are bladed.

17. A 24-year study of 1,500 adults showed that those subjects with a high intake of foods rich in beta-carotene were much less likely to die from cancer or heart disease than were those with a low intake of such foods. On the other hand, taking beta-carotene supplements for 12 years had no positive or negative effect on the health of subjects in a separate study of 20,000 adults.

Each of the following, if true, would help to resolve the apparent discrepancy between the results of the two studies EXCEPT:

(A) The human body processes the beta-carotene present in foods much more efficiently than it does beta-carotene supplements.
(B) Beta-carotene must be taken for longer than 12 years to have any cancer-preventive effects.
(C) Foods rich in beta-carotene also tend to contain other nutrients that assist in the human body's absorption of beta-carotene.
(D) In the 12-year study, half of the subjects were given beta-carotene supplements and half were given a placebo.
(E) In the 24-year study, the percentage of the subjects who had a high intake of beta-carotene-rich foods who smoked cigarettes was much smaller than the percentage of the subjects with a low intake of beta-carotene-rich foods who smoked.

GO ON TO THE NEXT PAGE.

18. If there are sentient beings on planets outside our solar system, we will not be able to determine this anytime in the near future unless some of these beings are at least as intelligent as humans. We will not be able to send spacecraft to planets outside our solar system anytime in the near future, and any sentient being on another planet capable of communicating with us anytime in the near future would have to be at least as intelligent as we are.

The argument's conclusion can be properly inferred if which one of the following is assumed?

(A) There are no sentient beings on planets in our solar system other than those on Earth.
(B) Any beings that are at least as intelligent as humans would want to communicate with sentient beings outside their own solar systems.
(C) If there is a sentient being on another planet that is as intelligent as humans are, we will not be able to send spacecraft to the being's planet anytime in the near future.
(D) If a sentient being on another planet cannot communicate with us, then the only way to detect its existence is by sending a spacecraft to its planet.
(E) Any sentient beings on planets outside our solar system that are at least as intelligent as humans would be capable of communicating with us.

19. Doctor: Medical researchers recently examined a large group of individuals who said that they had never experienced serious back pain. Half of the members of the group turned out to have bulging or slipped disks in their spines, conditions often blamed for serious back pain. Since these individuals with bulging or slipped disks evidently felt no pain from them, these conditions could not lead to serious back pain in people who do experience such pain.

The reasoning in the doctor's argument is most vulnerable to the criticism that it fails to consider which one of the following possibilities?

(A) A factor that need not be present in order for a certain effect to arise may nonetheless be sufficient to produce that effect.
(B) A factor that is not in itself sufficient to produce a certain effect may nonetheless be partly responsible for that effect in some instances.
(C) An effect that occurs in the absence of a particular phenomenon might not occur when that phenomenon is present.
(D) A characteristic found in half of a given sample of the population might not occur in half of the entire population.
(E) A factor that does not bring about a certain effect may nonetheless be more likely to be present when the effect occurs than when the effect does not occur.

20. Many workers who handled substance T in factories became seriously ill years later. We now know T caused at least some of their illnesses. Earlier ignorance of this connection does not absolve T's manufacturer of all responsibility. For had it investigated the safety of T before allowing workers to be exposed to it, many of their illnesses would have been prevented.

Which one of the following principles most helps to justify the conclusion above?

(A) Employees who are harmed by substances they handle on the job should be compensated for medical costs they incur as a result.
(B) Manufacturers should be held responsible only for the preventable consequences of their actions.
(C) Manufacturers have an obligation to inform workers of health risks of which they are aware.
(D) Whether or not an action's consequences were preventable is irrelevant to whether a manufacturer should be held responsible for those consequences.
(E) Manufacturers should be held responsible for the consequences of any of their actions that harm innocent people if those consequences were preventable.

21. It is virtually certain that the government contract for building the new highway will be awarded to either Phoenix Contracting or Cartwright Company. I have just learned that the government has decided not to award the contract to Cartwright Company. It is therefore almost inevitable that Phoenix Contracting will be awarded the contract.

The argument proceeds by

(A) concluding that it is extremely likely that an event will occur by ruling out the only probable alternative
(B) inferring, from a claim that one of two possible events will occur, that the other event will not occur
(C) refuting a claim that a particular event is inevitable by establishing the possibility of an alternative event
(D) predicting a future event on the basis of an established pattern of past events
(E) inferring a claim about the probability of a particular event from a general statistical statement

GO ON TO THE NEXT PAGE.

22. Researchers have found that children in large families—particularly the younger siblings—generally have fewer allergies than children in small families do. They hypothesize that exposure to germs during infancy makes people less likely to develop allergies.

Which one of the following, if true, most supports the researchers' hypothesis?

(A) In countries where the average number of children per family has decreased over the last century, the incidence of allergies has increased.
(B) Children in small families generally eat more kinds of very allergenic foods than children in large families do.
(C) Some allergies are life threatening, while many diseases caused by germs produce only temporary discomfort.
(D) Children whose parents have allergies have an above-average likelihood of developing allergies themselves.
(E) Children from small families who entered day care before age one were less likely to develop allergies than children from small families who entered day care later.

23. Film preservation requires transferring old movies from their original material—unstable, deteriorating nitrate film—to stable acetate film. But this is a time-consuming, expensive process, and there is no way to transfer all currently deteriorating nitrate films to acetate before they disintegrate. So some films from the earliest years of Hollywood will not be preserved.

Which one of the following is an assumption on which the argument depends?

(A) No new technology for transferring old movies from nitrate film to acetate film will ever be developed.
(B) Transferring films from nitrate to acetate is not the least expensive way of preserving them.
(C) Not many films from the earliest years of Hollywood have already been transferred to acetate.
(D) Some films from the earliest years of Hollywood currently exist solely in their original material.
(E) The least popular films from the earliest years of Hollywood are the ones most likely to be lost.

24. In a recent study of arthritis, researchers tried but failed to find any correlation between pain intensity and any of those features of the weather—humidity, temperature swings, barometric pressure—usually cited by arthritis sufferers as the cause of their increased pain. Those arthritis sufferers in the study who were convinced of the existence of such a correlation gave widely varying accounts of the time delay between the occurrence of what they believed to be the relevant feature of the weather and the increased intensity of the pain. Thus, this study _______.

Of the following, which one most logically completes the argument?

(A) indicates that the weather affects some arthritis sufferers more quickly than it does other arthritis sufferers
(B) indicates that arthritis sufferers' beliefs about the causes of the pain they feel may affect their assessment of the intensity of that pain
(C) suggests that arthritis sufferers are imagining the correlation they assert to exist
(D) suggests that some people are more susceptible to weather-induced arthritis pain than are others
(E) suggests that the scientific investigation of possible links between weather and arthritis pain is impossible

GO ON TO THE NEXT PAGE.

25. Cities with healthy economies typically have plenty of job openings. Cities with high-technology businesses also tend to have healthy economies, so those in search of jobs should move to a city with high-technology businesses.

The reasoning in which one of the following is most similar to the reasoning in the argument above?

(A) Older antiques are usually the most valuable. Antique dealers generally authenticate the age of the antiques they sell, so those collectors who want the most valuable antiques should purchase their antiques from antique dealers.
(B) Antique dealers who authenticate the age of the antiques they sell typically have plenty of antiques for sale. Since the most valuable antiques are those that have had their ages authenticated, antique collectors in search of valuable antiques should purchase their antiques from antique dealers.
(C) Antiques that have had their ages authenticated tend to be valuable. Since antique dealers generally carry antiques that have had their ages authenticated, those collectors who want antiques that are valuable should purchase their antiques from antique dealers.
(D) Many antique collectors know that antique dealers can authenticate the age of the antiques they sell. Since antiques that have had their ages authenticated are always the most valuable, most antique collectors who want antiques that are valuable tend to purchase their antiques from antique dealers.
(E) Many antiques increase in value once they have had their ages authenticated by antique dealers. Since antique dealers tend to have plenty of valuable antiques, antique collectors who prefer to purchase the most valuable antiques should purchase antiques from antique dealers.

26. Sociologist: A recent study of 5,000 individuals found, on the basis of a physical exam, that more than 25 percent of people older than 65 were malnourished, though only 12 percent of the people in this age group fell below government poverty standards. In contrast, a greater percentage of the people 65 or younger fell below poverty standards than were found in the study to be malnourished.

Each of the following, if true, helps to explain the findings of the study cited by the sociologist EXCEPT:

(A) Doctors are less likely to correctly diagnose and treat malnutrition in their patients who are over 65 than in their younger patients.
(B) People over 65 are more likely to take medications that increase their need for certain nutrients than are people 65 or younger.
(C) People over 65 are more likely to suffer from loss of appetite due to medication than are people 65 or younger.
(D) People 65 or younger are no more likely to fall below government poverty standards than are people over 65.
(E) People 65 or younger are less likely to have medical conditions that interfere with their digestion than are people over 65.

S T O P

IF YOU FINISH BEFORE TIME IS CALLED, YOU MAY CHECK YOUR WORK ON THIS SECTION ONLY.
DO NOT WORK ON ANY OTHER SECTION IN THE TEST.

LSAT® Writing Sample Topic

Directions: The scenario presented below describes two choices, either one of which can be supported on the basis of the information given. Your essay should consider both choices and argue for one over the other, based on the two specified criteria and the facts provided. There is no "right" or "wrong" choice: a reasonable argument can be made for either.

The Wangs must arrange summer child care for their ten-year-old child. They have found two summer-long programs that are affordable and in which friends of their child would also be participating. Using the facts below, write an essay in which you argue for one program over the other based on the following two considerations:

- The Wangs want their child to enjoy activities that would add variety to the regular school experience.
- Transportation to the program must be easy for the Wangs to accommodate to their work situations.

City Summer is located at a college near Mrs. Wang's job but a considerable distance from Mr. Wang's. It offers early arrival and late pick-up times for parent convenience. Mrs. Wang has somewhat flexible work hours, but must travel overnight occasionally. City Summer offers classes in the visual arts, dance, drama, music, swimming, and gymnastics, as well as gym activities like basketball and volleyball. In addition, there are organized field trips to museums, plays, and historical sites. The program concludes with a presentation of student work from the classes.

Round Lake Camp is located 30 minutes outside the city. Bus transportation is provided to and from several city schools, one of which is next door to Mr. Wang's job. Pick-up and drop-off are at set times in the early morning and late afternoon. Mr. Wang has flexibility in his work starting time but often must work late. The camp has classes in swimming, sailing, archery, nature study, crafts, and outdoor skills. It also has regular free periods when campers can choose among outdoor activities or just explore the woods. At the end of the summer the campers have an overnight camping trip at a nearby state wilderness area.

Scratch Paper

Do not write your essay in this space.

Directions:

1. Use the Answer Key on the next page to check your answers.
2. Use the Scoring Worksheet below to compute your raw score.
3. Use the Score Conversion Chart to convert your raw score into the 120-180 scale.

Scoring Worksheet

1. Enter the number of questions you answered correctly in each section.

	Number Correct
SECTION I............	________
SECTION II............	________
SECTION III...........	________
SECTION IV...........	________

2. Enter the sum here: ________

This is your Raw Score.

Conversion Chart:
For Converting Raw Score to the 120-180 LSAT Scaled Score
LSAT Form 0LSN85

Reported Score	Raw Score Lowest	Raw Score Highest
180	99	102
179	98	98
178	97	97
177	96	96
176	95	95
175	94	94
174	93	93
173	91	92
172	90	90
171	89	89
170	88	88
169	86	87
168	85	85
167	83	84
166	82	82
165	80	81
164	79	79
163	77	78
162	75	76
161	74	74
160	72	73
159	70	71
158	69	69
157	67	68
156	65	66
155	63	64
154	62	62
153	60	61
152	58	59
151	57	57
150	55	56
149	53	54
148	52	52
147	50	51
146	48	49
145	47	47
144	45	46
143	43	44
142	42	42
141	40	41
140	39	39
139	37	38
138	36	36
137	35	35
136	33	34
135	32	32
134	30	31
133	29	29
132	28	28
131	27	27
130	25	26
129	24	24
128	23	23
127	22	22
126	21	21
125	20	20
124	18	19
123	17	17
122	16	16
121	15	15
120	0	14

SECTION I

1. A	8. D	15. A	22. D
2. C	9. A	16. B	23. C
3. E	10. E	17. A	24. B
4. B	11. E	18. B	25. E
5. B	12. D	19. D	26. E
6. E	13. C	20. C	27. C
7. D	14. B	21. D	

SECTION II

1. D	8. A	15. B	22. D
2. E	9. C	16. E	23. C
3. B	10. B	17. A	24. E
4. E	11. A	18. D	25. A
5. C	12. E	19. D	26. E
6. A	13. D	20. C	
7. C	14. B	21. E	

SECTION III

1. D	8. C	15. A	22. A
2. D	9. B	16. A	23. D
3. E	10. B	17. D	
4. E	11. A	18. E	
5. B	12. C	19. B	
6. A	13. E	20. E	
7. B	14. C	21. A	

SECTION IV

1. C	8. C	15. D	22. E
2. D	9. C	16. B	23. D
3. A	10. B	17. D	24. C
4. C	11. B	18. D	25. C
5. B	12. D	19. B	26. D
6. A	13. C	20. E	
7. C	14. E	21. A	

Chapter Three: The December 2010 LSAT Deconstructed

The explanations below are presented in the same order that the questions are given on the exam. Please keep in mind that all explanations draw on methods discussed in *The PowerScore LSAT Reading Comprehension Bible*. Please refer to that text if you desire a more detailed discussion of a particular concept or approach. If you encounter any unknown terms, a glossary is provided at the end of the book.

December 2010 Section 1: Reading Comprehension

Overview: In recent years, as Logic Games has been somewhat easier overall, Reading Comprehension sections have often been of above-average difficulty level, and this section was no exception. Test-takers were faced with two Science-oriented passages (#1 and #3) whose subject matter was relatively esoteric (lichenometry and dental caries). These were also the longest passages in the section, with 8 and 7 questions each. The first passage included a significant number of Global Reference Must Be True questions, requiring solid understanding of passage structure and organization. In the comparative passage set, the relationship between the two shorter passages was more complex than usual. As a result, many of Concept Reference questions exploited the subtle differences in perspective between the two authors, and required a good grasp of causal reasoning.

The second and the fourth passages were relatively straightforward. The Law-oriented passage discussed the controversial practice of allowing custom-made medical illustrations to be presented as evidence in legal cases, and most of the questions tested your ability to compare and contrast the arguments against the use of such illustrations with the arguments in favor of their use. Similarly, the fourth passage compared the work of Sarah Jewett, a female fiction writer, to the domestic novels of the 1850s. Your main job was to understand the author's explanation of the differences between them, and compare that explanation to the opposing viewpoint. Predictably, the attitude towards Jewett was one of affirmative commendation, which was a fact you could use to attack some of the questions.

Passage #1. Science: Lichenometry

The passage compares two methods used by seismologists to date past earthquakes—radiocarbon dating and lichenometry. After briefly describing each method, the author discusses why lichenometry is more accurate than radiocarbon dating, but warns that lichenometry is not without limitations.

Paragraph 1 Overview

This passage begins with a description of radiocarbon dating, an established procedure for detecting and dating past earthquakes. When fault-line sediments shift during an earthquake, they usually trap wood or other organic material, which contain naturally occurring radioactive isotope carbon 14. Since carbon 14 decays at a constant rate, seismologists can reconstruct the age of the organic material trapped inside the sediments by measuring the amount of isotope remaining in it. This, in turn, shows the location and frequency of past earthquakes.

Paragraph 2 Overview

Whenever a passage begins by describing an established theory or method, you can be almost sure that the second paragraph will introduce a new theory or method. Indeed, the second paragraph discusses lichenometry, a new method developed by Bull and Brandon for dating past earthquakes. Since earthquakes generate rockfalls, and lichens grow at a constant rate on exposed rocks, measuring the size of the lichens can help determine the age and location of the earthquake. Pay special attention to the example of North American lichen at the end of this paragraph, which adds to our understanding of how lichenometry is used to determine and date past earthquakes.

Paragraph 3 Overview

This paragraph compares the advantages and disadvantages of radiocarbon dating and lichenometry. A savvy test-taker should anticipate that the author would favor the new method (lichenometry) over its predecessor. Predictably, we are told that lichenometry has "distinct advantages" over radiocarbon dating, which summarizes the author's main point in this passage. The problem with radiocarbon dating has to do with the varying amounts of carbon 14 in the environment. Since the amount of carbon 14 depends on the intensity of radiation striking Earth's upper atmosphere, and this intensity has fluctuated over the past 300 years, radiocarbon dating of any event over that period is unreliable. Note that lichenometry has its own set of limitations. Because certain factors might impede or promote lichen growth, using lichenometry requires careful site selection to minimize the influence of such factors, and is best used for earthquakes that occurred within the last 500 years.

Summary

The passage compares two methods for dating past earthquakes—radiocarbon dating and lichenometry. The author's viewpoint is consistent with that of Bull and Brandon, who favor lichenometry over radiocarbon dating due to the former's superior ability to accurately date earthquakes that occurred within the past 500 years. The structure of the passage is as follows:

Paragraph 1: Introduce radiocarbon dating as an established method for dating past earthquakes.
Paragraph 2: Describe lichenometry, a new method for dating past earthquakes, and provide an example of how lichenometry has been put into practice.
Paragraph 3: Discuss the advantages of lichenometry over radiocarbon dating, and introduce the potential limitations of each method. Examples of environmental conditions that affect lichen growth are given.

Question #1: Global Reference, Main Point. The correct answer choice is (A)

Since this is a Main Point question, you should attempt to form a prephrase before beginning to assess the answer choices. The main point of this passage, roughly, is to examine two methods for dating past earthquakes and argue that one of them—lichenometry—has distinct advantages over the other.

Answer choice (A): This is the correct answer choice. It is consistent with our prephrase, and repeats almost verbatim the first sentence of the third paragraph, which contains the main point of the passage.

Answer choice (B): This answer choice contains an exaggeration. There is no evidence that lichenometry has been proven to be more accurate than *any* other method of discerning the dates of past earthquakes. We only know that lichenometry is more accurate than radiocarbon dating.

Answer choice (C): Although the author claims lichenometry to be a superior method, there is no evidence that *most* seismologists share the same view. The first paragraph suggests that radiocarbon dating is a well-established method, and there is no evidence that seismologists have abandoned it for the sake of its competitor.

Answer choice (D): This answer choice is both exaggerated and inaccurate. First, it would be a stretch to regard Bull and Brandon's method as revolutionary. Second, the third paragraph provides no evidence that lichenometry is particularly easy to apply. On the contrary—it requires "careful site selection and accurate calibration of lichen growth rates" (lines 51-52).

Answer choice (E): Even though radiocarbon dating is not as reliable as lichenometry, we cannot consider it "unreliable." Furthermore, the author never advocated abandoning radiocarbon dating altogether.

Question #2: Global Reference, Must Be True. The correct answer choice is (C)

For this question, we need to consider which of the following five questions can be answered using the information provided in the passage. Often the most efficient approach to this sort of question is to review the choices and quickly eliminate any that cannot be answered using the information in the passage. Then examine the remaining responses more closely.

Answer choice (A): From the last paragraph, we know that lichens exist in a diverse range of conditions that need to be factored into any calibration of lichen grown rates. However, the precise method for measuring lichen growth rates under such conditions is unclear. Since this question cannot be answered with the information provided, this answer choice is incorrect.

Answer choice (B): From the last paragraph, we know that the intensity of the radiation striking Earth's upper atmosphere affects the amount of carbon 14 contained in the environment. The precise method for determining the intensity of this radiation is never discussed. Therefore, this answer choice is incorrect.

Answer choice (C): This is the correct answer. In line 57, Bull and Brandon give examples of some of the conditions that encourage lichens to grow at a more rapid rate than usual (shade and wind). By knowing exactly where this information appears, it is relatively easy to verify that there is sufficient information to answer this question. Therefore, answer choice (C) is correct.

Answer choice (D): The use of lichenometry is discussed in the second paragraph of the passage, which provides no information as to the approximate date of the earliest earthquake that lichenometry has been used to identify. From the last paragraph we know that lichenometry is best used for earthquakes that occurred within the last 500 years. This does not, however, mean that the earliest earthquake identified by the use of lichenometry occurred 500 years ago.

Answer choice (E): Although the techniques used in radiocarbon dating may well be applicable in areas other than studying past earthquakes, no such applications were discussed in this passage. Be careful not to rely on your own knowledge of the topic when answering Must Be True questions.

Question #3: Specific Reference, Purpose. The correct answer choice is (E)

Although this question specifically refers to lines 29-30, it is advantageous to have an understanding of the role each paragraph plays in the overall context of the passage. Since the second paragraph describes the use of lichenometry in dating past earthquakes, the author's primary purpose in referring to the growth rate of North American lichen species is to help us understand how fast lichens grow. This is important, since lichen growth rate can help us associate the diameter of lichens with the timing of past earthquakes.

Answer choice (A): The author never intended to emphasize the rapidity with which lichen colonies establish themselves on newly exposed rock surfaces. The fact that they do so rather quickly is mentioned in line 25, but the rate of 9.5 millimeters per century measures lichen growth rate *after* they have colonized the rock surface.

Answer choice (B): There is no reason to suspect that the North American lichen species has a particularly slow rate of growth. We have no information to determine its growth rate relative to other lichen species.

Answer choice (C): Environmental conditions can indeed alter lichens' rate of growth; however, that discussion takes place at the very end of the passage, not in the second paragraph.

Answer choice (D): Although lichenometry does work best for dating earthquakes that occurred in the last 500 years, the rate of growth of North American lichen species does not support that statement. According to the second paragraph, lichens grow at a slow but constant rate for as long as 1,000 years, if left undisturbed. The reason why lichenometry works best for dating more recent earthquakes is because a shorter timeframe can minimize the influence of factors that affect lichen growth rates. That discussion takes place much later in the passage, not in the middle of the second paragraph.

Answer choice (E): This is the correct answer. By understanding the timescale on which lichen growth occurs, we can get a better sense of why lichen size is a useful indicator of the frequency and location of past earthquakes.

Question #4: Global Reference, Must Be True. The correct answer choice is (B)

This question asks for a response that is most strongly supported by the passage, so we must find an answer choice that is consistent with the author's reasoning. Because the question stem does not contain a location indicator, the most efficient approach would be to review the answer choices and quickly eliminate any that are inconsistent with the passage. When examining the remaining responses more closely, consider passage organization first—this will help you locate the specific paragraph(s) that validate your answer.

Answer choice (A): At the end of the first paragraph, the author indicates that radiocarbon dating can provide hints about the likelihood and location of future earthquakes. However, we are given no information as to how lichenometry compares to radiocarbon dating in this respect. A direct comparison between the two methods is made in the third paragraph of the passage, but only with respect to each method's accuracy of dating *past* earthquakes, not of predicting *future* ones.

Answer choice (B): This is the correct answer. According to the information presented in the first paragraph, radiocarbon dating involves digging "trenches along visible fault lines, looking for sediments that show evidence of having shifted" (lines 3-4). Clearly, without identifiable fault lines, seismologists would have difficulty finding sediments in which organic material was trapped during an earthquake. The fact that radiocarbon dating requires fault-line sediments can also be inferred from its comparison to lichenometry in the second paragraph (lines 21-23).

Answer choice (C): The passage provides no evidence to support the claim that radiocarbon dating and lichenometry are currently the *only* viable methods of detecting and dating past earthquakes. Just because no other methods were discussed does not mean that such methods do not exist.

Answer choice (D): According to lines 45-48, radiocarbon datings of events that occurred during the past 300 years are of little value. Lichenometry, on the other hand, is best used for earthquakes that occurred within the last 500 years (lines 53-54). On the basis of this information, we can conclude that both lichenometry and radiocarbon measurements would be relatively accurate in dating earthquakes that occurred approximately 400 years ago, but there is no evidence to support the claim that radiocarbon dating would be *more* accurate than lichenometry in this respect.

Note that just because lichenometry is *best used* for earthquakes that occurred within the last 500 years does not make it *the best* method for dating such earthquakes. Nevertheless, there is no evidence that radiocarbon dating would be any more accurate than lichenometry.

Answer choice (E): At first glance, this seems like an attractive answer. In the third paragraph, Bull and Brandon urge caution in carefully selecting sites that minimize the influence of "disturbances that would affect lichen growth" (lines 55-57). However, this does not mean that lichenometry is altogether useless in regions where such disturbances do occur. Furthermore, note that the occurrence of conditions that accelerate lichen growth does not preclude the usefulness of lichenometry, as long as such conditions can be "factored in" (line 58).

Question #5: Specific Reference, Must Be True, Purpose. The correct answer choice is (B)

Since this question specifically refers to the first paragraph, it is once again advantageous to have an understanding of the structure of the passage. The first paragraph provides a description of radiocarbon dating, a method for dating past earthquakes that will later be compared to another method—lichenometry. This prephrase is consistent with answer choice (B).

Answer choice (A): Although the first paragraph does describe a well-known procedure, this is a classic half-right, half-wrong answer, as radiocarbon dating is not examined on a step-by-step basis in the rest of the passage.

Answer choice (B): This is the correct answer. The rest of the passage compares lichenometry, a new procedure for dating past earthquakes, to radiocarbon dating, an established procedure for dating past earthquakes.

Answer choice (C): Although Bull and Brandon argue that lichenometry is more accurate than radiocarbon dating, this does not mean that radiocarbon dating is entirely obsolete. Recall that lichenometry is best used for dating events that occurred within the last 500 years (line 54). It is entirely possible that radiocarbon measurements would still be very useful in dating earthquakes that occurred earlier.

Answer choice (D): While radiocarbon dating is indeed a traditional procedure, lichenometry is not another traditional procedure. Rather, lichenometry is described as a *new* method for dating past earthquakes (line 16). Furthermore, radiocarbon dating is contrasted with only one other procedure.

Answer choice (E): The passage provides no evidence to support the claim that radiocarbon dating has resulted in erroneous conclusions about earthquakes. Just because such dating is accurate only to within plus or minus 40 years does not make its findings erroneous; they are simply not as accurate as those derived through the use of lichenometry.

Question #6: Specific Reference, Assumption, Subject Perspective. The correct answer choice is (E)

Although assumption questions are far more common in Logical Reasoning than in Reading Comprehension, our approach will be the same. The answer you select must contain a statement upon which Bull and Brandon's argument depends, i.e. a statement that is *necessary* for their conclusion to be true.

In lines 50-58, Bull and Brandon argue that lichenometry requires careful site selection and accurate calibration of lichen growth, concluding that their method is "best used for earthquakes that occurred within the last 500 years" (line 53-54). The rest of the paragraph provides additional information regarding the specific environmental conditions that must be avoided or "factored into" the calibration of lichen growth rates. This assumes, of course, that seismologists can properly factor in the effect of these conditions when calibrating lichen growth rates.

Answer choice (A): Although this answer choice supports the position that lichenometry produces more accurate results than radiocarbon dating, this is not an assumption upon which Bull and Brandon's argument depends. To double-check if this is an assumption, simply apply the Assumption Negation Technique as if it were a Logical Reasoning question—logically negate the answer and ask yourself if the following statement would undermine their argument:

> Lichenometry is just as accurate as other methods for dating earthquakes that occurred within the past 500 years.

Bull and Brandon merely stated that lichenometry is *best used* for dating such earthquakes that occurred within the last 500 years, not that it is the absolute best method for dating such earthquakes. Since the logical opposite of Answer choice (A) does not weaken Bull and Brandon's conclusion, this answer choice does not contain an assumption upon which their argument depends.

Answer choice (B): The statements made by Bull and Brandon concern lichenometry, not radiocarbon dating, which is sufficient to eliminate this answer choice from consideration. If you are having trouble with this answer choice, apply the Assumption Negation Technique:

> There *is* a reliable method for detecting the intensity of the radiation now hitting Earth's upper atmosphere.

Even if there were a reliable method for determining the intensity of the radiation *now* hitting Earth's upper atmosphere, this would not help us overcome the problem of fluctuating radiation during the past 300 years. Since this fluctuation is the reason why radiocarbon datings of events during this period are of little value (lines 45-48), it is still possible that lichenometry is more accurate than radiocarbon measurements for dating such events.

Answer choice (C): Hopefully, you were able to eliminate this answer choice relatively quickly. The types of rocks where lichens can grow are irrelevant to the statements made by Bull and Brandon in the third paragraph.

Answer choice (D): If the mountain ranges that produce the kinds of rockfalls studied in lichenometry are also subject to more frequent snowfalls and avalanches, it may prove difficult to minimize the effect of various disturbances affecting normal lichen growth. This would undermine the feasibility of calibrating lichen growth rates at these sites, and weaken the argument that lichenometry is more accurate than radiocarbon dating. Since the question does not ask us to weaken Bull and Brandon's statements, this answer choice is incorrect.

Answer choice (E): This is the correct answer, as it agrees with our prephrase of a Defender Assumption. If this answer is troubling you, use the Assumption Negation Technique and ask yourself if the following statement would undermine Bull and Brandon's argument:

> The extent to which conditions like shade and wind have affected the growth of existing lichen colonies *cannot* be determined.

If the effect of environmental conditions affecting lichen growth cannot be determined, it would be difficult to factor them into our calibration of lichen growth rates. As a result, lichenometry may prove unreliable in dating past earthquakes, which would weaken Bull and Brandon's argument.

Question #7: Concept Reference, Must Be True. The correct answer choice is (D)

This question asks us to identify a reason why radiocarbon dating may be unreliable. Passage organization is once again key. Since the author compared radiocarbon dating to lichenometry in the third paragraph, any potential downsides to the use of either method can be found there.

Answer choice (A): Although radiocarbon dating does involve measuring the quantity of radioactive isotopes present in a variety of organic material (line 6), this was never presented as a downside to its use.

Answer choice (B): The author never discussed the variable quantity of organic material caught in shifted sediments. Rather, the problem with radiocarbon dating was determining the variable quantity of *carbon 14 isotope* contained in such material.

Answer choice (C): If fault lines related to past earthquakes are not always visible, this would certainly be an obstacle to using radiocarbon dating of fault-line sediments to date such earthquakes. However, this issue was never raised in the passage, which makes answer choice (C) incorrect.

Answer choice (D): This is the correct answer. The amount of carbon 14 isotope depends on the intensity of the radiation striking Earth's upper atmosphere, which has fluctuated greatly during the past 300 years. This causes many radiocarbon datings to be of little value (lines 45-48).

Answer choice (E): The possibility that radiation has not always struck the upper atmosphere was never mentioned in the passage, which makes this answer choice incorrect.

Question #8: Global Reference, Must Be True. The correct answer choice is (D)

This question asks us to identify an area (other than the dating of past earthquakes) to which lichenometry would be particularly applicable. Recall that the process of using lichen shape and size as clues to the location and frequency of earthquakes was described in the second paragraph. Using that information, look for an answer choice describing an analogous situation where lichen size would be of value in gauging the occurrence of some past event.

Answer choice (A): Recall that lichenometry involves measuring the size of lichens growing on exposed rocks at a slow but constant rate *if left undisturbed* (lines 26-28). Since each flooding of the river would disturb the normal growth of lichens in the flooded area, it is unlikely that lichenometry can be used to identify the number of times a particular river has flooded. Lichenometry may help identify the timing of the most recent flooding, but not the number of times the river has flooded over the years.

Answer choice (B): Since lichens grow at a constant rate for no more than 1,000 years (line 28), it is unlikely that we can use them to identify the age of a fossilized skeleton of a mammal that lived *thousands* of years ago.

Answer choice (C): Given that lichenometry involves measuring the size of lichens growing on exposed rocks, it is unclear how we can use it to identify the age of an ancient beach that is currently underwater.

Answer choice (D): This is the correct answer. Since lichens grow radially at a constant rate, the diameter of the largest lichen would provide direct evidence of the initial position of the glacier at the bottom of the mountain valley. As the glacier recedes, the lichens would have less and less time to develop and therefore decrease in size and abundance. Thus, if we know the rate of lichen growth, we can also calculate the rate at which the glacier has been receding up the valley.

Answer choice (E): Although lichenometry is best used for earthquakes that occurred within the last 500 years, do not be misled by the analogous time frame in this answer choice. Given what we know about lichenometry, it is unclear how this method can be used to identify trends in annual rainfall rates, especially since the varying amounts of rainfall can potentially affect the growth rate of lichen colonies in the valley.

Passage #2. Law: Medical Illustrations

The passage discusses the controversial practice of allowing custom-made medical illustrations depicting personal injury to be presented as evidence in legal cases. The author considers and rejects several arguments against this practice, concluding that custom-made illustrations are objectively accurate and especially valuable in cases involving complex testimonies by medical experts.

Paragraph 1 Overview

This passage begins by outlining the objection that illustrations from medical textbooks are adequate in representing injuries that are mostly generic in nature. Although the author does not dispute this claim directly, you should notice the use of phrases such as "some opponents…argue" (line 6) and "they say" (line 11). By creating a rhetorical "distance" between thc author's viewpoint and the opponents of custom-made illustrations, such phrases imply that the author will ultimately argue *in favor of* using such illustrations in the courtroom. This presentation style also mixes the various opponent arguments with the author's rebuttals, and this "compare-and-contrast" format generates greater complexity in the passage. To combat this, always make sure to carefully track each viewpoint within the passage.

Paragraph 2 Overview

The second paragraph considers the argument that custom-made illustrations can misrepresent the facts to help lawyers bolster a weak case. The author rejects this claim, ("but this is mistaken"—line 25), arguing that deceptive illustrations would be inadmissible as evidence in the courtroom unless a medical expert testified to their accuracy.

Paragraph 3 Overview

In the beginning of the third paragraph, the author addresses the complaint that even if custom-made illustrations are technically accurate, they can still distort the issues. The author rejects this view, arguing that (1) custom-made illustrations are objectively accurate; (2) illustrators strive to avoid devices that have inflammatory potential; and (3) custom-made illustrations include only information relevant to the particular case.

The author specifically compares custom-made illustrations to medical textbook illustrations, noting that the latter often include superfluous details that may confuse jurors. It is important to closely examine (and notate) such comparisons, as you are likely going to be asked about them later on. In fact, Questions #10 and #12 directly test your understanding of the comparison between the two types of illustrations.

Paragraph 4 Overview

The final paragraph outlines the author's argument in favor of using custom-made medical illustrations in legal cases, particularly those involving complex expert testimonies.

Summary

The author considers and rejects several major arguments against the use of custom-made medical illustrations (CMI) in personal injury cases. Make sure to understand each argument and counter-argument before proceeding to the questions:

Arguments Against CMI (Opponent's View)	Counterarguments in Favor of CMI (Author's View)
Illustrations from medical textbooks are usually sufficient (¶1)	No, medical textbooks often provide unnecessary detail and confuse the issue (¶3)
	Also, CMIs are especially valuable as a visual representation of data in complex cases (¶4)
CMIs can be deceptive (¶2)	No, because deceptive illustrations would be inadmissible as evidence (¶2)
Even if accurate, CMIs can subtly distort the issues (¶3)	No, because CMIs are designed to be (1) objectively accurate; (2) not inflammatory; and (3) contain only information relevant to the particular case (¶3)

Question #9: Global Reference, Parallel, Author's Perspective. The correct answer choice is (A)

This question asks us to identify a scenario that is most analogous to the role played by custom-made medical illustrations in personal injury cases. Although Parallel Reasoning questions are far more common in Logical Reasoning than in Reading Comprehension, our approach will be the same. Recall that in the fourth paragraph, the author describes custom-made illustrations as "visual representations of data whose verbal description would be very complex" (lines 54-55). By applying the Test of Abstraction, you will look for a scenario in which a visual device facilitates our understanding of verbal communication.

Answer choice (A): This is the correct answer choice. The schematic drawings accompanying an engineer's oral presentation function in the same way as custom-made medical illustrations do when used alongside expert testimony. In both cases, the pictorial device helps "translate" technical terminology into visual imagery.

Answer choice (B): Although road maps are visual devices that facilitate our ability to orient ourselves, their purpose is to save us from having to ask for directions. The role of custom-made medical illustrations, however, is to *supplement* expert testimony, not replace it altogether.

Answer choice (C): Using children's drawings to detect wishes and anxieties not apparent in the children's behavior is not analogous to the use of custom-made medical illustrations. The purpose of medical illustrations is not to detect or reveal hidden injuries, but rather to explain the nature of these injuries to judges and jurors.

Answer choice (D): Custom-made medical illustrations offer a unique visual representation of the injury relevant to a particular case, not a reproduction of something famous or unique that is then disseminated to a wider audience.

Answer choice (E): Since custom-made medical illustrations are designed to be objectively accurate depictions of an injury that has already occurred, they clearly represent a finished product, not a preliminary sketch.

Question #10: Global Reference, Must Be True, Author's Perspective. The correct answer choice is (E)

For this question, we need to consider which of the following responses most accurately captures the author's position regarding illustrations in medical textbooks. Having a solid grasp of passage organization is key. A direct comparison between medical textbook illustrations and custom-made illustrations is made in the third paragraph, which you should use as evidence to prove your response.

Answer choice (A): This is an Opposite answer. It is the custom-made medical illustrations that are "sometimes even eschewing the use of color" (line 36), not the illustrations found in medical textbooks. If you found this answer choice attractive, you failed to differentiate between the author's viewpoint and that of her opponents, who argue that "custom-made illustrations may subtly distort the issues through the use of emphasis, coloration, and other means" (lines 30-32).

Answer choice (B): This answer choice is incorrect, since it refers to the use of custom-made medical illustrations, not illustrations found in medical textbooks (lines 26-29).

Answer choice (C): The passage offers no evidence to support the claim that the same individuals draw both custom-made and textbook illustrations.

Answer choice (D): At first glance, this may seem like an attractive answer choice. Indeed, the opponents of custom-made medical illustrations do consider textbook illustrations to be less prone to misrepresentation than custom-made medical illustrations (lines 17-21 and 30-33). However, there is no reason to suspect that *most lawyers* agree with the opponents of custom-made illustrations. Furthermore, the question specifically asks about the *author's* view regarding illustrations in medical textbooks, not the opponents' view.

Answer choice (E): This is the correct answer choice. In the third paragraph, the author compares the two types of illustrations, noting that "the more complex details often found in textbooks can be deleted [from custom-made illustrations] so as not to confuse the issue" (lines 44-46). Therefore, it would be reasonable to conclude that textbook illustrations are more apt to confuse jurors than are custom-made medical illustrations.

Question #11: Concept Reference, Must Be True. The correct answer choice is (E)

This question asks us to identify the role of medical experts in relation to custom-made medical illustrations. Having a solid grasp of the argument—counterargument structure underlying the passage is once again key. The author describes the role of medical experts in the second paragraph, claiming that deceptive illustrations would be inadmissible as evidence unless an expert testified to their accuracy (lines 26-29).

Answer choice (A): Although medical experts do play a role in establishing the admissibility of medical illustrations, they are not the ones making the *decision* as to which custom-made medical illustrations should be admissible. Read carefully—medical experts only "testify to their accuracy" (line 29); they do not decide questions of law.

Answer choice (B): This answer choice is incorrect, because medical experts are not the ones who temper the impact of medical illustrations. Professional medical illustrators do (lines 33-36).

Answer choice (C): This is a reverse answer. The role of medical experts is not to make medical illustrations understandable; rather, the role of medical illustrations is to make medical experts understandable (lines 55-64).

Answer choice (D): The passage offers no evidence to support the claim that medical experts provide opinions to attorneys as to which illustrations would be useful.

Answer choice (E): This is the correct answer choice, as the author's statements in lines 26-29 directly support it.

Question #12: Global Reference, Must Be True. The correct answer choice is (D)

This question asks us to identify one of the ways in which medical textbook illustrations differ from custom-made medical illustrations. The most efficient way to approach this question would be to review the answer choices and quickly eliminate any that are inconsistent with the passage. When examining the remaining responses more closely, refer to the third paragraph of the passage, which compares the two types of illustrations. As mentioned earlier, whenever the author makes a direct comparison between two items, it is advantageous to notate that section of the passage so you can quickly refer to it when needed.

Answer choice (A): There is no evidence to suggest that medical textbook illustrations fail to accurately represent human anatomy. The fact that they contain "extensive detail required by medical students" (line 38) certainly does not make them inaccurate (just confusing).

Answer choice (B): Although custom-made medical illustrations sometimes eschew the use of color (line 36), it is an exaggeration to say that they *must* avoid color. Moreover, there is no evidence to suggest that just because medical textbooks include extensive detail, they also employ color freely.

Answer choice (C): The passage does not differentiate between textbook illustrations and custom-made illustrations on the basis of whether they are objective or not.

Answer choice (D): This is the correct answer choice. According to the information contained in the third paragraph, medical textbook illustrations "include [...] extensive detail" (line 38), whereas custom-made illustrations contain "only the information that is relevant for those deciding a case" (lines 40-41).

Answer choice (E): This is an Opposite answer. The problem with medical textbook illustration is precisely that they contain *too much* detail, making them difficult to comprehend by nonmedical audiences. Custom-made medical illustrations, on the other hand, include only the information relevant to the particular case, making them more easily understandable.

Question #13: Concept Reference, Author's Prespective. The correct answer choice is (C)

This question requires us to describe the author's attitude toward the testimony of medical experts in personal injury cases. Since expert testimony was primarily discussed in the fourth paragraph of the passage, pay particular attention to the language used in that paragraph to quickly validate your response.

Answer choice (A): This is a classic half-right, half-wrong answer, since the author is indeed skeptical about the effectiveness of expert testimony in the absence of illustrations designed to facilitate its comprehension. However, even though the author clearly appreciates the difficulty involved in *understanding* medical data (lines 56-58), there is no evidence that she appreciates the difficulty of trying to *explain* it.

Answer choice (B): Even if medical professionals may be unable to explain complex data in the clearest of terms, it would be a stretch to suggest that the author harbors "disdain" for their communications skills. Likewise, there is no evidence that the author admires their technical knowledge.

Answer choice (C): This is the correct answer choice. The author does not dispute the accuracy of the testimony by medical experts, but clearly has reservations regarding their ability to verbally communicate complex medical data to people who are not specially trained in the field (lines 56-59).

Answer choice (D): This answer choice is quite attractive, since the author does exhibit apprehension concerning the tendency of judges and jurors to be overwhelmed by technical details. However, there is no evidence that the medical professionals *try* to overwhelm their audience with technical details. Read carefully—this nuance is crucial and sufficient to make answer choice (D) incorrect.

Answer choice (E): Although there is no reason to doubt the author's respect for expert witnesses, the claim that she is *intolerant* of technical terminology is an exaggeration. The author is simply aware of its limitations.

Question #14: Specific Reference, Must Be True, Purpose. The correct answer choice is (B)

This question specifically refers to the primary purpose of the third paragraph. Recall that the third paragraph begins by outlining the argument that even if custom-made depictions are technically accurate, they can still distort the issues. The author's counterargument consists of three premises, namely, that custom-made medical illustrations are designed to: (1) be objectively accurate; (2) avoid inflammatory potential; and (3) contain only information relevant to the particular case. In short, the primary purpose of the third paragraph is to reply to the objection that even technically accurate custom-made medical illustrations can be deceiving. Note that this objection is a slightly different variant on the complaint made in the second paragraph, which claims that custom-made illustrations are *factually* deceptive.

Specific Reference/Purpose questions test your ability to describe not only the purpose of the element referenced in the question itself, but also its overall function in the passage. It would be a mistake to focus only on the third paragraph when answering this question—make sure you understand how it relates to the rest of the passage.

Answer choice (A): Although the overall purpose of the passage may be to argue for a greater use of custom-made medical illustrations in personal injury cases, this is not the primary purpose of the third paragraph. If anything, answer choice (A) better describes the purpose of the fourth paragraph of the passage, not the third.

Answer choice (B): This is the correct answer choice. The third paragraph addresses (and rejects) the allegation that even technically accurate illustrations can still subtly distort the issues (lines 30-33). This is a variant of the objection raised in the second paragraph, namely, that custom-made medical illustrations often misrepresent the facts (lines 17-18). Answer choice (B) agrees with our prephrase and is therefore correct.

Answer choice (C): At first, this may seem like an attractive answer. Without doubt, the author is not convinced that illustrations from medical textbooks are well suited for use in the courtroom, given that they often contain extensive and confusing details (lines 36-46). This, however, is not the *primary* purpose of the third paragraph; it is a secondary point supporting the argument that custom-made medical illustrations are objectively accurate and valuable as evidence in the courtroom.

Answer choice (D): Although the third paragraph begins by outlining a possible objection to the use of custom-made medical illustrations, its primary purpose is not to discuss *why* they are controversial, but rather to respond to one particular objection to their use.

Answer choice (E): While the third paragraph compares custom-made illustrations to illustrations from medical textbooks, the author's primary purpose is not simply to describe how they are different, but rather to convince the reader that custom-made illustrations are not deceptive and therefore superior.

Passage #3, Science: Dental Caries and Agriculture

Passage A

The passage argues that since carbohydrate consumption causes dental caries (decay), prehistoric human teeth can provide clues about when a population made the transition from a hunter-gatherer diet to a carbohydrate-rich agricultural one.

Paragraph 1 Overview

This paragraph introduces several factors that can affect the formation of dental caries (decay)—tooth structure, bacteria in the mouth, and diet. Of these factors, diet is especially important to the author's argument. Carbohydrate-rich foods are common staples in agricultural diets. Because the formation of dental caries is strongly linked to the consumption of carbohydrates, the author believes that prehistoric human teeth can provide evidence about when a population made the transition from a hunter-gatherer diet to an agricultural one.

Paragraph 2 Overview

The second paragraph brings in additional evidence to support the correlation between a population's dependence on agriculture and its rate of caries formation. In particular, the author describes a study by Leigh comparing indigenous populations in North America that primarily consumed meat (low rate of caries formation) to those heavily dependent on cultivated maize (high rate of caries formation). Other researchers have also confirmed this correlation.

Paragraph 3 Overview

In the final paragraph, the author concedes that some nonagricultural populations, such as those in western North America as well as the Hopi, may also exhibit high caries rates due to their consumption of foods with high cariogenic potential (as an aside, do not be put off by the word "cariogenic"; it simply means "decay causing"). Although this information does not disprove the correlation cited in the second paragraph, it shows that the correlation is not perfect.

Summary

Overall, the author believes that a population's dependence on agriculture tends to increase its rate of caries formation, due to our consumption of cariogenic carbohydrate-rich foods. This hypothesis is not without limitations, as some nonagricultural populations can also exhibit high caries rates. Nevertheless, the author is confident that prehistoric human teeth can be used as evidence to determine when a population transitioned from a hunter-gatherer diet to an agricultural one.

As a whole, the passage is not overly complex, especially if you recognized the causal reasoning framework inherent in the author's logic. Although we study causal reasoning primarily in the context of Logical Reasoning questions, causality in Reading Comprehension is often used to explain why certain events occurred, and is not typically viewed as flawed reasoning.

Passage B

The second passage focuses on the archeological findings at the Ban Chiang site in Thailand. Although the site's early inhabitants appear to have had a hunter-gatherer-cultivator economy, the population gradually became dependent on agriculture. Surprisingly, the rate of caries formation decreased over time, suggesting that increased reliance on agriculture does not necessarily lead to an increase in caries frequency.

Paragraph 1 Overview

The first paragraph opens with a description of the passage's central focus: the inhabitants of the prehistoric Ban Chiang site in Thailand, who transitioned from a hunter-gatherer-cultivator diet to an agricultural one.

Paragraph 2 Overview

For the most part, the research findings described in the second paragraph agree with those in Passage A—agricultural intensification can lead to increased caries frequency. Note, however, that consumption of carbohydrate-rich foods is not the only way to explain this relationship; alterations in tooth wear can also play a role. Since agricultural diets reduce our intake of fiber, they can diminish tooth wear and promote caries formation. Interestingly, too much tooth wear may also result in caries.

Paragraph 3 Overview

Here the author describes the diet of Ban Chiang's inhabitants in greater detail. Since they consumed a varied diet that initially included some carbohydrate-rich foods, the author alleges that increased reliance on such foods should *theoretically* result in increased caries frequency. Note the speculative language in the last sentence, suggesting that agricultural intensification did not *actually* result in increased caries frequency, as shown in the next paragraph.

Paragraph 4 Overview

The fourth paragraph compares caries frequency in the Early and Late Ban Chiang Groups. Surprisingly, the rate of caries formation among the Ban Chiang's inhabitants did not increase as they transitioned into a predominantly agricultural diet; on the contrary—caries frequency was slightly greater in the Early Group than in the Late Group. Since no alterations in tooth wear were observed, the author proposes two ways to explain the unexpected results:

1. The diet in the Late period remained varied enough that no single food dominated;
2. There may have been a shift from sweeter carbohydrates (yams) toward rice, a less cariogenic carbohydrate.

Summary

Overall, the author does not dispute the prevailing view that agricultural intensification can result in declining dental health. However, the counterexample of the Ban Chiang population presents a scenario in which the cause occurs without the effect, suggesting that agricultural diets do not always result in increased caries frequency. The passage is slightly more difficult than Passage A, but you can still rely on your understanding of causal reasoning to break it down.

Passage Similarities:

There is considerable agreement on the relationship between carbohydrate consumption and caries formation between the two authors. Both believe that the consumption of carbohydrate-rich foods can increase the incidence of dental caries, a view both passages support by observing that dental caries is uncommon in nonagricultural populations. The two authors also agree that some carbohydrate-rich foods have a higher cariogenic potential than others. Both passages examine the prevailing view that agricultural intensification tends to increase the incidence of caries formation in a population, and both express reservations suggesting that the correlation is not perfect.

Passage Differences:

While the topics of the passages are similar, the first author exhibits a slightly higher degree of confidence in the prevailing view that increased dependence on agriculture leads to higher rates of caries formation. Unlike the second passage, Passage A cites specific studies confirming this correlation, and only briefly describes any exceptions in the last paragraph.

By contrast, the main focus of Passage B is the counterexample of the Ban Chiang inhabitants, suggesting that a population's dependence on agriculture may actually decrease its rates of caries formation. Interestingly, Passage A presents a counterexample in which the effect occurs without the cause, whereas Passage B describes a scenario in which the cause occurs without the effect. Passage B also offers a more elaborate view of the causal relationship between agricultural diets and caries formation, suggesting that carbohydrate consumption and alterations in tooth wear can each play a role in caries formation.

Question #15: Global Reference, Must Be True, Passage Commonality, Purpose. The correct answer choice is (A)

The first question is a Passage Commonality question, forcing you to evaluate the primary purpose that is common to both passages. To successfully solve this question, use the Fact Test—the correct answer must be proven by referring to the facts stated in both passages. Quickly examine the five answer choices and eliminate those that cannot be proven by referring to both passages.

Answer choice (A): This is the correct answer choice. The primary purpose of both passages it to examine the topic of prehistoric human teeth, and the extent to which they provide archaeological evidence of agricultural intensification (lines 4-5 and 39-41). Although this answer choice is relatively vague, remember that the correct answer to a Purpose/Function question is often an abstract version of the main point.

Answer choice (B): This answer choice is incorrect for two reasons. First, Passage A never mentions the topic of overall human health (only Passage B does, in line 40). Second, each passage is concerned with examining the impact of agriculture on *dental* health, not *overall* health.

Answer choice (C): While both passages examine the effects of carbohydrate-rich foods on caries formation, the scope of each passage extends beyond strictly agricultural societies. Recall that the last paragraph of Passage A discusses caries rates in nonagricultural populations, while the Ban Chiang populations are described as having a hunter-gatherer-cultivator economy before becoming dependent on agriculture (lines 35-38).

Answer choice (D): This is a classic Shell Game answer. Although each passage is concerned with the extent to which human teeth provide archaeological evidence of agricultural development, there is no reason to believe that the populations described were the *first* agricultural societies to emerge.

Answer choice (E): Hopefully you were able to eliminate this answer choice relatively quickly, since the extent to which pre-agricultural populations were able to obtain carbohydrate-rich foods is not discussed in either passage.

Question #16: Specific Reference, Must Be True, Passage Relationship. The correct answer choice is (B)

This question asks us to identify a distinguishing characteristic of the Ban Chiang populations discussed in Passage B and the populations discussed in the last paragraph of Passage A. To do so, we need to consider the information from both passages in the aggregate, and eliminate any answers that contain facts inconsistent with those presented in the passages.

Answer choice (A): This answer choice is incorrect, since the wild plants collected by the Hopi included several species with high cariogenic potential (lines 30-31). The Ban Chiang populations, on the other hand, consumed some cariogenic foods, though the Late Group may have shifted toward rice, a less cariogenic carbohydrate (lines 68-69).

Answer choice (B): This is the correct answer. Since the populations discussed in the last paragraph of Passage A were nonagricultural, we can infer that they did not eat cultivated foods. The diet of the Ban Chiang populations, on the other hand, included some cultivated rice and yams (lines 51-52).

Answer choice (C): This is an Opposite answer, as the Ban Chiang populations did not consume a diet consisting primarily of carbohydrates; their diet was varied and included wild plant and animal foods (line 55). Some of the nonagricultural populations discussed in the last paragraph of Passage A did consume highly processed flour, a carbohydrate-rich food, though it is unclear whether such foods predominated in their diet.

Answer choice (D): Hopefully you were able to eliminate this answer choice rather quickly, since Passage A does not mention tooth wear as a factor contributing to caries formation. Also, with respect to the Ban Chiang populations, we only know that their tooth wear patterns did not change between Early and Late Groups (lines 61-62).

Answer choice (E): This is a Reverse answer. It is the populations in western North America that ate the highly processed foods, not the Ban Chiang.

Question #17: Concept Reference, Must Be True, Passage Exclusivity. The correct answer choice is (A)

Passage Exclusivity questions ask about information contained in only one of the two passages. Since this question refers to fiber and grit in a diet, recall that their role was discussed in the second paragraph of Passage B. A thorough understanding of passage organization allows for quick access to the information necessary to attack questions involving a concept reference.

Answer choice (A): This is the correct answer choice. While too little fiber and grit diminish tooth wear and increase caries frequency, too much fiber and grit can expose a tooth's pulp cavity and can also result in caries (lines 47-50). Therefore, fiber and grit can either limit or promote caries formation, depending on their prevalence in the diet.

Considering the unusual effect of fiber and grit on caries formation, it would have been wise to highlight or underline lines 47-50 in Passage B, especially since the topic of fiber and grit is unique to that passage.

Answer choice (B): This is a Shell Game answer. Although increased reliance on agriculture increases the consumption of carbohydrate-rich foods, there is no evidence that it also increases the consumption of fiber and grit. As far as we know, there were no changes in the tooth wear between Early and Late Ban Chiang Groups (lines 61-63).

Answer choice (C): Since the nutritional value of fiber and grit was never addressed in either passage, this answer choice is incorrect.

Answer choice (D): This is an Opposite answer. Recall that tooth wear removes fissures on tooth surfaces, whereas the reduction of fiber and grit diminishes tooth wear (lines 45-48). Clearly, as long as tooth wear is not severe, fiber and grit would not contribute to the formation of fissures in tooth surfaces; on the contrary—they may help wear down the tooth surfaces enough to *remove* the fissures in them.

Answer choice (E): The effect of fiber and grit on the stickiness of carbohydrate-rich foods was never addressed in either passage. This answer choice is incorrect.

Question #18: Concept Reference, Must Be True, Passage Commonality. The correct answer choice is (B)

This Passage Commonality question asks us to identify evidence mentioned in both passages in support of the prevailing view that carbohydrate consumption causes dental caries. Items appearing in only one of the passages are common traps in such questions; the correct answer must describe evidence mentioned in *both* passages.

Once again, a thorough understanding of passage organization allows for quick access to the information necessary to attack Concept Reference questions. Recall that the second paragraph in each passage focuses on the research findings that establish a link between carbohydrate consumption and caries. Since research findings are often used as evidence to support various viewpoints, we can use this location element to prove the correct answer to this question.

Answer choice (A): The effect of consuming highly processed foods on caries formation is only discussed in the context of early nonagricultural populations in western North America (lines 25-29). Consumption of highly processed foods is never addressed in Passage B.

Answer choice (B): This is the correct answer choice. Although some nonagricultural populations, such as the Hopi, do exhibit high caries rates, both passages mention the relatively low incidence of caries among nonagricultural people as evidence suggesting that carbohydrate consumption results in caries formation (lines 13-22 in Passage A; lines 41-42 in Passage B).

Answer choice (C): The effect of fiber and grit on caries formation was only discussed in Passage B, not Passage A (lines 47-50). Items appearing in only one of the passages are common traps in Passage Commonality questions.

Answer choice (D): This answer choice mixes elements from both passages, but appears in neither passage. Although both the Hopi and the Ban Chiang populations consumed wild plants, there is no evidence that such consumption affected their tooth wear. Furthermore, recall that Passage A never mentioned the role of tooth wear on caries formation (only Passage B did), making answer choice (D) relatively easy to eliminate.

Answer choice (E): The effect of agricultural intensification on overall human health was only mentioned in Passage B, not Passage A (line 40).

Question #19: Concept Reference, Must Be True, Author Agreement. The correct answer choice is (D)

Since there is considerable agreement on the frequency and causes of dental caries between the two authors, the most efficient way to approach this question would be to review each answer choice and quickly eliminate those that contain information extraneous to either passage.

Answer choice (A): If you found this answer choice attractive, you may have assumed that populations are bound to become increasingly dependent on agriculture over time. This may have been true for prehistoric societies, but there is no evidence that the trend would continue indefinitely. Furthermore, since caries frequency among the Ban Chiang populations actually decreased over time, we can easily eliminate answer choice (A).

Answer choice (B): The difficulty of detecting dental caries in prehistoric human teeth is not discussed in either passage, making this answer choice incorrect.

Answer choice (C): This is an Opposite answer. Both authors generally agree with the prevailing view that dental caries tend to be more prevalent in agricultural societies. Although there are clear exceptions to this correlation, neither author is arguing that the exceptions disprove the correlation.

Answer choice (D): This is the correct answer. The last paragraph of Passage A asserts that some nonagricultural populations exhibit high caries rates, suggesting that the frequency of dental caries does not necessarily correspond directly to the population's degree of dependence on agriculture. Likewise, Passage B describes comparisons of caries frequency in the Early and Late Ban Chiang Groups, indicating that overall caries frequency is slightly greater in the Early Group (line 59-60), despite the increased dependence on agriculture in the Late period.

Answer choice (E): We can quickly eliminate this answer choice from consideration, since Passage A never discussed the link between dental caries and tooth wear. Likewise, Passage B never compared the relative impact of tooth wear and carbohydrate consumption on caries formation.

Question #20: Concept Reference, Must Be True, Passage Commonality. The correct answer choice is (C)

Although we know from each passage that carbohydrate-rich foods tend to cause caries, this prephrase is quite obvious and unlikely to be particularly helpful in identifying the correct answer. Nevertheless, the answer to a Passage Commonality question must pass the Fact Test; both passages will provide sufficient information to prove only one of the statements regarding carbohydrate-rich foods.

Answer choice (A): If you found this answer choice attractive, you probably relied on outside information when answering a Must Be True question. Varieties of foods that are cultivated may indeed have a greater tendency to cause caries than varieties that grow wild. However, neither passage presents evidence to support this observation. On the contrary—the last paragraph of Passage A specifically refers to certain wild plants, such as pinyon nuts and wild tuber, that are highly cariogenic (lines 29-31).

Answer choice (B): Although it may be tempting to conclude that foods requiring substantial processing do not play a significant role in hunter-gatherer diets, recall that early nonagricultural populations in western North American consumed large amounts of highly processed stone-ground flour made from gathered acorns. Furthermore, Passage B never mentioned the topic of processed foods, making answer choice (B) easier to eliminate.

Answer choice (C): This is the correct answer choice. The wild plants consumed by the Hopi, described in lines 29-31 of Passage A, suggest that some carbohydrate-rich foods have higher cariogenic potential than others. Similarly, at the very end of Passage B, the author describes a possible shift in the diet of the Late Ban Chiang period from sweeter carbohydrates toward less cariogenic carbohydrates (lines 66-68). These two observations imply that some carbohydrate-rich foods have a greater tendency to cause caries than others.

The fact that answer choice (C) can only be proven by facts presented at the very end of each passage is neither trivial nor accidental. Such information is often forgotten because the average student is eager to move on to the next passage or jump to the questions.

Answer choice (D): Although high fiber content may indeed increase tooth wear and reduce caries formation (lines 44-50), the effects of fiber and grit on dental health are discussed only in Passage B, not Passage A. This type of trap is common in Passage Commonality questions.

Answer choice (E): This answer choice is almost identical to answer choice (A). Neither passage provides evidence to support a correlation between the cultivation of a given variety of food and its cariogenic potential.

Question #21: Specific Reference, Must Be True, Passage Relationship. The correct answer choice is (D)

This Passage Relationship question asks us to identify the abstract relationship between the evidence from Ban Chiang discussed in Passage B and the generalization reported in the second paragraph of Passage A (lines 20-22). Recall that the generalization reported in Passage A concerned the positive correlation between a population's dependence on agriculture and its rate of caries formation. By contrast, as the Ban Chiang populations became increasingly dependent on agriculture, their caries frequency decreased. This suggests that the evidence from Ban Chiang is *inconsistent* with the generalization reported in Passage A.

Answer choice (A): This is an Opposite answer, since the evidence from Ban Chiang does not confirm the correlation between agricultural intensification and caries formation.

Answer choice (B): This is an Opposite answer, similar to answer choice (A). The evidence from Ban Chiang does not support the correlation described in Passage A.

Answer choice (C): The evidence from Ban Chiang is inconsistent with the generalization reported in Passage A, not irrelevant to it.

Answer choice (D): This is the correct answer. The Ban Chiang exhibited a negative correlation between caries rates and agricultural dependence, which is inconsistent with the positive correlation reported in the second paragraph of Passage A. Therefore, the evidence from Ban Chiang does not conform to the generalization.

Answer choice (E): This answer choice contains an exaggeration. Just because some facts are inconsistent with a particular generalization does not mean that the generalization is thereby disproven.

Passage #4. Humanities: Sarah Orne Jewett

The passage examines the work of writer Sarah Orne Jewett in the literary context of 19th century United States and discusses its relationship to the domestic novels of the previous generation.

Paragraph 1 Overview

The first paragraph compares the work of Sarah Orne Jewett, an American writer of regional fiction in the nineteenth-century, to the domestic novelists of the 1850s:

- Similarities: both focus on women and their concerns, with men relegated to the periphery (lines 6-8).
- Differences: domestic novels revolve around children and contain religious themes, whereas Jewett's fiction does not.

Whenever you encounter a compare-and-contrast section in a Reading Comprehension passage, make sure to notate the similarities and differences between the items being compared. Equally important is the juxtaposition between two competing viewpoints: the critics, who seek to align Jewett's work with the domestic novelists of the previous generation, and the author's arguing that it "differs markedly from these antecedents" (line 8). The ability to differentiate between contrasting viewpoints is an important skill that is frequently tested on the LSAT.

Paragraph 2 Overview

The second paragraph seeks to explain the differences between Jewett's fiction and the domestic novels of the previous generation. The author cites several possible explanations, but discounts them as mere reflections of a more fundamental shift in the conception of fiction held by Jewett and her predecessors:

Cause		Effect
Differing conceptions of fiction	⟶	Differences b/w Jewett and the domestic novel

The domestic novel, the author asserts, was based on a conception of fiction as a continuum that also included writings devoted to piety and domestic instruction. As such, novels were indistinguishable from other forms of writing. By contrast, Jewett's work embodies a new "high-cultural" conception of fiction as an autonomous sphere with value in and of itself.

This causal relationship is the crux of the author's argument, and must be fully understood before proceeding to the next paragraph. Although we study causal reasoning primarily in the context of Logical Reasoning questions, causality in Reading Comprehension is often used to explain why certain events occurred, and is not typically viewed as flawed reasoning.

Paragraph 3 Overview

In the final paragraph, the author elaborates on Jewett's conception of fiction as "pure art." Unlike the domestic novelists, Jewett intended her work not as a means to an end but as an end in itself. This, the author concludes, is the fundamental difference between Jewett and her predecessors, overriding any superficial similarity in subject matter between them. Make sure to highlight the last two sentences of the passage, as they summarize the main point at issue between the author and the critics.

Summary

Despite the subject matter similarities between Jewett's fiction and the domestic novels of the 1850s, the author argues that they reflect differing conceptions of fiction. There are two viewpoints you should keep in mind as you attack the questions:

Critics:	Due to its focus on women and domestic occupations, Jewett's work belongs to the same literary tradition as the domestic novel.
Author:	Jewett's fiction inhabits a secular world without didactic aims, and embodies the high-cultural conception of fiction as an autonomous sphere with a value in and of itself.

The structure of the passage is as follows:

Paragraph 1:	Provide an account of the similarities and differences between Jewett's fiction and the domestic novels of the mid-nineteenth century.
Paragraph 2:	Propose and reject several ways of explaining the differences between them, concluding that such differences ultimately reflect conflicting conceptions of fiction held by Jewett and the domestic novelists.
Paragraph 3:	Examine the meaning and implications of the high-cultural aesthetic and summarize the main argument of the passage.

Question #22: Global Reference, Must Be True. The correct answer choice is (D)

For this question, we need to consider which one of the following five questions can be answered using the information provided in the passage. Often the most efficient approach to this sort of question is to review the choices and quickly eliminate any Losers that cannot be answered using the information in the passage. Then examine the remaining Contenders more closely.

Answer choice (A): Just because the domestic novels focused primarily on women does not mean that women were also the only writers of such novels. Since the passage does not indicate whether any men wrote domestic novels in the 1850s, this is not a question that we can answer using the information given.

Answer choice (B): Even though the high-cultural aesthetic became the dominant conception of fiction later in the nineteenth century (lines 42-43), it is entirely plausible that some widely read domestic novels were still written after the 1860s. Since the author limited the scope of her discussion to the domestic novels of the 1850s, we cannot answer this question using the information provided.

Answer choice (C): This is a classic Shell Game answer. The rural youth's migration to the cities is cited as a possible explanation of the differences between Jewett's fiction and the domestic novels of the 1850s (line 23). However, it is unclear how (or whether) such migration affected the development of domestic fiction in the 1850s.

Answer choice (D): This is the correct answer choice. Because of her new conception of literary art as an autonomous sphere with value in and of itself, Jewett created a secular world that was devoid of didactic (or instructive) aims. The first two paragraphs provide sufficient information to help answer this question.

Answer choice (E): Hopefully you were able to eliminate this answer choice quickly, since the passage does not specify the region of the United States with which Jewett's writings were concerned.

Question #23: Specific Reference, Must Be True, Author's Perspective. The correct answer choice is (C)

This question asks us to identify the author's perspective in evaluating the criticism of Sarah Orne Jewett mentioned in line 1. The author initially concedes the point that Jewett's work resembles the domestic novels of the 1850s, but immediately follows that statement by saying that it also differs markedly from these antecedents (line 8). Therefore, we can infer that the author probably views the recent criticism as initially plausible but ultimately mistaken—a prephrase that agrees with answer choice (C).

Answer choice (A): Although the author initially concedes that Jewett's work resembles the domestic novels of the 1850s, the remainder of the first paragraph functions as a counterargument against that claim. Judging from the argument developed in the second and third paragraphs, the fundamental differences between Jewett and her predecessors outweigh any superficial similarity in subject matter (lines 51-54). To say that the author would view the critics' position as "essentially correct" is to miss entirely the main point of the passage.

Answer choice (B): We have no reason to suspect that the author would view the critics' claims as "true." On the contrary—the author rejects the critics' attempt to align Jewett with the domestic novelists of the 19th century, arguing that Jewett's work embodies a new conception of fiction.

Answer choice (C): This is the correct answer choice. The claim that Jewett's work resembles the domestic novels of the 19th century is indeed based on some reasonable evidence, such as the shared focus on women and their concerns. The author concedes that this evidence is initially plausible, but later argues that it supports a mistaken conclusion.

Answer choice (D): This is a classic half-right, half-wrong answer. The author would most likely view the recent criticism as "questionable," but not for the reasons cited here, which have no bearing on the argument at stake.

Answer choice (E): To say that the critics' claims are based on speculation for which there is no reasonable support is to ignore the discussion in lines 4-7. Clearly, the superficial similarity in subject matter does lend *some* support to the critics' position.

Question #24: Specific Reference, Must Be True, Author's Perspective. The correct answer choice is (B)

To properly understand the author's use of the term "continuum" in line 30, it is important to examine the context in which it appears. The information needed to answer Specific Reference questions often resides elsewhere in the passage, in a section that also touches on the issue in the Specific Reference.

In the second paragraph, the author argues that the domestic novel is based on a conception of fiction "as part of a continuum that also included writings devoted to piety and domestic instruction, bound together by a common goal of promoting domestic morality and religious belief" (lines 28-33). In other words, this conception of fiction blurs the lines between several literary genres in order to achieve a particular extraliterary objective. This prephrase agrees with answer choice (B), which is the correct answer choice.

Answer choice (A): Domestic fiction may indeed be part of an ongoing tradition; however, the goal of the second paragraph is not to examine such fiction from a historical or a temporal perspective.

Answer choice (B): This is the correct answer choice. The domestic novel is indistinguishable from other categories of writing, such as the child-rearing manual or the tract on Christian duty (lines 33-35). As such, it is based on a conception of fiction that does not treat fiction as clearly distinct from other categories of writing.

Answer choice (C): You should be able to eliminate this answer choice relatively quickly, since the passage contains no evidence suggesting that domestic novels were published in serial form.

Answer choice (D): Although the passage as a whole may indicate that conceptions of fiction are constantly evolving, the term "continuum" refers to a particular conception of fiction, not to its evolving nature.

Answer choice (E): Domestic fiction may have promoted societal morality and religious belief, but the cohesiveness and continuity of society are entirely unrelated to the author's use of the term "continuum" on line 30. If you found this answer choice attractive, you were probably misled by one of the dictionary definitions of the term "continuum." Remember—specific reference questions often test your contextual understanding of the term, not your knowledge of its dictionary definition(s).

Question #25: Global Reference, Must Be True, Purpose. The correct answer choice is (E)

Global Reference Purpose questions ask you to describe why the author wrote the passage, and the correct answer is often an abstract version of the main point. Think of it this way—a Main Point question is primarily concerned with a summary of *what* the author said; a Global Reference Purpose question wants to know *why* the author said it. A good prephrase is always important when answering such questions.

Answer choice (A): While the author proposes and defends a redefinition of Jewett's work, there is no reason to suspect that this redefinition would extend to entire categories of literary style. The author does not seek to redefine domestic fiction or the high-cultural aesthetic of the late 19th century.

Answer choice (B): Jewett may indeed be an example of the high-cultural aesthetic; however, the purpose of the passage is not merely to evaluate a new style of writing and give an example. Recall that the description of the high-cultural aesthetic in the third paragraph serves to support the argument regarding Jewett's work, not the other way around.

Answer choice (C): This answer choice may seem attractive, since the author does question the assumptions connecting Jewett to the domestic novelists of the 1850s. However, the primary function of the passage is not merely to question these assumptions, but to defend an alternative view that reclassifies Jewett's work.

Answer choice (D): Even though the author juxtaposes two different conceptions of the nature of fiction, her purpose is not to weigh their merits but rather to argue that a particular writer embodies a certain conception of fiction.

Answer choice (E): This is the correct answer choice. The primary purpose of the passage is to reject classifying Jewett's work as a domestic novel, and defend an alternative view arguing that it belongs to the high-cultural aesthetic of the late 19th and 20th centuries.

Question #26: Specific Reference, Must Be True, Organization. The correct answer choice is (E)

This question asks us to identify the structure of the second paragraph. In many ways, this question is similar to Method of Reasoning questions in the Logical Reasoning section, and you should attempt to "match" the answer choices to what you already know occurred in the second paragraph of the passage. Read closely—the incorrect answer choices often contain some elements that can be matched, but also contain new information for which there is no support in the passage.

Answer choice (A): This is a classic half-right, half-wrong answer choice. Although the second paragraph does consider several possible explanations for the differences between Jewett's work and the domestic novels, the author never suggested that any attempt at explanation would be impossible, or that it would do violence to the unity of a phenomenon.

Answer choice (B): This is another half-right, half-wrong answer choice. Indeed, the author provides reasons for preferring one explanatory hypothesis to another: the differences between Jewett and the domestic novelists of the 1850s are the result of a fundamentally different conception of fiction, not just the historical transformations described in lines 22-24. However, there is no evidence suggesting that these explanations are incompatible with each other. The author acknowledges that historical factors *may help to explain* the differences between Jewett and her predecessors (line 25), but proceeds to defend an alternative explanation seen as more fundamental.

Remember—Organization questions belong to the Must Be True family of questions, requiring you to provide textual evidence supporting each and every element in the correct answer.

Answer choice (C): This is an Opposite answer, since the explanatory hypotheses presented are clearly distinct from one another.

Answer choice (D): The third paragraph elaborates upon the argument presented in the second paragraph; it does not reject it.

Answer choice (E): This is the correct answer choice. The author mentions the historical transformations in lines 22-24, giving them a mildly favorable comment ("such factors may help to explain the differences" [lines 24-25]). The remainder of the second paragraph presents the differing conceptions of fiction held by Jewett and the domestic novelists as another, more fundamental explanation for the difference between their works.

Question #27: Concept Reference, Must Be True. The correct answer choice is (C)

For this question, we need to consider which of the following five questions can be answered by the differing conceptions of fiction held by Jewett and the domestic novelists. Recall that the author presents the differing conceptions of fiction as a way of explaining why Jewett's work does not feature children and religious themes as prominently as the domestic novels do. This is yet another question that tests your ability to understand the cause and effect relationship that underlies the author's main argument.

Answer choice (A): This answer choice may seem attractive, but we have no reason to suspect that Jewett was *unwilling* to feature children and religious themes in her works. She understood the nature and purpose of fiction differently from her predecessors, but there is no evidence that she made the conscious choice of not featuring the same topics as the domestic novelists. Our conceptions may guide our actions, but not necessarily in a conscious or deliberate way.

Answer choice (B): Hopefully you were able to eliminate this answer choice quickly, since there is no evidence suggesting that Jewett and the domestic novelists focused primarily on rural as opposed to urban concerns.

Answer choice (C): This is the correct answer choice. Since Jewett's conception of fiction was different from that of her predecessors, she was not constrained by the requirement that fiction be part of a continuum that included writings devoted to piety and domestic instruction. Consequently, she did not need to feature children and religion as prominently in her works as did the domestic novelists.

Answer choice (D): The passage provides no explanation as to why Jewett and the domestic novelists focused predominantly on women and their concerns.

Answer choice (E): This answer choice is similar to answer choice (A). Once again, we have no reason to believe that Jewett was *unable* to feature children or religion. Just because her conception of fiction was different does not mean that she suddenly lost the ability to feature the same topics as the domestic novelists.

CHAPTER FOUR: THE DECEMBER 2010 LSAT DECONSTRUCTED

The explanations below are presented in the same order that the questions are given on the exam. Please keep in mind that all explanations draw on methods discussed in *The PowerScore LSAT Logical Reasoning Bible*. Please refer to that text if you desire a more detailed discussion of a particular concept or approach. If you encounter any unknown terms, a glossary is provided at the end of the book.

LOGICAL REASONING I

DECEMBER 2010 SECTION 2: LOGICAL REASONING

Overview: This section is probably the less difficult of the two Logical Reasoning sections, but it does have its share of challenging questions. The ordering of the questions is somewhat distinctive; half of the section's six Strengthen questions are presented in sequence (#2, #3, and #4), and all four of this section's Flaw in the Reasoning questions are tightly distributed between question #5 and question #11. In standard LSAT form, the majority of the hardest questions appear in the second half of the section, including two particularly challenging examples of Conditional Reasoning in questions #15 and #17, and some potentially tricky Formal Logic in questions #19 and #21.

Question #1: Must Be True—Principle. The correct answer choice is (B)

In this stimulus the author discusses a study in which young children learned the word "stairs" as they walked up and down a flight of actual stairs. When they later saw a video of a ladder being used, the children also referred to the ladder, incorrectly, as stairs. It seems clear that the children misconstrued the new word as more generally referring to some means of travelling upwards and downwards.

There is no real conclusion drawn in this discussion; rather, the author provides a set of facts about the recent study. Given the lack of any conclusion, it is not surprising that the stimulus is followed by a Must Be True question stem—specifically, a question stem which asks for the principle illustrated by the study. The general idea seems to be that in some cases, children might learn a new word, and mistakenly use that word for something similar.

Answer choice (A): Although the study does deal with children who mistakenly apply a given word to the wrong object, this incorrect answer choice discusses children who repeatedly hear a word without seeing the object denoted. In the study discussed by the author, the children learned the word "stairs" *as they were using actual stairs*. Since the first part of this answer choice is completely inapplicable, this cannot be the principle illustrated.

Answer choice (B): The study discussed by the author does exemplify this method of teaching—the children did learn the word "stairs" by seeing them used. However, the author does not make the claim that this is the *best* way to learn words. In fact, this would be a rather questionable assertion considering the fact that after the learning in precisely this manner, they all used the word incorrectly.

Answer choice (C): The author provides no basis for this proposition. Only one study is discussed, with one group of young children, so there is no way to assess whether older or younger children would have learned better or worse.

Answer choice (D): This is the correct answer choice. The study clearly illustrates the principle that in some cases, children learn a given term through observation and mistakenly apply that term to a different object that is similarly used—the children learned about stairs as a means of ascending and descending; then the children mistakenly applied the term to a different means of comparable movement.

Answer choice (E): The problem in the study was not that other objects were *simultaneously* present. Rather, the children learned "stairs" as referring to something one climbs in order to go up and down, and later mistakenly applied the word to a different means of achieving the same results of ascension and descension.

Question #2: Strengthen, CE. The correct answer choice is (E)

Here we are told of a correlation between people who live past the age of 100 and those who have led lives that we would generally consider to be unhealthy—drinking, smoking, eating poorly and doing little exercise. Based on the fact that such behavior often leads to shorter lives, the author concludes that those who have enjoyed long lives, despite unhealthy habits, probably have some kind of genetic predisposition to living longer:

Premise:	A large portion of people who live to be 100 or more are known to have led unhealthy lives: drinking, smoking, eating poorly, and getting little exercise.
Premise:	Such unhealthy behavior often leads to a shortened lifespan.
Conclusion:	Those who live for exceptionally long periods must have been genetically predisposed to having longer lifespan.

The argument presented here is a causal one. The effect being considered is that of living past the age of 100. The author believes that the cause must not be lifestyle, because a large proportion of those with such long life spans have lifestyles that are known to be associated with shorter lives. Instead, the author asserts that the likely cause is a genetic predisposition to a longer lifespan:

<u>Cause</u>		<u>Effect</u>
Genes	⟶	Long lifespan

The question stem requires that we find the answer choice that strengthens the author's causal assertion that those who live past 100, despite unhealthy lifestyle choices, probably have their genes to thank for their long lives. The correct answer choice will probably either directly strengthen the argument for a causal link between genetic makeup and long life, or perhaps rule out other possible causes of the 100+ year lifespans of the people discussed.

Answer choice (A): This answer choice may provide some insight as to how one could eat fatty foods and drink alcohol without suffering the detriment one might expect; while it may help to explain how some individuals with such habits could still enjoy long lives, however, this choice does not strengthen the link between genetics and long life.

Answer choice (B): First of all, the word "some" is quite vague—it could refer to one or more of the individuals referenced in the stimulus. Further, the people described in this answer choice are not members of the same group discussed in the stimulus. The author of the stimulus discusses those engaged in drinking, smoking, eating poorly and getting little exercise. The fact that some people with long lives do only some of these bad things does not strengthen the argument that genetics likely plays a role in cases where people are long-lived despite very unhealthy lifestyles.

Answer choice (C): This answer choice is much like answer choice (B). The stimulus deals with people who live long despite drinking, smoking, eating poorly and not exercising, whereas this choice deals with a different population—the one or more people who make some good lifestyle choices and some bad ones. In any case, this choice does not strengthen the case for genetics playing a role, as asserted by the author.

Answer choice (D): This choice deals with a population that is completely irrelevant to the subject matter of the stimulus. We would probably expect that there would be cases of unhealthy people dying before the age of 100, but this does not strengthen the author's assertion that those with poor lifestyles, but long lives, probably enjoy some genetic predisposition to longevity.

Answer choice (E): This is the correct answer choice, as it bolsters the argument that the long lives are attributable to genetics: if the individuals discussed all had siblings who had similarly long lifespans, then this would certainly strengthen the case for genetics' having played some significant role in their longevity.

Question #3: Strengthen. The correct answer choice is (B)

This stimulus opens with information about medications that have an unpleasant taste, which can be produced in the form of tablets, capsules, or soft-gels. The author points out that medication M has a low tolerance for heat and thus cannot be made into tablet form. Further, the company that manufactures medication M produces all of its own medications and is not technologically capable of making soft-gels. Based on these premises, the author concludes that medication M will most likely be produced in capsule form. The argument can be broken down simply as follows:

Premise:	Medications with an unpleasant taste are generally produced only as tablets, capsules, or soft-gels.
Premise:	Medication M cannot be made into tablet form because of its low melting point.
Premise:	The company developing medication M does all of its own manufacturing, and it does not have the capability to manufacture soft-gels.
Conclusion:	M will most likely be produced in capsule form.

Overall this appears to be a nicely structured argument: the author lays out three possible forms of unpleasant tasting medication, rules out two possibilities, and concludes that the third will thus be the most likely form. The problem, however, is that the three possible forms of medication refer *only* to those with an unpleasant taste. Although the medicine is referred to as "waxy," the author never claims that M has an unpleasant taste; establishing that M tastes bad would certainly strengthen the author's reasoning. In the alternative, establishing that medication M has the same possible forms as unpleasant tasting medications would bolster the author's argument as well.

Answer choice (A): This is an Opposite answer. Because the author never establishes that medicine M has an unpleasant taste, providing another option for the form of medication M actually weakens the author's conclusion that the medication will most likely be produced in capsule form.

Answer choice (B): This is the correct answer choice, and the one which restates the prephrased answer discussed above. If medication M has an unpleasant taste, then this would certainly strengthen the author's conclusion that if neither tablet nor soft-gel forms of the medicine could be produced, the medicine would likely then take capsule form.

Answer choice (C): Since it looks as though medication M will not be produced in soft-gel form, this choice does not strengthen the author's conclusion that the medicine will likely be produced as a capsule.

Answer choice (D): Medication M does have a low melting point, but since the author has established that it will not be produced in soft-gel form, this choice is irrelevant to the question, and does not strengthen the assertion that capsule form will be the most likely for medication M.

Answer choice (E): The stimulus provides no information regarding the level of unpleasantness in the tastes of various forms of medication. Since this answer choice makes it no more likely that medication M will be produced as a capsule, it cannot be the correct answer to this Strengthen question.

Question #4: Strengthen. The correct answer choice is (E)

Here we are told of the aspirations of Carol Morris, who wishes to become the majority shareholder of the city's biggest paper, The Daily. Azedcorp, the current majority shareholder, is the only thing standing in the way of Morris' goal, and has thus far refused to sell. Despite these facts, however, industry analysts predict that Morris will soon achieve the goal of becoming majority shareholder.

The stimulus is followed by a Strengthen question, so the correct answer choice will help the analysts' prediction that Carol Morris' goal will soon be achieved. The right answer will likely either explain why analysts believe that Azedcorp will soon be selling shares, or provide some other explanation as to how Morris would be able to amass enough shares to become the majority shareholder.

Answer choice (A): The other holdings in Azedcorp's portfolio are irrelevant to the analysts' prediction; this choice does not lend any strength to the assertion that Morris will soon be majority shareholder, so this choice can be quickly eliminated.

Answer choice (B): This choice does not strengthen the assertion that Morris will soon be able to purchase sufficient shares to become majority shareholder. If anything, this choice would weaken the analysts' assertion, because if Azedcorp has turned down such an appealing offer, this really speaks to the notion that Azedcorp does is not interested in selling its shares to Morris.

Answer choice (C): Since Azedcorp has steadfastly refused to sell its shares in the past, the fact that there are no other interested buyers is irrelevant to the question. This choice does not strengthen the prediction that Morris will soon be majority shareholder, so it cannot be the correct answer choice to this Strengthen question stem.

Answer choice (D): The author of the stimulus established the fact that Morris is a significant shareholder in The Daily, and that Azedcorp is the only thing standing in the way of Morris' becoming majority shareholder. So this choice, which provides that Morris is currently the second largest shareholder, does not strengthen the prediction that Morris will soon be the majority shareholder.

Answer choice (E): This is the correct answer choice, and the one which significantly strengthens the analysts' argument that Morris will soon be majority shareholder. If Azedcorp is on the brink of bankruptcy, and will soon be forced to part with its newspaper holdings, then this would allow Morris to purchase the Azedcorp shares that she has thus far been unable to buy. This choice explains how, despite Azedcorp's steadfast refusals in the past, they will soon be forced to concede, allowing Morris to purchase their shares.

Question #5: Flaw in the Reasoning, CE. The correct answer choice is (C)

In this stimulus, the area resident begins by pointing out the successful reduction in child lead poisoning that has taken place since the early 1970s. When the country stopped using leaded gas and banned lead paint, lead poisoning dropped, but apparently there are still lead paint hazards in 25% of local homes. The area resident then jumps to the conclusion that getting rid of the lead paint in those homes would completely eradicate the entire lead poisoning problem:

Premise:	Since the 1970s, when lead was eliminated from both gasoline and paint, cases of childhood lead poisoning have declined steadily.
Premise:	According to recent statistics, 25% of the homes in this area still have lead paint which is hazardous.
Conclusion:	If we eliminate lead paint from the homes mentioned, then childhood lead poisoning will finally be completely eradicated.

The stimulus is followed by a Flaw question, the answer to which should certainly be prephrased: the problem with the argument in the stimulus is that the area resident presumes that taking care of the lead paint problem will solve the more general problem of lead poisoning.

Answer choice (A): There is no basis for the claim presented in this answer choice; the stimulus does not provide any reason to presume that the referenced statistics are probably unreliable.

Answer choice (B): This incorrect answer choice describes the logical flaw of circular reasoning: when a premise and its conclusion are logically equivalent, nothing has been proven. This, however, is not the problem in this case. Instead, the resident's mistake is in assuming that eradicating lead paint will eradicate all hazardous lead.

Answer choice (C): This is the correct answer choice. The area resident doesn't seem to realize that lead might exist in hazards other than paint—although the stimulus mentions only gas and paint, there is no suggestion that these are the only two sources.

Answer choice (D): The author does not take this for granted. Rather, the resident's claim is based on a condition: "if we eliminate lead paint…" There is no discussion of economic viability.

Answer choice (E): The area resident does not presume that every lead paint-hazardous home is inhabited by a child, but rather that getting rid of all lead paint will eliminate the whole problem.

Question #6: Must Be True. The correct answer choice is (A)

The author of this stimulus begins by introducing the fact that soft drinks do not list their exact caffeine content on their labels. If the exact caffeine content were listed, this would make it easier for people to limit their caffeine intake without cutting it out altogether. If this were possible, then many people would start to limit their caffeine intake, and would improve their health as a result.

The stimulus is followed by a Must Be True question, so the correct answer choice must pass the Fact Test: The correct answer will be the one confirmed by the facts presented in the stimulus.

Answer choice (A): This is the correct answer choice. The stimulus points out that many would derive health benefits from the ability to limit their caffeine intake without eliminating it entirely. Since this could be accomplished by listing exact caffeine content on soda labels, it must be true that at least some people would enjoy health benefits as a result.

Answer choice (B): The stimulus only points out that listing sodas' exact caffeine content would make it easier to limit caffeine intake. This does not mean that limiting caffeine intake would be impossible without such listings, or that anyone will be unable to do so. Perhaps doing so without label listings would merely be more difficult.

Answer choice (C): The stimulus does not discuss people who want to eliminate their caffeine intake entirely, and this group would not have to guess at the exact caffeine content regardless: anyone looking to eliminate caffeine entirely would avoid all soft drinks with *any* caffeine.

Answer choice (D): The stimulus is mostly concerned with those who wish to moderate rather than eliminate. Those who wish to completely eliminate caffeine from their diets would not benefit from knowing the *exact* caffeine content—they would only need to know if there was any caffeine content at all.

Answer choice (E): There is no suggestion in the stimulus that any detrimental effects would come from providing such listings. So, although we can safely say that at least some people would benefit from listing exact caffeine content, we cannot presume that anyone would suffer as a result. Since this choice fails the Fact Test, it cannot be the correct answer.

Question #7: Parallel Flaw. The correct answer choice is (C)

Here we are presented with a discussion about Vidmar, whose individual private collection was among the most valuable ever assembled. After Vidmar died, and her collection was to be auctioned off, "art lover MacNeil" believed that it would be impossible to afford any of the works in Vidmar's collection:

Premise: Vidmar's is among the most valuable art collections ever assembled by a single individual.

Conclusion: Thus, claims MacNeil, MacNeil cannot possibly afford any of the works being auctioned.

But is this valid? The problem with this conclusion is in MacNeil's presumption that what is true of the whole is also true of each component—just because the collection as a whole is one of the most expensive in existence, that does not mean that every single work in the collection is priceless. This is a classic Error of Division—the flawed presumption that what is true of the whole must be true of each part. Vidmar might have had varied tastes, and may have had many inexpensive works in her collection. Hypothetically, the collection could even have been comprised exclusively of inexpensive works (even if each painting in a collection were valued at only $50, a collection of a million such paintings would still be worth $50 million).

The stimulus is followed by a Parallel Flaw question, so the correct answer choice will reflect the mistaken presumption that what is true of a whole is also true of each of its parts.

Answer choice (A): In a sense this is the reverse of what we're looking for. In this choice, the author considers an attribute of each component (that is, each word), and draws a conclusion about the whole (the entire book). This is an Error of Composition, which does not provide a parallel flaw. In the stimulus, the premise was an attribute of the whole, and the conclusion wrongly presumed each part to share that attribute.

Answer choice (B): If the vote was unanimous, it would seem that councilperson Martinez was indeed among those who voted to adopt the plan. This is actually a scenario in which (if everyone on the council voted) it would actually be valid to presume that what is true of the whole is also true of the sum of the parts; if the vote was unanimous, then it would be valid to conclude that everyone who voted had voted in favor of the decision. Since this reasoning is not necessarily flawed, it cannot provide the parallel flawed reasoning in this case.

Answer choice (C): This is the correct answer choice, as it is the one that reflects the mistaken notion that what is true of a whole is therefore also true of each of its component parts. In the same way that it was incorrect to presume that every work in an expensive collection must itself be expensive, it is also wrong to conclude that every sentence in a long paragraph must itself be long.

Answer choice (D): This answer choice is similar to answer choice (A) in that it references an Error of Composition, not Division. While it is invalid to conclude that a company is old based on a number of old employees, the flawed reasoning reflected in the stimulus is different from that reflected in this answer choice. Again, the flaw that would parallel that of the stimulus must involve the presumption that what is true of the whole is also true of each constituent part.

Answer choice (E): The reasoning in this answer choice is the mistaken presumption that if it is true of the parts, it must also be true of the whole (again, another Error of Composition). Although this reasoning is flawed, it does not parallel that of the stimulus, which asserts that if it is true of the whole, it must also be true of each part.

Question #8: Flaw in the Reasoning. The correct answer choice is (A)

This stimulus takes a very familiar LSAT form: it begins with an assertion, concludes that the assertion is not valid, and then provides support for this conclusion (although in this case that support is questionable). In this example, the author opens with the contention of a leading critic of space exploration, who claims that it would be wrong to send a manned expedition to Mars, because current technology would make their survival unlikely.

The author asserts that this characterization is an exaggeration of the risk, because back-up security systems exist at every stage, each making a fatal accident unlikely at any given stage of the trip:

Claim:	With current technology, those who try to go to Mars are unlikely to survive the trip.
Author's conclusion:	This is an exaggeration.
Author's premise:	With back-up systems in place, a fatal accident is unlike at any given stage.

The problem with this argument is known as an Error of Composition: the flawed presumption that what is true of each part is also true of the whole—that if each individual stage of the trip is safe, then the overall trip must be safe as well.

The stimulus is followed by a Flaw question, so the correct answer choice will describe the flawed presumption that what is true of each part must also be true of the whole.

Note: It is probably no coincidence that this question, which displays an Error of Composition, is placed immediately after another question dealing with the related but distinguishable Error of Division.

Answer choice (A): This is the correct answer choice, and an accurate description of the Error of Composition displayed in the reasoning of the stimulus. The author wrongly infers that something (crew safety) is true of a whole (the entire trip to Mars) merely from the fact that it is true of each individual part (each stage of the trip).

Answer choice (B): The author of this stimulus does not infer that something cannot happen, but that something (a fatal catastrophe) would be quite unlikely. Since there is no such inference, this choice cannot reflect the flawed reasoning found in the stimulus.

Answer choice (C): Much like wrong answer choice (B), this incorrect answer describes an unjustified leap from probability to certainty. The author of the stimulus, however, does not make this leap to certainty; the assertion is merely that a fatal accident is unlikely.

Answer choice (D): The author does not infer that anything will definitely work. Rather, the author discusses backup safety measures that make an accident unlikely at any given stage of the trip discussed. Since the stimulus deals with likelihood rather than certainty, this cannot be the correct answer choice.

Answer choice (E): The author does not reject the critic's concern based on the critic's inadequate argument. Rather, the author rejects the concern based on the safety measures in place at each stage of the trip (and the flawed conclusion that an accident is unlikely to occur at *any* given stage of the trip).

Question #9: Justify the Conclusion, CE. The correct answer choice is (C)

Retrospective studies are those which seek to link a participant's past experiences (from before the beginning of such a study) with his or her present characteristics, looking for connections to show the causes that led to current attributes. Based on the fact that these studies rely on participants to report on their own past experiences, however, the author of this stimulus concludes that such studies cannot reliably determine the causes of present characteristics:

Premise: Retrospective studies rely on subjects to report on past experiences

Conclusion: Retrospective studies can't reliably determine causes of present characteristics

The author clearly believes that studies that rely on people to report their past experiences cannot provide reliable information regarding the past causes of participants' present characteristics.

The question stem that follows the stimulus is one that is often mistaken for an Assumption question, because it asks for the assumption that will enable the author's conclusion to be properly drawn. What this really means, though, is that the correct answer choice will Justify the author's Conclusion.

Applying the Justify Formula, we can pinpoint the rogue elements that must be linked for the conclusion to be properly drawn: The right answer will likely provide that studies which rely on subjects to report on their past experiences cannot reliably determine the causes of participants' present characteristics.

Answer choice (A): This answer choice might look quite enticing at first, because it opens with a discussion of reliable determination of a cause. However, this choice is not applicable because it deals with inaccurate reports. The author does not assert that such reports (which are self-reported by subjects) are necessarily *inaccurate*, but rather that they are *unreliable* (a subtle but important distinction: if, based on a coin flip, someone claims that tomorrow will be rainy, I would probably take issue with the reliability of such a method, even if it does actually rain the following day).

Answer choice (B): This confusingly worded and incorrect answer choice basically says that the causes of present characteristics cannot be determined unless such characteristics correlate with past experiences. This choice fails to link the element of self-reporting with the element of unreliability, so it cannot be the correct answer choice to this Justify the Conclusion question.

Answer choice (C): This is the correct answer choice, and the one which links the prephrased element of self reporting with that of lacking reliability. If, as this answer choice provides, self-reported information is likely to be inaccurate, this justifies the author's conclusion that retrospective studies (which use such self-reported information) cannot reliably determine the causes of present attributes.

Answer choice (D): In the stimulus the author asserts that self-reported experiences are of questionable reliability, rendering retrospective studies unreliable as well:

Self-reported info ⟶ can NOT reliably determine past causes of present attributes

This incorrect answer choice presents something similar to a Mistaken Negation of that statement:

Accurate info ⟶ can reliably determine past causes of present attributes

The author of the stimulus asserts that retrospective studies, based on self-reported information, cannot reliably determine past causes of present characteristics. This is certainly not the same as asserting that accurate information will *guarantee* reliable causal determinations.

Answer choice (E): The stimulus deals only with retrospective studies, and the author has already established that such studies must rely on subjects' reports of past experiences in determining the causes of current attributes, so this choice does provide the link we seek between self-reported information and a lack of reliability of that information.

Question #10: Main Point. The correct answer choice is (B)

Despite the fact that enormous passenger planes under development will have sufficient room to contain shops and lounges for the passengers, the author of this stimulus asserts that this extra room will more likely be used for extra passenger space. The author bases this conclusion on the premise that since passenger numbers are expected to triple over the next two decades, airports will be unable to accommodate so many passengers in existing, standard sized jets.

The question that follows asks for the main conclusion of the argument. This stimulus took a fairly standard form: background information (new passenger planes will have more room), followed by the author's conclusion (that this extra space will more likely be used to fly more passengers), which is then followed by the supporting premises.

In this case, the author's conclusion that extra space will probably be used for more seats rather than for lounges, etc., is based on two premises which are introduced immediately after the conclusion. First, the number of air passengers is expected to double over the next two decades, and second, airports cannot meet the needs of that many passengers using normal-sized jets. Reorganized in a more intuitive order, the argument breaks down as follows:

Premise:	The number of air travelers is expected to double over the next 20 years.
Premise:	Airports will not be able to accommodate that many passengers using standard-sized jet planes.
Conclusion:	The extra space that will be available in the gigantic planes under development is more likely to be used for extra passenger seating than for shops and lounges.

Since the stimulus is followed by a Main Point question stem, the conclusion discussed above provides a pre-phrased answer.

Answer choice (A): Although this statement is accurate, it does not represent the conclusion of the author's argument, as discussed above.

Answer choice (B): This is the correct answer choice, which basically restates the prephrased conclusion above.

Answer choice (C): This is one of the two premises on which the author bases the conclusion, which is that the extra room that will be available on future passenger planes is more likely to be used for additional seating than for shops and lounges.

Answer choice (D): Like incorrect answer choice (C), this choice provides one of the premises provided in support of the author's conclusion. Since this choice does not reflect the author's conclusion, it cannot be the right answer choice.

Answer choice (E): Not only does this answer choice fail to reflect the prephrased conclusion above, it doesn't even pass the Fact Test. Since the author does not make any reference to whether or not the majority of passengers will be flying in gigantic planes, this choice is not confirmed by the information provided in the passage, and it certainly cannot reflect the main point of the argument.

Question #11: Flaw in the Reasoning, SN. The correct answer choice is (A)

The scientist begins this dialogue by describing a study of experimental medications involving two groups of people with athlete's foot. One of the groups of athlete's foot sufferers was given only medication M, and the other was given only medication N. The only people to be cured had been given medication M. In other words, if any given study participant was cured, that person was on medication M. This conditional statement can be diagrammed as follows:

Cured ⟶ On medication M

The reporter responds with a statement that indicates that he has made an inaccurate assessment of the scientist's statement. The reporter's invalid conclusion is that anyone who was not cured was not on medication M. This is actually a Mistaken Negation of the scientist's statement, which can be diagrammed as follows:

Mistaken Negation: ~~Cured~~ ⟶ On ~~medication~~ M

This is not a valid conclusion because all we know from the scientist's statements is that anyone who *was* cured was on medication M. This could mean that just one person was cured from a large group of participants that had been on medication M. So it is not valid to conclude, as the reporter does, that everyone on M had been cured.

Thus, we know the flaw in the reasoning of the reporter is conditional in nature, and in seeking the correct answer choice, we need an answer that describes the conditional error (preferably using conditional terms such as "necessary" or "sufficient," although that is not a requirement).

Answer choice (A): This is the correct answer choice. The reporter considers the premise that M *can* possibly cure athlete's foot (perhaps even in just one person), and incorrectly concludes that M always cures athlete's foot. This answer is tricky because it actually describes the contrapositive of the Mistaken Negation above:

Contrapositive of Mistaken Negation: On medication M ⟶ Cured
(a.k.a. the Mistaken Reversal)

The contrapositive of a Mistaken Negation is the Mistaken Reversal of the original statement (remember, the Mistaken Negation and the Mistaken Reversal of the same original statement are contrapositives of each other). Thus, because this answer choice describes a relationship that is functionally identical to error in the reporter's statement, it is correct.

Answer choice (B): The reporter's error is not in drawing invalidly broad conclusions based on a small sample, but rather in misunderstanding the conditional statement provided by the scientist.

Answer choice (C): The reporter's statement only concerns people involved in the study, reflecting no mistaken presumptions about those who were not involved in the study.

Answer choice (D): The reporter's response deals only with study participants, so there is no reason to consider the circumstances of those who may be cured without either of the two medications studied.

Answer choice (E): This potentially confusing incorrect answer choice provides a fairly convoluted conditional point—that the reporter wrongly presumes that there are not many people who can be cured only by *avoiding* medication M. But the reporter's actual conclusion regards those who took medication M, and the reporter's mistake is in presuming that all of those participants were cured.

Question #12: Assumption. The correct answer choice is (E)

This paleontologist's discussion surrounds "plesiosauromorphs." Hopefully you didn't bother pronouncing that one—as long as you can just recognize the word refers to a large animal from the dinosaur era, your energy and focus are probably better spent elsewhere. Most believe that these big reptiles (we'll refer to them as "plesi-reptiles") hunted by hiding and ambushing their prey, but this author believes that they probably hunted their prey by long-distance chase. This conclusion is based on a single premise, presented in the final sentence of the stimulus: these plesi-reptiles had long, thin fins, much like the wings of birds that are specialized for long flight. This simple argument can be diagrammed as follows:

> Premise: Plesi-reptiles had fins that resembled long distance birds' wings.
>
> Conclusion: Plesi-reptiles must have hunted by chasing their prey over long distances.

The paleontologist's conclusion presumes that these plesi-reptiles must have used their fins in the same way that birds use their similarly shaped wings—for the purpose of long distance travel, and that this was a strategy they used for hunting.

The stimulus is followed by an Assumption question, so the correct answer choice will probably reflect one of the Supporter assumptions discussed above.

Answer choice (A): The argument does not depend on the assumption that birds and reptiles share many common features, but rather that one common feature affects the two in a similar fashion.

To confirm that this answer choice is incorrect, we can apply the Assumption Negation technique, knowing that the right answer choice, when logically negated, will weaken the author's argument. The negated form of this answer choice would be something like "Birds and reptiles don't share many physical features based on common ancestry." This would not weaken the author's argument, which deals with only one common physical feature of birds and reptiles—the wings and fins, respectively.

Note that you do not need to negate every answer choice, but we shall do so in the analysis of each answer choice in order to explain each answer as fully as possible.

Answer choice (B): This stimulus deals exclusively with this one type of reptile, so there is no need for the author to presume that it was the only reptile of the time that had long, thin fins. Negating this choice yields the following:

> During the age of dinosaurs, plesiosauromorphs were NOT the only marine reptiles that had long, thin fins.

Even if there were many other such reptiles at the time, this would not weaken the author's conclusion, so this cannot be the correct answer choice.

Answer choice (C): This choice basically says that something the size of the plesi-reptile could *only* have survived by hunting over long distances. This assumption is not required by the paleontologist's conclusion. If this stimulus had instead been followed by a Justify the Conclusion question stem, this choice would have worked, since it would justify the author's conclusion that the reptile probably hunted prey over long distances. However, since this assumption is not required by the argument, it is not the right answer to this Assumption question.

To confirm that this is not the correct answer choice, we can again apply the Assumption Negation technique. Even if there had been other ways for the plesi-reptile to survive, this would not hurt the author's conclusion, which is based not on the animal's needs but on a feature similar to one of long distance flight birds.

Answer choice (D): The author's argument does not require presuming anything about "most marine animals that chase prey over long distances," because this is not the basis of the author's conclusion. To confirm that this is not the correct answer choice, we can again apply the Assumption Negation technique: even if most long-distance-prey-chasing marine animals are not specialized for long distance swimming, this would not weaken the paleontologist's argument, which deals only with one particular reptile.

Answer choice (E): This is the correct answer choice. Since the conclusion is based on the similarity between the plesi-reptile's fins and long distance birds' wings, the paleontologist must assume that there is some significant similarity between their uses.

Again, since this is an Assumption question, the correct answer can always be confirmed with the Assumption Negation technique: the right answer choice will provide an assumption which, when negated, weakens the conclusion in the stimulus. If we logically negate answer choice (E), the result is, "the shape of a marine animal's fin does not affect the way the animal swims in the same way that the shape of a bird's wing affects the way a bird flies." This would defeat the paleontologist's argument, which is based on the presuming that this similarity exists.

Question #13: Parallel—Principle. The correct answer choice is (D)

This stimulus deals with the issue of elaborate screensavers, and the pros and cons that might come with purchase. The benefit of such programs, which produce moving images onto a monitor in order to prevent long term screen damage, is sometimes outweighed by the detriment, as employees are often mesmerized by these incredible screensavers when they could be spending their time more productively:

Premise: Employees cannot resist spending time looking at screensavers

Conclusion: The purchase of elaborate screensavers can end up costing more in time than it saves in energy efficiency and monitor damage control.

The stimulus is followed by a Parallel—Principle question, so the correct answer choice will contain a scenario that reflects the same principle that is at work in the stimulus: Sometimes the benefits of safety or efficiency measures can be outweighed by the detriments associated with those well-intended precautionary actions.

Answer choice (A): The stimulus regards investments in precaution, and how such purchases may result in a net loss, but does not deal with user preferences or getting the most economical package. This choice has nothing to do with precautionary measures, so it is not the choice that most closely conforms to the principle in the stimulus.

Answer choice (B): This choice starts out in the right direction, as an energy efficient insulation system is something of a precautionary investment. But this choice has a happy outcome—long term savings—whereas the principle in the stimulus deals with situations where the burden may outweigh the benefit.

Answer choice (C): The stimulus deals with situations in which an investment is made in the interest of precaution but may end up having greater cost than benefit. This choice reflects no such principle, so it cannot be the right answer to this Parallel—Principle question.

Answer choice (D): This is the correct answer choice, as it perfectly reflects the principle in the stimulus. A complicated hotel security system is purchased as a precaution against theft, but these benefits might be outweighed by the detriments that come with it—namely, the loss of customer goodwill.

Answer choice (E): Unlike the stimulus, this answer deals with the choice between two different products, where one is less expensive to purchase but more expensive to repair. This is different from the stimulus, which is that an investment in prevention can sometimes end up having greater cost than benefit.

Question #14: Method of Reasoning. The correct answer choice is (B)

In this two-speaker stimulus, the music professor puts forth a fairly straightforward argument, presenting two supporting premises followed by a conclusion about rap as a musical form. First, rap musicians can work alone in a studio, without having to keep any other musicians happy. Second, learning rap is a fairly informal process when compared to the process of learning an instrument. Based on these two premises, the music professor concludes that rap is a non-traditional and very individualistic form of music. The argument can be broken down simply as follows:

Premise: Rap musicians can work alone in a studio, without the need to collaborate with other musicians.

Premise: Learning to rap is a relatively informal process.

Conclusion: Thus, rap is both individualistic and nontraditional.

The music critic's response begins with the word "but," and proceeds to take issue with both of the music professor's supporting premises. First, on the topic of whether rap is nontraditional: rap samples small pieces of older songs, thus appealing to tradition, and regardless, rap has developed its own musical tradition in terms of theme and style. Second, in response to the issue of rap as an extremely individualistic musical form, the critic points out that if a rap musician wishes to be successful, his or her style must conform to the preferences of the public to some extent. The critic's response can be broken down simply as follows:

Refuting the professor's first premise with a new premise: Rap does have its own tradition, and also appeals to tradition by sampling bits of older songs.

Refuting the professor's second premise with another new premise: Even though learning to rap might be an informal process, rappers are not completely idiosyncratic—rather, successful rappers must conform their styles to public preference.

By refuting both of the music professor's supporting premises, the critic effectively undermines the professor's conclusion about rap being both non-traditional and extremely individualistic.

The dialogue in the stimulus is followed by a Method of Reasoning question, so the correct answer choice will accurately describe the music critic's response. As a possible prephrase of this answer, we might note that the critic responds by providing two new premises in order to undermine the professor's conclusion about rap.

Answer choice (A): This might have been a tempting answer choice, especially placed first, but this choice is not entirely accurate. The music critic challenges the professor's argument by refuting both of the professor's premises with new considerations (as opposed to presenting evidence to disprove one of the professor's premises).

Answer choice (B): This is the correct answer choice, and the one which restates the answer prephrased above. The critic's response to the professor's argument is to point to two new premises in order to refute the professor's supporting premises and undermine the professor's conclusion.

Answer choice (C): Both the professor and the critic discuss rap music in particular. The professor does not generalize to a broader context, but rather confines his or her claims to the topic of rap as a musical form.

Answer choice (D): The critic does not provide an alternative explanation of a given phenomenon. Rather, the critic points to two new premises which conflict with the professor's stated opinion.

Answer choice (E): The statements made by the music professor are not broad claims about tradition and individuality in music—they deal with rap music specifically, in support of the professor's conclusion that rap is both extremely individualistic and nontraditional.

Question #15: Justify the Conclusion, SN. The correct answer choice is (B)

In this challenging stimulus, the speaker opens by recounting Smith's argument: the true meaning of an author's statements can *only* be understood through insight into the social circumstances of the author. This conditional statement, that full understanding *requires* such insight, dictates that in this case the sufficient condition is "full understanding of an author's true meaning," and the necessary condition is "insight into the author's social circumstances." This conditional relationship is diagrammed below, followed by the statement's contrapositive:

Statement: Understand author's true meaning ⟶ Insight into author's social circumstance

Contrapositive: Insight into ~~author's~~ circumstance ⟶ Can understand ~~author's~~ true meaning

The speaker then jumps to the conclusion that if we have insight into Smith's circumstances, then we should, to some extent, understand the true meaning of Smith's words
(Insight into Smith's social circumstance ⟶ understand true meaning of Smith's words).

In the final sentence, the speaker asserts this all points to the conclusion that Smith herself is not aware of the true meaning of Smith's own words. Putting this together with the contrapositive diagrammed above, we can arrive at the following:

Premise: Insight into ~~author's~~ circumstance ⟶ Can understand ~~author's~~ true meaning

Conclusion: Smith ⟶ Can understand ~~author's~~ (her) true meaning

Because this is a Justify question, we can solve this question mechanistically by examining the "rogue" elements in the argument. As is clear from the two diagrams above, the rogue elements that must be linked to justify the speaker's conclusion are "Smith" and "no insight into author's circumstance." In other words, the speaker must be presuming that Smith has no insight into Smith's social circumstances.

Answer choice (A): The speaker does not discuss the subject of understanding the author's intended meaning, only the true meaning of the author's words, which require insight into the author's social circumstances. Since the intended meaning does is not a part of the stimulus, it cannot be one of the rogue elements that we need to link, and this answer choice cannot be correct.

Answer choice (B): This is the correct answer choice, and the one that is prephrased in the discussion above. If Smith lacks insight into her own social circumstance, then the speaker is justified in the conclusion that Smith cannot truly understand the meaning of her own words.

Answer choice (C): Even if it is Smith's intent for her work to have only one meaning, this would not justify the speaker's conclusion that Smith herself is not aware of the true meaning of her own words. Since this choice fails to justify the speaker's conclusion, this cannot the correct answer choice.

Answer choice (D): The speaker does not criticize Smith's *theory* as lacking insight, but instead criticizes Smith herself as such. This statement would not justify the speaker's conclusion that Smith is unaware of her own words—in fact, this answer choice would weaken the speaker's conclusion, which is based on Smith's theory.

Answer choice (E): The author's intent is not discussed by the speaker, nor is the question of whether such evidence can tell us the true meaning of the work. In any case, this answer choice does not align with the prephrased answer in the discussion above, nor does it justify the speaker's conclusion regarding Smith's lack of awareness of the true meaning of her own words.

Question #16: Strengthen, CE. The correct answer choice is (E)

Among patients who have undergone throat surgery, frequent snorers were much more likely to have significant abnormalities in their throat muscles than those who snored rarely, or not at all. The author concludes based on this premise that snoring can damage one's throat:

Premise: Based on biopsies of patients who have undergone throat surgery, those who snore frequently are much more likely to have abnormalities in their throat muscles than those who snore rarely or not at all.

Conclusion: Snoring can cause damage to the throat of the snorer.

The problem with this conclusion, much like the problem with many flawed causal arguments, is that the evidence provided speaks only to a correlation. That is, if we were to look at the population with abnormalities in their throat muscles, and we were to look at the population that snores heavily, we would see some significant overlap—there would be many people with both throat muscle abnormalities and heavy snoring habits. This does not necessarily mean, of course, that a *causal* relationship actually exists.

Although this conclusion is flawed, in this case the stimulus is followed by a Strengthen question. There are several ways that we could strengthen such a causal claim (as covered in the *PowerScore LSAT Logical Reasoning Bible*):

A. Eliminate any alternate causes for the stated effect

Because the author believes there is only one cause (the stated cause in the argument), eliminating one or more of the other possible causes strengthens the conclusion.

B. Show that when the cause occurs, the effect occurs

Because the author believes that the cause always produces the effect, any scenario where the cause occurs and the effect follows lends credibility to the conclusion. This type of answer can appear in the form of an example.

C. Show that when the cause does not occur, the effect does not occur

Using the reasoning in the previous point, any scenario where the cause does not occur and the effect does not occur supports the conclusion. This type of answer also can appear in the form of an example.

D. Eliminate the possibility that the stated relationship is reversed

Because the author believes that the cause and effect relationship is correctly stated, eliminating the possibility that the relationship is backwards (the claimed effect is actually the cause of the claimed cause) strengthens the conclusion.

E. Show that the data used to make the causal statement are accurate, or eliminate possible problems with the data

   If the data used to make a causal statement are in error, then the validity of the causal claim is in question. Any information that eliminates error or reduces the possibility of error will support the argument.

Answer choice (A): This answer choice weakens the credibility of the study overall, since self-reporting might not be as accurate as monitoring (many people might not even realize that they snore). Since this answer choice calls into question the existence of even a correlation between throat abnormalities and snoring, it certainly does not strengthen the author's causal argument that snoring can damage one's throat.

Answer choice (B): This choice is entirely irrelevant to the question of whether or not heavy snoring can have a damaging effect on the muscles of the throat. Regardless of the reasons behind the throat surgeries, the author's points to the correlation between heavy snoring and throat muscle irregularities, and asserts a causal relationship. This choice does not strengthen that causal argument, so it cannot be the correct answer choice to this question.

Answer choice (C): Regardless of the similarities between test subjects, the point of this stimulus is to assess the relationship between two factors—snoring and throat muscle irregularities. The author argues that this reflects a particular causal relationship, and this choice fails to strengthen that conclusion.

Answer choice (D): This would be a tempting answer choice if the stimulus concerned the relationship between snoring and *throat surgery*, but this author is concerned only with the relationship between snoring and throat muscle irregularities. All of the subjects in this case had undergone throat surgery, so this choice does not strengthen the author's argument that snoring can damage the throat.

Answer choice (E): This is the correct answer choice, because it rules out the reverse explanation of the correlation between snoring and throat abnormalities (thus meeting the strengthening method described in point D described on the previous page). If we can confidently rule out the possibility that the throat abnormalities cause heavy snoring, then this strengthens the argument for the author's conclusion that it's actually the other way around—that snoring leads to the throat abnormalities discovered in the biopsies.

Question #17: Justify the Conclusion, SN. The correct answer choice is (A)

Although this is a short stimulus, it can still be extremely challenging (many consider this question to be one of the most difficult in the section). The author opens with the conclusion, which is that one should never sacrifice one's health in order to acquire money. This is based on the single premise presented in the second half of the single-sentence stimulus (the premise is introduced by the word "for"), which is that if you don't have health, happiness is unobtainable. More simply diagrammed and restated:

Premise: sacrifice health ⟶ ~~happiness~~ obtainable

Conclusion: acquiring money doesn't justify the sacrifice of one's health.

So, something that should be traded for money should not require the sacrifice of your health, because without health, you cannot obtain happiness.

The stimulus is followed by a Justify question stem, so the correct answer choice will provide a premise that justifies the author's conclusion that one should not sacrifice one's health in order to acquire money. If we are to use the mechanistic approach to respond to this question, we can see that the element that recurs in both the premise and the conclusion is that of "sacrifice one's health." The two rogue elements are those of "happiness obtainable" and "acquisition of money." Some link between these two elements is necessary to justify the author's conclusion, and this connection is provided by correct answer choice (A). Note that those elements do not have to be negative (consider what would occur if the contrapositive of both statements above were used—then each "rogue" element would be positive instead of negative).

Answer choice (A): This is the correct answer choice. This answer should be an immediate Contender because it contains both "rogue" elements in the argument. And, as discussed above, if something should be traded for the acquisition of money, it should not come at the cost of your health, because this would make happiness unobtainable. Ultimately, it is the only answer that contains both "rogue" elements, so even you were a bit uncertain of the meaning of this answer, you should still choose it based on your mechanistic analysis.

Answer choice (B): This incorrect answer choice provides a conditional rule that would not justify the author's conclusion. Since this choice fails to deal with the issue of whether something should be traded for money, it is not the correct answer choice.

Answer choice (C): The author has already provided that health is necessary for happiness. This choice would make happiness the only outcome of good health, which plays no role in the argument.

Answer choice (D): This incorrect choice allows for the possibility that some wealthy people are not happy. This would not justify the claim that health (and thus happiness) shouldn't be traded for money.

Answer choice (E): The author of the stimulus has already provided that health is a necessary precondition for happiness, so this answer choice, which says that health is better than money at providing happiness, adds nothing to the argument, and fails to justify the author's conclusion.

Question #18: Cannot Be True—Principle (same as Could Be TrueX—Principle). The correct answer choice is (D)

In this dialogue, Vanessa opens with her conclusion: that all computer code has to be co-written by two programmers, to avoid creating programs that only a single original programmer could understand. Jo replies that, considering the fact that the best programmers are at least 100 times more productive than the worst, the most productive workers must be allowed to work alone.

The question stem that follows is an unusual one. The stem references consistency, the two principles expressed by the speakers in the stimulus, and "except." An important note on consistency: if two statements are consistent with one another, this simply means that they are not contrary to one another, and thus they both could be true. When "except" is added in, four of the answer choices will be consistent with the principle expressed by the two speakers (Could Be True), and one will not (Cannot Be True). With the principle considered, this question is thus classified as a Could Be TrueX—Principle question, which is identical to a Cannot Be True—Principle question.

Operationally, the four incorrect answer choices in this case will be consistent with the speakers' principles, and one will explicitly violate at least one of the rules set forth, or provide a scenario that is contrary to at least one of the speakers' two statements:

I. All code must be co-written.
II. The most productive programmers must be allowed to work alone.

In order to violate one of the two rules above, an answer choice will likely present a scenario in which either some of the referenced code is not co-written, or in which some of the most productive workers are not allowed to work alone.

Answer choice (A): This answer choice is not contrary to either of the principles discussed in the stimulus, because the programmers are working together, staying in line with Vanessa's directive, and as neither Olga nor Kensuke is one of the most productive programmers they can work together without offending Jo's principles.

Answer choice (B): These two programmers work together in the same work station, which Vanessa requires, and neither one is one of the *most* productive programmers, so Jo would not require that either John or Tyrone work alone. Since this scenario is consistent with the principles of both speakers from the stimulus, it cannot be the correct answer to this question.

Answer choice (C): Much like the other incorrect answer choices, the scenario presented here would offend neither speaker's principles. They work together, as Vanessa asserts they must, and neither one is among the most productive programmers, so neither one needs to be left alone according to Jo. Since this choice is consistent with the principles of both speakers, it should be ruled out as a contender in this Except question.

Answer choice (D): This is the correct answer choice, because it is the only one which provides a scenario that violates one of the principles established in the stimulus. According to Jo, the most productive programmers must be able to work alone. Regardless of the fact that Mike is also productive, Yolanda, as the most productive programmer on the team, should be allowed to work alone, according to Jo's statements. Since this choice is the only one that is not consistent with the principles expressed in the stimulus, it is the correct answer choice to this Except question.

Answer choice (E): This scenario is consistent with both Vanessa's and Jo's principles, because the two programmers discussed are assigned to work together, which should make Vanessa happy, and since neither one is among the most productive programmers, Jo would not argue that either one needs to be left to program alone.

Question #19: Must Be True, FL. The correct answer choice is (D)

The author presents several statements about the pet stores in West Calverton. These can be diagrammed as follows:

Most pet stores in the area sell exotic birds:	Pet stores —M→ Exotic birds
Most that sell exotic birds also sell tropical fish:	Exotic birds —M→ TFish

These two statements can be linked as follows:

Pet stores —M→ Exotic birds —M→ TFish

The author then presents a somewhat complicated conditional rule: that if a pet store sells tropical fish, but not exotic birds, then it must sell gerbils. Further, any store that sells gerbils is not an independently owned West Calverton pet store:

Tropical fish and ~~Exotic birds~~ ——→ Gerbils ——→ ~~Independently owned WC pet store~~

The author draws no conclusion in this stimulus, and this fact set is followed by a Must Be True question stem, so we know that only one answer choice will be dictated to be true by the statements in the stimulus.

Answer choice (A): The only thing we know about independently owned pet stores in West Calverton is that they never sell gerbils (this is true from last clause of the final sentence of the stimulus). Since there is no way to confirm whether or not the majority of such stores sell exotic birds, this choice does not pass the Fact Test and should thus be eliminated.

Answer choice (B): The only information we have regarding gerbil selling is that it is not done by independently owned pet stores in West Calverton. The author has provided some information about stores that have tropical fish and *no* birds, but nothing about the pet stores that carry both. Since this choice is not confirmed by the information in the stimulus, it cannot be the correct answer to this Must Be True question.

Answer choice (C): Regarding the pet stores in the area that sell gerbils, all we can say is that they are not independently owned. It is possible that some (perhaps one) do sell exotic birds, but this is not dictated to be true, so this choice should be ruled out.

Answer choice (D): This is the correct answer choice; it is confirmed by the conditional statements presented in the second half of the stimulus. From those statements we know that a store selling tropical fish with no exotic birds must also sell gerbils—and any store that sells gerbils is *not* an independently owned West Calverton pet store.

Answer choice (E): The final sentence in the stimulus tells us that no independently owned pet stores in the area sell gerbils. This is the only reference to independently owned pet stores and can be diagrammed as follows:

Gerbils ⟶ ~~Independently owned West Calverton pet store~~

The contrapositive of this statement would be diagrammed as follows:

Independently owned West Calverton pet store ⟶ ~~Gerbils~~

Since the author has provided no information about the independent pet stores that do not sell tropical fish, we cannot confidently assert that such stores sell exotic birds, and this cannot be the correct answer choice.

Question #20: Resolve the Paradox. The correct answer choice is (C)

The discussion comes from an astronomer, who presents some seemingly paradoxical information, and also claims to have the solution. Earlier estimates of some stars' distance from Earth would dictate that some stars are roughly a billion years older than the universe itself, which of course is impossible. The astronomer believes that these stars are much farther away from the Earth than previously estimated, meaning that these stars also must be much brighter than previously thought. These newer estimates, we are told, help to resolve the apparent paradox that resulted from the older estimates.

This is a unique Resolve the Paradox question, in that the Astronomer actually provides the resolution, and our task is to determine how the new information helps to solve the prior paradox. As we know, earlier approximations had to have overestimated the age of certain stars, because there is no way that any star in the universe could be older than the universe. This tells us that the Astronomers' more recent estimates must either:

I. Estimate those stars to be younger than previously thought; or
II. Estimate the universe to be older than previously thought.

Since the new information provided concerns the distance of the stars from the Earth, and their brightness, the astronomer's resolution of the issue is more likely to deal with the age of the stars, which means that the new information in some way points to those stars' being younger than previously believed.

Answer choice (A): The paradox under discussion deals with the issue of stars within the universe that appear to be a billion years older than the universe itself. Even if the stars under discussion are the oldest objects discovered so far, this would not allow them to be older than the universe.

Answer choice (B): The paradox discussed in the stimulus could be solved either by estimating the stars to be younger than previously thought, or by approximating the universe to be older than previously estimated. This choice, which might support the notion of a younger universe, would actually worsen the original paradox: the stars discussed had already been believed to be older than the universe itself, so if the universe is actually younger than previously believed, this would make for an even greater age gap, and stars that are even more than a billion years older than the universe.

Answer choice (C): This is the correct answer choice. If it is true that the brighter a star is, the younger it is, then the astronomer's more recent approximations, which estimate the stars to be farther away and brighter than previously thought, would also point to the stars' being younger than previously thought. This of course helps to resolve the issue of the stars' appearing to have been older than the universe itself.

Answer choice (D): In the stimulus the astronomer alludes to this point with the words, "given their appearance to us on Earth." Since this choice provides no new information, it cannot possibly explain how the paradox has been resolved.

Answer choice (E): This choice would help to explain how astronomers might see such stars, but provides no resolution to the paradox of stars which in the past had been estimated to predate the universe itself.

Question #21: Must Be True, FL. The correct answer choice is (E)

This stimulus provides only a fact set, since the author draws no conclusions. First, we are provided with two general pieces of information about *most* large nurseries:

I. Most large nurseries sell primarily to commercial raspberry growers.
II. Most large nurseries sell only plants that are guaranteed to be disease-free

It is important to understand that "most" refers to the majority—over 50%.

The author goes on to discuss a particular shipment: the shipment of raspberry plants that Wally's Plants sent to Johnson carried a common virus.

The stimulus is followed by a Must Be True question, so the correct answer choice will be the one that passes the Fact Test, and can be confirmed by the information provided in the stimulus.

Answer choice (A): If Wally's is not a large nursery, then the information provided by the author is not very helpful—we know two things about most large nurseries, but nothing about smaller nurseries (such as Wally's, in this case). If Wally's is not a large nursery, there is no way to assess the likelihood that the raspberry plants were guaranteed disease free.

Answer choice (B): The conditional answer presented here is that if the shipment was not entirely as guaranteed, Johnson is probably not a commercial raspberry grower:

Shipment not as guaranteed ⟶ Johnson probably not a commercial grower

This choice is not confirmed by the information provided in the stimulus. We know that *most* large nurseries sell only plants that are guaranteed to be disease-free, but the most relationship creates a one-sided "most" arrow:

large nurseries —M⟶ sell only plants guaranteed to be disease free

When we consider the relationship from the other side, all we really know about the nurseries that sell only plants that are guaranteed to be disease free is that *some* are large nurseries:

Sell only plants guaranteed disease free ⟵S⟶ large nurseries

Since this choice cannot be confirmed by the information provided in the stimulus, it cannot be the correct answer choice in this case.

Answer choice (C): All we know from the stimulus is that most large nurseries sell *primarily* to commercial raspberry growers—not *exclusively*. Since we know nothing about non-commercial raspberry growers (they might still deal with large nurseries), knowing that Johnsons is not a commercial raspberry grower would not allow us to determine the likelihood of Wally's Plants' being a large nursery.

Answer choice (D): Although the author of the stimulus provides that most large nurseries sell primarily to commercial raspberry growers, knowing that a particular store sells primarily to commercial raspberry growers does not tell us whether or not that store is a large nursery. And although the recent shipment of raspberries carried a virus, we cannot conclude based on this information that Wally's is not well run (it is important to note that the no-virus guarantee merely puts the responsibility on the guarantor—this is <u>not</u> the same as asserting that virus-free raspberries are an absolute certainty).

Answer choice (E): This is the correct answer choice. If the sender is indeed a large nursery, then the first piece of information is relevant. That means that Wally's plants is *likely* to sell primarily to commercial growers, and is *likely* to sell only plants that are guaranteed to be disease-free (these two points are both likely because we know that they are true for *most* large nurseries). If this is the case, and the shipment was *probably* guaranteed to be disease-free, then we can also safely say that the shipment was *probably* not entirely as guaranteed.

Question #22: Weaken. The correct answer choice is (D)

The drug company manager quoted here discusses a new product that is failing to sell. The manager points out that a marketing campaign would not guarantee success, but would provide "one chance" to rescue the failing product, and concludes that the company should try the campaign:

Premise: A marketing campaign would not be certain to work, but it would provide one chance to save a failing product.

Conclusion: The company should try the new marketing campaign.

Note that the manager does not say that the advertising campaign is the "only" chance of saving the campaign. Instead, the manager uses language indicating that the advertising campaign offers "a" chance.

The stimulus is followed by a Weaken question, so the correct answer choice will hurt the author's argument, and somehow show that the suggested marketing campaign would be inadvisable—likely referencing some sort of previously unmentioned detriment that would be associated with such a campaign or perhaps the existence of better options for saving the drug.

Answer choice (A): Losses from any product are likely to be harmful to the company's profits, but this choice would strengthen the argument of the manager, who seems willing to try anything to save this single failing product. This choice certainly does not weaken the manager's argument, so it cannot be the correct answer choice.

Answer choice (B): This answer choice provides little new information, because the drug company manager has already pointed out that a marketing campaign's success would not be guaranteed.

Answer choice (C): The manager said merely that the campaign was not guaranteed to be a success, not that the campaign had no chance to succeed. Since this choice does not necessarily apply to the manager's suggested campaign, it does not weaken the argument presented in the stimulus.

Answer choice (D): This is the correct answer choice. If the marketing campaign suggested by the manager would hurt the company's overall position, then it would be much more difficult to justify an expensive marketing campaign in order to have "one chance" at helping out a single failing product.

Answer choice (E): The correct answer choice to this question should provide a reason to avoid the suggested marketing campaign. This choice fails to do so, and should thus be ruled out.

Question #23: Strengthen—Principle. The correct answer choice is (C)

In this stimulus, a consumer advocate provides information regarding a pesticide called TMD that is used on peaches. When ingested at the rate of the average person in the country, TMD shows no effect on people's health, but this is just an overall average, which accounts for those who eat no peaches and those who eat far *more* peaches than the national average, meaning they ingest far more TMD than those who eat peaches at the average rate for the country. Thus, even though TMD use on peaches is largely a non-issue for most of the population, because of concerns over the individuals that eat a large number of peaches, the consumer advocate notes that using TMD on peaches has not been shown to be an acceptable practice.

The question that follows is sometimes mistaken for a Justify the Conclusion question, but it asks for the principle which *most* helps to justify the advocate's argumentation. Since we are looking for the answer choice that lends most strength to the argument advanced in the stimulus, this a Strengthen question. Remember, Justify questions require an answer that strengthens the argument 100%; if there are any words in the question stem that lessen the completeness of the justification, then the question is a Strengthen question.

Given that a principle is also referenced in the question stem, you must select the answer choice which most strongly supports the author's conclusion that using TMD on peaches has not been shown to be an acceptable practice.

Answer choice (A): This choice fails to strengthen the author's argument, because it suggests cautious assessment, but does not support the notion that TMD use is not acceptable.

Answer choice (B): The consumer advocate's argument is not based on the fact that a majority of the population uses TMD; the argument is based on the fact that the level of use for some has not been shown to be an acceptable practice.

Answer choice (C): This is the correct answer choice, because it provides a principle which, if adopted, would strengthen the assertion that TMD has not been shown to be an acceptable practice. The pesticide has not been shown to be safe when ingested in greater quantities, so, according to this principle, it is not acceptable.

Answer choice (D): This principle would not apply to the consumer advocate's argument, because the average amount of TMD ingested in peaches *has* been shown to be safe. This choice would not support the conclusion that TMD use has not been proven an acceptable practice.

Answer choice (E): The consumer advocate does point out that TMD, though safe in average quantities, is in some cases ingested in much greater quantities. The principle in this answer choice, provides that protective measures are sometimes detrimental to certain segments of the population. This principle does not, however, support the advocate's conclusion that TMD use has not been shown to be an acceptable practice.

Question #24: Cannot Be True. The correct answer choice is (E)

The legal commentator provides a fairly straightforward discussion of a recently enacted workplace smoking ban, intended to protect employees from secondhand smoke. "But," the commentator says, the law could never be interpreted to prohibit people from smoking in their homes. The implication is that this follow-up point modifies (or perhaps contradicts) the author's first point in some way. Regardless, there is no conclusion present, just a fact set, meaning that you are likely looking at a Must Be True, Cannot Be True, or Resolve the Paradox question.

The question stem which follows asks for the claim that can be rejected based on the information from the stimulus. In other words, we must find the answer choice that cannot be true based on the commentator's statements.

Answer choice (A): This choice provides that the law will be interpreted in a way that is inconsistent with the intent of the law's supporters. Since from the legal commentator's statements there is no way to ensure that the new law will always be interpreted in a manner *consistent* with the intentions of the supporting lawmakers, this choice cannot be rejected based on the information in the stimulus. Thus, it cannot be the correct answer choice.

Answer choice (B): This answer choice provides that the new legislation's supporters believe the law will significantly impact the health of many workers. Since there is no way to refute this claim, which deals with the beliefs of the supporters, based on any of the information provided by the political commentator, this choice can be confidently ruled out.

Answer choice (C): The commentator specifically points out that the law could never be interpreted to prohibit smoking inside the home. This choice, which provides that the new law would never extend beyond people's workplaces, is not inconsistent with the commentator's argument, so this choice cannot be the correct answer to this Cannot Be True question stem.

Answer choice (D): The legal commentator's second point is that the new law could not be interpreted to prohibit people from smoking inside their homes. This answer choice provides that most people believe in a fundamental right to smoke inside one's home. Since there is no inconsistency between these two ideas, this choice cannot be rejected based on the legal commentator's claims.

Answer choice (E): This is the correct answer choice, and one which explains why the author chose to use the word "but" in the stimulus. Although the recently enacted law was intended to protect workers from the dangers of secondhand smoke, the law has limited reach—it could not be interpreted to prohibit smoking inside the home, meaning that domestic workers such as housecleaners would not be protected by the new law. Since this is the only choice that can be rejected based on the information provided in the stimulus, it is the correct answer choice.

As a final point, notice how Cannot Be True questions are often more challenging than average, not because the stimulus is difficult to understand, but because the process of finding an answer choice that can be rejected is rather unusual. If this question was one you found to be difficult, make sure to study this question type closely and become comfortable with the process of finding the answer choice that does *not* follow from the statements in the stimulus.

Question #25: Assumption. The correct answer choice is (A)

In this stimulus a university president says that the application pool has been shrinking, and that one possible explanation is the low tuition and fees charged by the school. The president suggests that these low charges might not reflect well on the quality of the education offered by the school, from the perspective of visiting students and parents, when compared with more expensive schools. The president concludes that if the school wants to increase its applicant numbers, tuition and fees should be raised. This argument is fairly straightforward (though clearly not airtight) and can be diagrammed as follows:

Premise: The school's applicant pool has been decreasing over the last few years.

Premise: One possible explanation is that the school's low tuition and fees are perceived, by visiting students and parents, as a reflection of lower quality.

Conclusion: In order to increase the size of the school's applicant pool, the university should raise its tuition and fees.

The stimulus is followed by an Assumption question, so the university president's argument will rely upon the correct answer choice. As with all Assumption questions, we can apply the Assumption Negation Technique to certain answers in order to confirm that a given answer choice is correct or incorrect. In this question, we will negate every answer choice for the purpose of clarity; on the LSAT you would only negate those answers that you could not eliminate, or to confirm the correct answer if you were uncertain.

Answer choice (A): This is the correct answer choice. The author's conclusion clearly relies upon the assumption that the excessively low tuition and fees are to blame for the school's diminishing pool of applicants. If these low costs are not the true culprit, then the author's conclusion would not make much sense.

In order to confirm that this is the correct answer, we can apply the Assumption Negation technique, which will also further clarify the argument's reliance on this assumption (again, the correct answer, when negated, or taken away, will hurt the author's argument. When we negate this answer choice, we arrive at the following:

The proposed explanation for the decline in applications does *not* apply in this case.

Clearly, when we take away the assumption provided by this answer choice, the argument fails: if the author's explanation is not applicable, there would be no basis for the assertion that an increase in tuition and fees would provide a remedy for the dwindling application numbers.

Answer choice (B): The author's conclusion does not rely on assuming that educational quality is dependent on the amount of a school's tuition (but rather on the *perception* of linking tuition to quality in the minds of students and parents). While this choice could conceivably be used to strengthen an argument for increased tuition and fees, it is not an assumption on which the author's argument relies. Again, for confirmation we can apply the Assumption Negation technique. The negated version of this choice would be as follows:

The quality of a university education is *not* dependent on the amount of tuition charged by the university.

This negated version does not hurt the author's argument, because the suggestion to increase tuition and fees is based on the premise that students and parents might *think* this reflects poorly on the quality of the institution (regardless of the validity of such conclusions).

Answer choice (C): This is a potentially tricky wrong answer choice; while it looks like something the author might *like* to assume, it is not an assumption that is absolutely *required* by the author's argument.

The application of the Assumption Negation Technique might be particularly valuable in the clarification of this analysis. The negated version of this answer choice is as follows:

An increase of tuition and fees would *not* guarantee a larger applicant pool.

Recall that the author's conclusion was that to increase the size of the university applicant pool, the school needs to increase tuition and fees. The assertion that the plan would not be *guaranteed* to work does not undermine the assertion that the need nonetheless exists.

Answer choice (D): The author's conclusion is based on the idea that the diminishing number of applications is potentially attributable to the perceptions of visiting students and parents. This does not require the assumption that the low tuition and fees are the only possible cause. To clarify, we can assess the negated version of this choice, as follows:

There *might be* additional explanations for the university's shrinking applicant pool.

Again, even if there are additional explanations, this does not completely undermine the assertion that an increase in tuition and fees might help to solve the problem.

Answer choice (E): Applying the Assumption Negation Process to this choice, we get the following negated version:

The amount the university charges for tuition *has* increased in recent years.

This does not undermine the author's argument, because the suggested increases in tuition and fees are made on the basis that overall the school charges too little.

Question #26: Strengthen—PR. The correct answer choice is (E)

This editorial has a very common LSAT structure of argumentation: the author begins by relaying an assertion, immediately refutes the assertion, and then closes with a premise to support the refutation. Specifically, the editorialist in this case discusses the suggested tactic of hiring private, for-profit companies to bring clean water to areas of the world where it is currently unavailable. The author concludes that water should not be supplied by private companies, and this assertion is based on the premises that water is necessary for health, and the purpose of private companies is not to promote health but rather to earn profits. The basis components of the editorialist's argument can be broken down as follows:

Premise:	Water is necessary for human health.
Premise:	The purpose of private companies is to produce profits, not to promote health.
Conclusion:	Private companies should not be hired to supply water to areas of the world where clean water is currently unavailable.

It would be easy to confuse the question that follows with a Justify the Conclusion question, but in this case we are not required to find the answer choice that fully justifies the conclusion from the stimulus; instead, we are asked to find the choice that *most* helps to justify the author's conclusion. Thus, this is a Strengthen question. Since this is a Principle question as well, the correct answer choice in this case will provide a principle that lends strength to the assertion that private companies should *not* be hired to supply clean water to areas where it is needed.

Answer choice (A): The principle presented in this incorrect answer choice is that private companies should only be allowed to supply essentials that are also supplied by government agencies. This would not strengthen the author's argument, because water is a necessity that is often supplied by such agencies. Since this choice fails to strengthen the author's argument against private companies as water suppliers, this cannot be the correct answer.

Answer choice (B): The stimulus does not deal with the lack of willingness or ability on the part of private companies to supply water to areas where it is unavailable. The author is only concerned with whether such companies *should* be hired to supply water, asserting that private companies should not, because their primary motivation is profit creation.

Answer choice (C): This incorrect answer choice would work better if the author's argument had been based on private companies' inability to supply safe, clean drinking water. However, author's argument is based on the premise that private companies would not be appropriate water suppliers because they are primarily motivated by profits. Thus, this cannot be the correct answer choice.

Answer choice (D): The author's argument, again, is that private companies are primarily motivated by profits, so they should not be hired to supply water, a health necessity, to areas where it is unavailable. The principle provided by this answer choice concerns promoting health, but fails to strengthen the author's argument that profit-motivated companies should not be hired for the purpose of health promotion.

Answer choice (E): This is the correct answer choice. If, as this principle states, necessities for human health (water included) should be provided by organizations whose primary purpose is the promotion of health, this lends strength to the argument advanced in the stimulus. If this principle is established, this strengthens the author's assertion that private companies should *not* be the ones to supply the needed water, since the primary motivation of such companies is to create profits, not health.

Chapter Five: The December 2010 LSAT Deconstructed

The explanations below are presented in the same order that the questions are given on the exam. Please keep in mind that all explanations draw on methods discussed in *The PowerScore LSAT Logic Games Bible*. Please refer to that text if you desire a more detailed discussion of a particular concept or approach. If you encounter any unknown terms, a glossary is provided at the end of the book.

December 2010 Section 3: Logic Games

Overview: Overall, this is a very challenging Logic Games section. In particular, the second and third games are notoriously difficult and caused widespread frustration for December 2010 LSAT takers.

Game #1: The first game appears to be a simple Basic Linear game, but there is a somewhat complex interaction between the first three days and last three days in the game. This interaction is extremely helpful to the students who recognized it during the setup, but for students who failed to recognize the interaction, the game was much more challenging. Thus, this game provided a point of separation to start the section, with some test takers gaining a significant advantage over other test takers.

Game #2: This game savaged many LSAT takers, and some of the questions—#9 and #10 in particular—are very difficult. But, like many infamous games, a clear understanding of the implications of certain rules makes this game somewhat more palatable than initially thought. Regardless, this game was not for the faint of heart. The students who did well had a clear grasp of the implication of the rules—especially the fourth rule—and they used that knowledge to move faster than other examinees.

Game #3: While many test takers lamented the toughness of the second game, it may be that the third game that was the most difficult on this exam. Both games are undeniably challenging, and after the relative toughness of the second game, the clearly difficult nature of the third game was a particularly unwelcome sight. This double blow in the middle of the section lead many test takers to cancel their score on this exam. However, as in the second game, there are elements you can identify in this game that help you attack the questions, and make the game a manageable experience.

Game #4: The final game of this test is a relatively easy Basic Linear game. However, the downside is that this game has only five questions, so test takers hoping to scoop up some late, easy points were a bit short-changed. And, unfortunately, many test takers never made it to this game because they became mired in the second and third games.

December 2010 Game #1: Questions 1-6

This is a Basic Linear: Balanced game.

The game scenario indicates that six service appointments will be scheduled for six consecutive days, exactly one per day, leading to the following Basic Linear setup:

G L P S T W [6]

1	2	3	4	5	6

From a quick analysis standpoint, this seems like a reasonable first game to attempt on the test.

The first rule establishes a basic sequence:

W > L

This rule leads to two Not Laws, one for W, which cannot be last, and one for L, which cannot be first:

G L P S T W [6]

1	2	3	4	5	6
~~L~~					~~W~~

The second rule also creates a conditional relationship, albeit one that is more complex than the relationship in the first rule:

```
      G
P > ------
      S
```

This rule leads to four Not Laws: G and S cannot be scheduled for the first day, and P cannot be scheduled for the fifth or sixth days:

GLPSTW ^{6}

1	2	3	4	5	6
~~L~~				~~P~~	~~W~~
~~G~~					~~P~~
~~S~~					

With the first two rules generating three Not Laws on the first day, we can infer that only P, T, or W can be scheduled for the first appointment:

GLPSTW ^{6}

P/T/W					
1	2	3	4	5	6
~~L~~				~~P~~	~~W~~
~~G~~					~~P~~
~~S~~					

The third rule establishes that G, S, and T cannot be scheduled for the second and third days, leading to six additional Not Laws:

GLPSTW ^{6}

P/T/W					
1	2	3	4	5	6
~~L~~	~~G~~	~~G~~		~~P~~	~~W~~
~~G~~	~~S~~	~~S~~			~~P~~
~~S~~	~~T~~	~~T~~			

Of course, with those three services eliminated from the second and third days, only L, P, and W can possibly be scheduled for those two days:

GLPSTW ^{6}

P/T/W	(L, P, W)				
1	2	3	4	5	6
~~L~~	~~G~~	~~G~~		~~P~~	~~W~~
~~G~~	~~S~~	~~S~~			~~P~~
~~S~~	~~T~~	~~T~~			

The third rule is extremely powerful, and there are two inferences that follow from this rule:

1. If one of L, P, or W is scheduled for a day other than the second or third day, then the remaining two services must be scheduled for the second and third days. For example, if W is scheduled for the first day, then L and P—not necessarily in that order—must be scheduled for the second and third days.

2. From the second rule G and S cannot be scheduled for the first day, and from the third rule G and S cannot be scheduled for the second and third days. Thus, G and S must be scheduled for days four, five, or six. More on this inference in a moment.

The fourth and final rule establishes that T cannot be scheduled for the sixth day, which leads to another Not Law on day six:

G L P S T W ^{6}

P/T/W	(L, P, W)				
1	2	3	4	5	6
~~L~~	~~G~~	~~G~~		~~P~~	~~W~~
~~G~~	~~S~~	~~S~~			~~P~~
~~S~~	~~T~~	~~T~~			~~T~~

With three Not Laws now present on the sixth day, we can infer that only G, L, or S can be scheduled for the sixth day:

G L P S T W ^{6}

P/T/W	(L, P, W)				G/L/S
1	2	3	4	5	6
~~L~~	~~G~~	~~G~~		~~P~~	~~W~~
~~G~~	~~S~~	~~S~~			~~P~~
~~S~~	~~T~~	~~T~~			~~T~~

At this point, all of the rules have been represented, along with several inferences. Let's delve into the game just a bit further before moving on to the questions.

An analysis of the diagram above shows that the game is composed of two interlocking systems:

1. Only T, L, P, and W can be scheduled for the first three days.

   With only four services available to fill the first three days, if any one of T, L, P, and W is scheduled for the *last* three days, then the remaining three must be scheduled for the first three days, in accordance with the restrictions already shown on the diagram. This is incredibly limiting and has a major effect on the game.

   Note that because only one of the three variables can be removed, that variable cannot be W, because then L would also be removed due to the first rule. Thus, W cannot be fourth or fifth, and that will be shown with Not Laws on the main diagram below.

2. G and S must be scheduled for the last three days.

   As established previously, G and S must be scheduled for the last three days. Thus, when another service aside from G and S is scheduled for the fourth, fifth, or sixth day, then G and S will fill the remaining two days. So, for example, if L is scheduled for the fourth day, then G and S—not necessarily in that order—must be scheduled for days five and six. Of course, because that other service must be T, L, P, or W, when one of those four is scheduled in the last three days, the composition (but not order) of the services in first three days and the last three days is fully determined.

The two points above will be shown "floating above" the main base of the diagram, leading to the final diagram for the game:

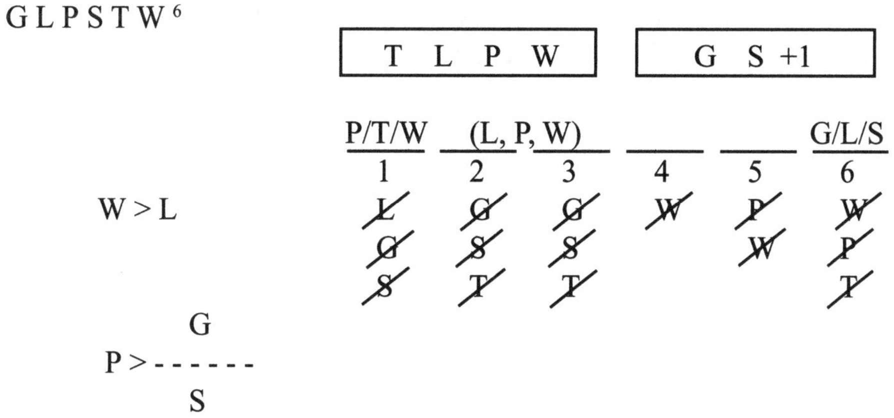

Thus, although this game appears to be relatively simple, there are some complex—and quite helpful—interactions occurring among the rules.

Question #1: Global, Could Be True, List. The correct answer choice is (D)

As with all complete List questions, simply apply the rules to the answer choices.

Answer choice (A): This answer choice is incorrect because it violates the second rule (G is scheduled earlier than P).

Answer choice (B): This answer choice is incorrect because it violates the fourth rule (T is scheduled for the sixth day).

Answer choice (C): This answer choice is incorrect because it violates the first rule (L is scheduled earlier than W).

Answer choice (D): This is the correct answer choice.

Answer choice (E): This answer choice is incorrect because it violates the third rule (T is scheduled for the second day).

Question #2: Local, Must Be True. The correct answer choice is (D)

The question stem stipulates that G, S, and T cannot be scheduled for the fourth day. This is a rather striking group of three services because it exactly matches the three services in the third rule that cannot be scheduled for the second and third days. When a similarity like this occurs, it is extremely unlikely to be a coincidence, and you should investigate the connection further.

With G, S, and T prohibited from being scheduled on the second, third, and fourth days, G, S and T must be scheduled for the first, fifth, and sixth days. Because there are three variables and three days, that fills the appointments for those three days. The other three services—L, P, and W—cannot be scheduled for any of those three days, and must instead be scheduled for the second, third, and fourth days:

G L P S T W [6]

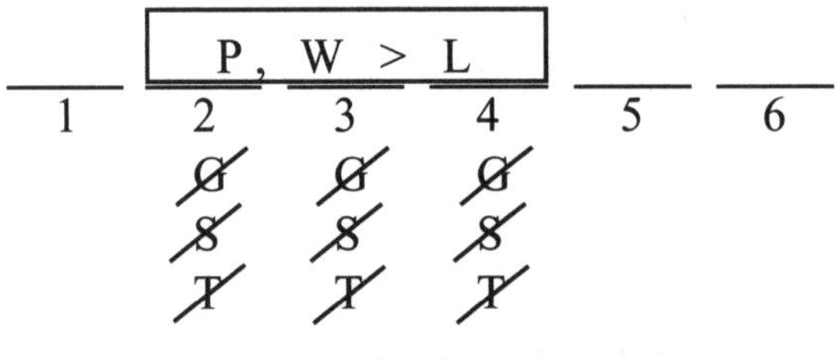

While G, S, and T are forced into the first, fifth, and sixth, their placement is not random. From the second rule, we know that G and S cannot be scheduled first. Thus, T must be scheduled first, and G and S must be scheduled for the fifth and sixth days, in some order:

GLPSTW[6]

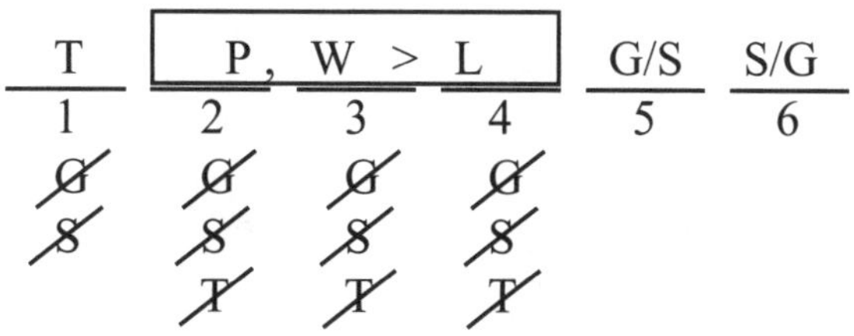

Answer choice (A): While this answer choice could be true, it does not have to be true since G can be scheduled for the sixth day. Thus, this answer choice is incorrect.

Answer choice (B): While P could be scheduled for the third day, P could also be scheduled for the second or fourth days, and thus this answer choice does not have to be true, and is incorrect.

Answer choice (C): This answer is the other half of answer choice (A). While this answer choice could be true, it does not have to be true since S can be scheduled for the fifth day. Thus, this answer choice is incorrect.

Answer choice (D): This is the correct answer choice. As revealed in the discussion of the conditions in the question stem, T must be scheduled for the first day.

Answer choice (E): W could be scheduled for the second day, but it could also be scheduled for the third day, and so this answer choice does not have to be true, and is incorrect.

Question #3: Global, Must Be True. The correct answer choice is (E)

Global Could Be True questions, such as this one, are often best left until the end of the game to complete because answering these questions is often much easier after you have seen several solutions to the game (for example, question #4 in this game contains three answers that can be used to eliminate answers in this question). Thus, unless the game is an Identify the Templates or Possibilities game, skip these questions and return to them at the end of the game. If you do attack this question in its natural position, make sure to use the hypotheticals produced by the first two questions. For example, the solution to question #1 eliminates answer choice (A), and the solution to question #2 eliminates answer choice (B). By using that approach, you will have reduced the amount of work you have to do to determine the correct answer.

Answer choice (A): As mentioned above, the solution to question #1 (answer choice (D)), shows that T can be scheduled earlier than L. The work in question #2 also proves the same point.

Answer choice (B): As mentioned above, the work in question #2 shows that L can be scheduled earlier than P.

Answer choice (C): This answer choice can be disproved by the following hypothetical:

GLPSTW [6]

P	W	L	G	T	S
1	2	3	4	5	6

As shown above, G can be scheduled earlier than T.

Answer choice (D): This answer choice can be disproved by the following hypothetical:

GLPSTW [6]

W	P	L	G	T	S
1	2	3	4	5	6

As shown above, W can be scheduled earlier than T.

Answer choice (E): This is the correct answer choice. G must be scheduled for one of the last three days, and, as discussed in the setup, W must be scheduled for one of the first three days. Because W must always be scheduled earlier than G, this is the correct answer choice. If the logic behind this is unclear, try a hypothetical: there is not enough room for G to be scheduled ahead of W because W must also be scheduled ahead of L, and S must be scheduled in the last three days as well.

Question #4: Global, Cannot Be True, List. The correct answer choice is (E)

Note the careful selection of the last three days in the question stem condition. As established in the game discussion, the last three days have a special characteristic, namely that G, S, and one other service will be scheduled in some order for the last three days. Answer choices (A), (B), (C), and (D) each contain both G and S, and so they at least meet the basic requirement for the placement of G and S. Answer choice (E), on the other hand, contains G but not S. This means that S would have to be scheduled for one of the first three days, a violation of the second and third rules. Thus, answer choice (E) cannot be true and is correct.

Answer choice (A): Because all of the incorrect answers could be possible, this answer choice can be used to confirm that answer choice (A) in question #3 is incorrect because it reveals that T would be scheduled for an earlier day than L (if G, S, and L are the last three services scheduled, then T would have to be on for the first three services scheduled).

The following full hypothetical proves that this answer choice could be true, and is therefore incorrect:

GLPSTW^6

T	P	W	G	S	L
1	2	3	4	5	6

Answer choice (B): The following full hypothetical proves that this answer choice could be true, and is therefore incorrect:

GLPSTW^6

T	P	W	L	S	G
1	2	3	4	5	6

Answer choice (C): This answer choice can be used to confirm that answer choice (B) in question #3 is incorrect because it reveals that L would be scheduled for an earlier day than P.

The following full hypothetical proves that this answer choice could be true, and is therefore incorrect:

GLPSTW^6

T	W	L	P	S	G
1	2	3	4	5	6

Answer choice (D): This answer choice can be used to confirm that answer choice (D) in question #3 is incorrect because it reveals that W would be scheduled for an earlier day than T.

The following full hypothetical proves that this answer choice could be true, and is therefore incorrect:

GLPSTW^6

W	P	L	T	S	G
1	2	3	4	5	6

Answer choice (E): This is the correct answer choice. As explained above, this is the correct answer.

Question #5: Local, Must Be True. The correct answer choice is (B)

The question stem eliminates two services—G and S—from being scheduled for the sixth day. As shown on the final diagram for the game, only G, L, and S can be scheduled for the sixth day, so when G and S are removed from consideration, we can conclude that L must be scheduled for the sixth day. Given that this is a Must Be True question, you should immediately seek this statement among the answer choices. Answer choice (B) states that inference, and answer choice (B) is correct.

Answer choice (A): This answer choice could be true, but it does not have to be true, and so it is incorrect. Note how question #4, answer choice (A) can be used to disprove this answer choice (A is actually the only answer from question #4 that can be used because neither G nor S is scheduled for the sixth day).

Answer choice (B): This is the correct answer choice.

Answer choice (C): This answer choice could be true, but it does not have to be true, and so it is incorrect.

Answer choice (D): This answer choice cannot true (there would not be enough room to schedule both G and S), and so it is incorrect.

Answer choice (E): This answer choice could be true, but it does not have to be true, and so it is incorrect.

Question #6: Local, Justify, Suspension. The correct answer choice is (A)

This is an interesting question stem, one that asks you to substitute a new condition for the fourth rule and still achieve the same effect. Thus, you must suspend the fourth rule, and then find an answer that replaces that rule and leads to or justifies an identical result.

The best way to solve a question of this type is to examine the direct effects of the rule on the variables addressed in the suspended rule, *as well as* the *other* characteristics of the variables affected by the rule. In addition, you must guard against additional limitations posed by an answer choice. Any new limitation that results from an answer will cause that answer to be incorrect.

In this case, the fourth rule addresses T only, so this rule is easier to analyze than some of the other rules. The fourth rule established that T could not be the appointment scheduled for the sixth day. That limitation was quite localized, and lead to the inference that G, L, or S had to be scheduled for the sixth day. T was still able to move freely over the first, fourth, and fifth days (the third rule eliminated T from the second and third days, and that rule is still in effect). Thus, we need an answer that matches the limitation on the sixth day while still allowing T no limitations on the first, fourth, and fifth days.

Answer choice (A): This is the correct answer choice. This answer choice properly limits T from being scheduled for the sixth day, but imposes no other limitation on T's movement.

Answer choice (B): This answer choice limits T to the fourth or fifth days. Thus, while it properly eliminates T from being scheduled on the sixth day, it improperly eliminates T from being scheduled on the first day. Thus, this answer choice is incorrect.

Answer choice (C): The condition in this question stem can be diagrammed as:

T > L

While this eliminates T from being scheduled on the sixth day and still allows L to be scheduled on the sixth day, T is improperly limited because, for example, if L is second then T is forced into the first day. The fourth rule had no such additional limitation, and thus this answer choice is incorrect.

Answer choice (D): While this answer choice eliminates T from being scheduled for the sixth day, it clearly adds a number of additional limitations on T by tying T to G when T is not scheduled for the first day. Thus, this answer choice is incorrect.

Answer choice (E): This is an extremely tricky answer choice, and one that is well-placed by the test makers in appearing at the end. While the condition in this answer eliminates T from being sixth and allows T to move freely among the first, fourth, and fifth days, this answer is incorrect because it establishes an extra limitation on the sixth day, namely that L cannot be scheduled for the sixth day. If only G and S can be scheduled for the sixth day, then L is also eliminated, which differs from the final setup of the game. Thus, this answer choice does not have the same effect as the fourth rule of the game, and is incorrect.

December 2010 Game #2: Questions 7-13

This is a Grouping: Partially Defined, Numerical Distribution, Identify the Templates game.

This game is extremely challenging, and it requires you to fully understand the implications of some relatively standard rules.

In the game scenario, an artisan is creating three stained glass windows from a selection of five colors. Each color is used at least once, and each window contains at least two colors. This leads to an initial setup as follows:

G O P R Y ^{5}

___	___	___
___	___	___
1	2	3

However, a major point of concern within this scenario is the use of "at least" in relation to both the use of the colors and the number of colors within each window. The use of "at least" opens the door to many more combinations than would exist if the word "exactly" had been used in each instance. For example, without considering the rules, initially each of the three windows could be made from all five colors. This use of "at least" is the first sign that this game may be harder than average.

The first rule establishes that exactly one window will contain both green and purple glass:

[G / P] One

Carefully note the wording in this rule however; it does not state that one of the windows will be *only* green and purple glass, just that exactly one of the windows contains both green and purple glass, which means that other colors could be present. Again, this allows for more options than would otherwise be the case.

The second rule is fairly straightforward, and it establishes that exactly two of the windows contain rose glass:

2R

This rule means that our minimum color set is now: G O P R R Y.

The third rule is actually two rules in one, and each rule is a negative grouping rule. Because we have a vertical component to our Grouping diagram, we will show these two rules as vertical not-blocks:

One of the implications of this rule is that none of Y, G, and O can be used three times. Because each color must be used in at least one window, if, for example, O was used three times (once in each window), then Y could not be used in any window. Thus, Y, G, and O are each used in one or two windows, and this numerical fact plays an important role in the game.

The final rule has a powerful effect on the game. This rule contains a negative sufficient condition, and most students initially diagram it as follows:

~~P~~ ⟶ O

Of course, the contrapositive of this rule is:

~~O~~ ⟶ P

When both representations are considered together, the rule means that when one of O or P is *not* used in a window, the other color *must* be used. Because every window must then contain O or P (or possibly both), this can be represented directly on the diagram as an O/P option for each window:

GOPRY [5]

___	___	___
O/P	O/P	O/P
1	2	3

Note that while P could be used in all three windows, O can only be used in at most two windows (see the discussion of the third rule above), so one window will always contain P and not O.

This is an incredibly powerful rule that must be accounted for in the making of each window, and by itself it answers question #8. Consider also what this rule means for Y. From the third rule Y cannot be used in a window that contains O, and thus whenever Y is used in a window, P must also be used:

Y ⟶ P

While this inference is not directly tested in the questions (how unfortunate!), it does play a role in answering questions such as #12.

At this juncture, our setup appears as follows:

GOPRY[5]

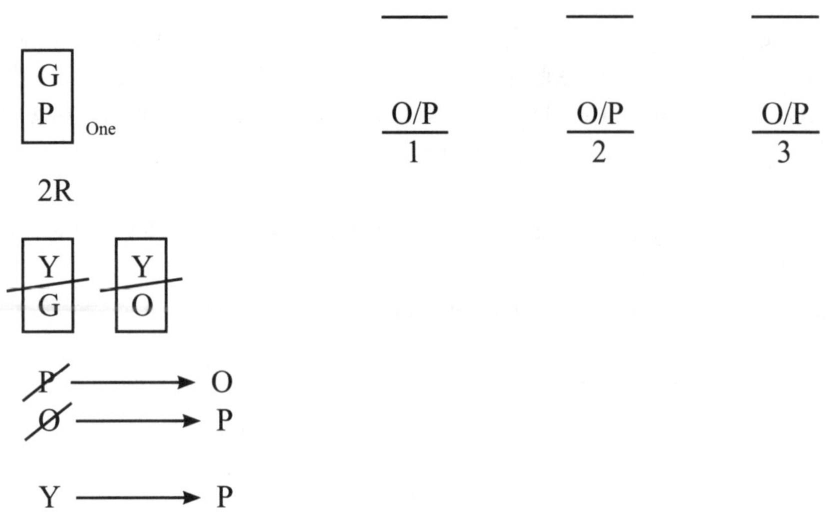

At this point, most students use this as the final setup and move on to the questions. And, with the information already derived from our cursory examination of the rules, they will answer questions #7 and #8 with relative ease. Plus, the inferences derived during our discussion will carry them to overall success on the game.

But, there is a further step that can be taken, and it is one that rests on recognizing that the specific window numbers are not that critical in this game. Take a moment to glance at the rules and the seven questions. You may notice that the composition of the windows is not attached to specific window numbers: none of the rules references a specific window number, and only question #7 references specific window numbers. Thus, we can also attack this came by considering the composition of each window irrespective of the window numbers. While this approach is not necessary for game success, it is worthwhile to consider from a strategic standpoint, and as an instructive lesson for future games that might be similar.

When the game is considered without referencing window numbers, the initial scenario would appear as follows:

GOPRY[5]

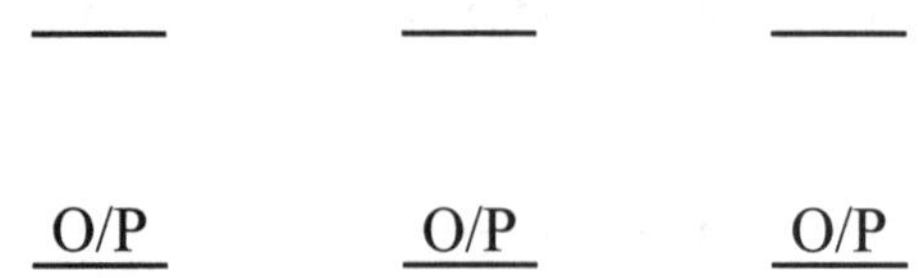

But, some of the rules—such as the first rule—establish further restrictions on the color combinations, such as the following:

GOPRY^{5}

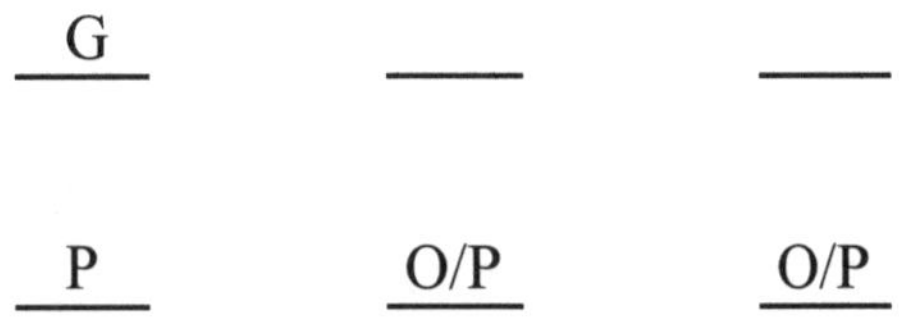

In addition, there is also the fact that Y is a very powerful variable in this game. Y must be used at least once, but it cannot be used in all three windows due to the third rule. Thus, Y must be used once or twice (and it correspondingly eliminates certain colors from being used and also requires P to be used). From this standpoint, the use of Y suggests a templating approach, one when Y is used once, and one when Y is used twice. Let's examine both:

<u>Template #1: Y used in exactly one window</u>

When Y is used in exactly one window, then the GP block from the first rule must be used in a different window (remember, from the third rule G and Y cannot be used in the same window). The "third" window then retains the choice of O or P. The use of each color must still be tracked, and the second rule involving R must also be tracked. This template thus provides a base, but it still allows for multiple options.

GOPRY^{5}

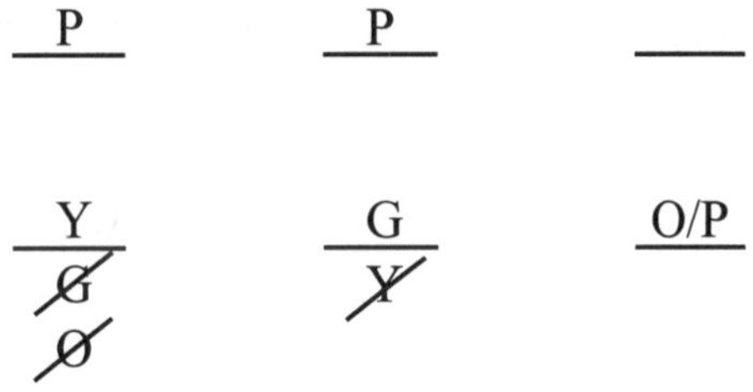

<u>Template #2: Y used in exactly two windows</u>

This template provides a bit more detailed information. Two of the windows contain Y, and thus they also contain P. The other window contains the GP block from the first rule, as well as O. The use of each color must still be tracked, and the second rule involving R must also be tracked.

GOPRY^{5}

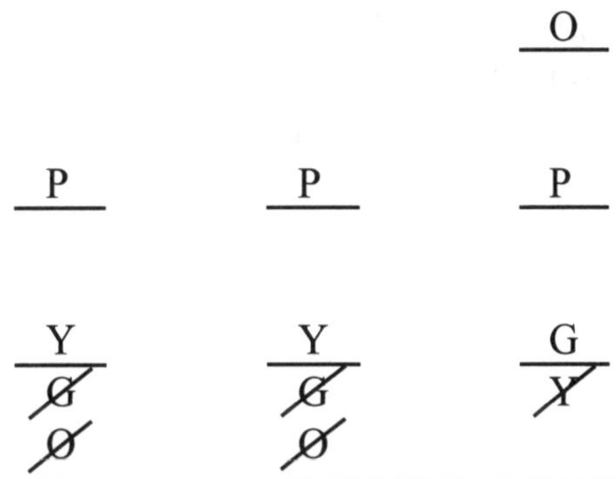

Is having the templates necessary to solving this game or even to solving it quickly? No, the rules and the resulting inferences will allow for success (thus, in the questions, we will generally use the rules to solve each problem and only occasionally reference the templates). But, again, this approach is slightly more efficient and gives you a better overall picture of the possible directions the game can take. Therefore, it is useful to consider, especially because a higher percentage of recent games have been best attacked by considering just the composition of the groups without reference to the specific names or numbers of the groups, and that at times suggests a template approach.

Question #7: Global, Could Be True, List. The correct answer choice is (B)

As with all complete List questions, simply apply the rules to the answer choices.

Answer choice (A): This answer choice is incorrect because window 2 violates the fourth rule (neither O nor P is used in window 2).

Answer choice (B): This is the correct answer choice.

Answer choice (C): This answer choice is incorrect because it violates the first rule (both windows 1 and 2 contain G and P).

Answer choice (D): This answer choice is incorrect because it violates the third rule (window 2 contains both Y and O).

Answer choice (E): This answer choice is incorrect because it violates the second rule (R is used in only one window).

Question #8: Global, Cannot Be True, List. The correct answer choice is (C)

In this question, four of the answers are viable window color combinations and one is not a viable color combination. Note that the question stem contains the word "complete" in reference to the listed color combinations, meaning that the two colors listed in each answer choice are the only two colors used in the window. This use of "complete" has a significant effect on the nature of the possible answers, because it limits the listed color combinations and forces you to find not just two colors that can be combined, but two colors that can be combined and be the only two colors present in a window. This restricts you ability to use hypotheticals such as the one produced in question #7. The word "complete" also appears in four of the next five questions stems, and this increases the difficulty of those questions.

This question was referenced in the setup during the discussion of the fourth rule. As established in that discussion, each window must contain either O or P, or both. Thus, to be a viable scenario, O or P must appear as one or both of the two colors. Answer choice (C), which contains neither O nor P as one of the two colors, therefore violates the fourth rule and cannot be a complete color combination in a window.

Question #9: Local, Could Be True, List. The correct answer choice is (B)

After two questions on the easier side, the test makers dramatically increase the difficulty with this question. The question stem first specifies that two of the windows are made with exactly two colors, and then asks for the possible color combination of one of those windows.

From our knowledge of the powerful fourth rule, answer choices (A) and (D) can immediately be eliminated because neither contains O or P. This leaves three answer choices, and the savvy test taker may realize that with two windows limited to just two colors and the second rule establishing that R must appear in two windows, that answer choice (B) is likely to be correct because it is the only remaining answer choice that contains R. However, let's turn to the templates to determine which answer choice is correct.

Template #2 is not possible because adding the two R's would create at least two windows with at least three colors, a violation of the condition in the question stem. Thus, Template #1 must be the applicable template for this question. When the two R's are added to the template, one must go with the O/P option, and the other must go with either the PY or PG blocks:

GOPRY [5]

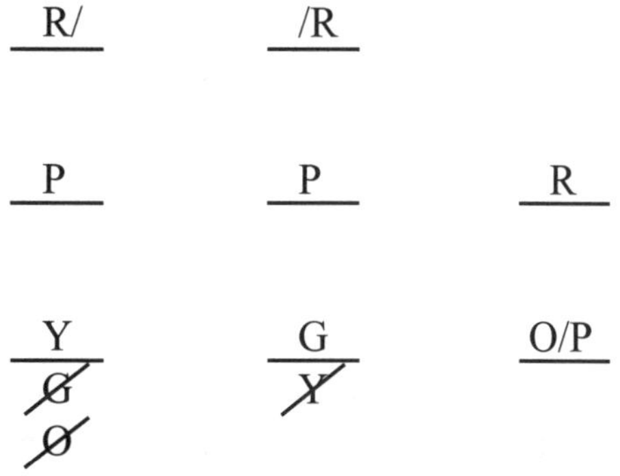

As O and R is one possible complete color combination, answer choice (B) is proven correct.

Question #10: Local, Could Be True, List. The correct answer choice is (B)

The question stem kindly provides the complete color combination in one of the windows—P, R, and O—and then asks you to identify a complete color combination that could be used in another window. The initial setup appears as follows, with no window numbers specified:

GOPRY [5]

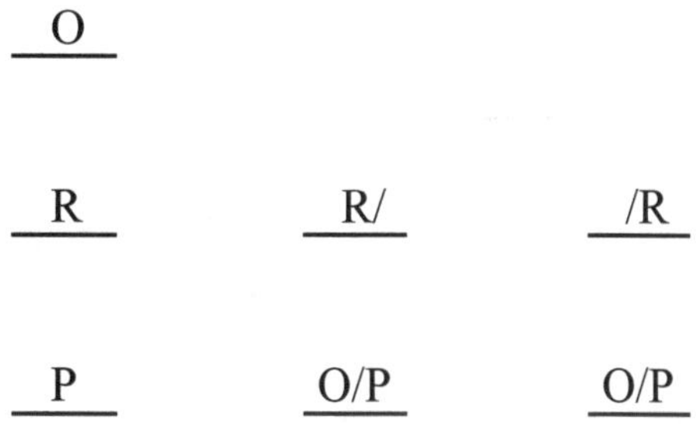

Of course, the first rule specifies that one of the windows must have G and P, and so that fact can be added to the diagram:

G O P R Y [5]

O	R/	
R	G	/R
P	P	O/P

Y must also be used in one of the windows, and from the third rule Y cannot be used with G or O, and so Y must be used in the remaining window, along with P:

G O P R Y [5]

O	R/	/R
R	G	Y
P	P	P

With the diagram above—which shows the *minimum* color usage in the other two windows—answer choices (C), (D), and (E) can each be eliminated. This is because each contains exactly two colors, and any two color window in under the above scenario would have to be GP or YP. As neither of those color combinations is listed in any of those three answers, each can be eliminated.

Answer choice (A) can also be eliminated because it does not contain P, and the diagram shows that each window must contain P. Thus, answer choice (B) is the correct answer, and under answer choice (B), the "third" window would have the remaining R:

G O P R Y [5]

O	O	R
R	G	Y
P	P	P

Question #11: Local, Could Be True, List. The correct answer choice is (A)

The question stem specifies that O is used in more windows than G. As discussed during the analysis of the third rule, G, and O are each used in one or two windows. Thus, in order to conform to the condition in this question, G must be used in exactly one window (with P in accordance with the first rule), and O must be used in exactly two windows.

At this point, many people are naturally inclined to assume that the G and O windows are separate, as in the following scenario:

G O P R Y ^{5}

P	___	___
G	O	O

However, this is impossible because from the third rule Y could not be used in a window. Thus, there *must* be an overlap and one of the windows must contain both G and O:

G O P R Y ^{5}

O		
P	___	___
G	O	___

This inference proves sufficient to answer the question by using process of elimination. From the condition in the question stem, G is used in only one window, and that window must also contain P and O. Answer choices (B), (C), (D), and (E) each contain G, but none of those answers also contains P and O. Consequently, each of those answer choices is incorrect. Only answer choice (A) remains, and is thus correct.

Note that the second diagram above is incomplete. For example, the "third" window must contain Y and P (Y must be used in one of the windows and P must also be used when Y is used), and the second rule involving 2 R's must also be accounted for. However, there is no need to continue to create the diagram when the initial inference allows you to eliminate each of the four incorrect answers.

Question #12: Global, Could Be True. The correct answer choice is (C)

As discussed during the analysis of the third rule, Y, G, and O are each used in one or two windows. Thus, none of them can be used in all three windows, and so answer choices (A), (B), and (E) can be eliminated.

Answer choice (D) can be eliminated because the second rule specifies that R is used in exactly two windows.

Answer choice (C) is thus proven correct by process of elimination. Additionally, the hypothetical from question #10 proves this answer choice correct as well.

Question #13: Local, Could Be True, List. The correct answer choice is (E)

If none of the windows contains O and R, then from the second rule two of the windows contain R, and O must be used in the remaining window:

$GOPRY^5$

___	___	___
R	R	O
		~~Y~~

Of course, from the fourth rule each window must contain O or P, and so the two windows with R (and thus not O) must both contain P:

$GOPRY^5$

P	P	___
R	R	O
		~~Y~~

One RP window must contain G in order to comply with the first rule, and the other RP window must contain Y because Y must be used and every time Y is used, P is used:

GOPRY [5]

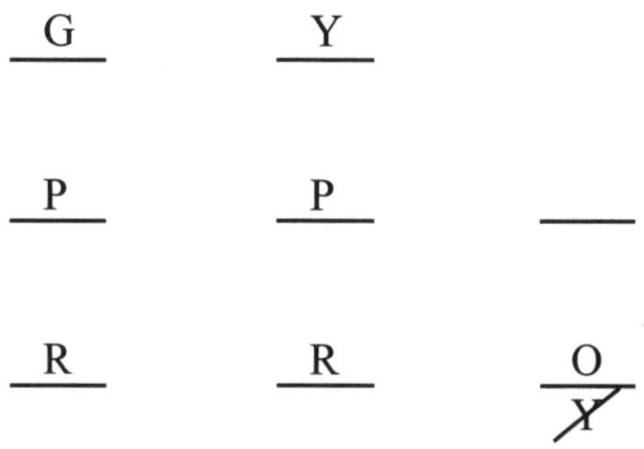

With one of the windows established as R, P, and Y (and containing no other colors since due to the third rule G and O cannot be used in that window), answer choice (E) must be correct.

As an aside, at least G or P must used in the "third" window.

Overall, this is a very challenging game, and it qualifies as one of the hardest games to ever appear on the modern LSAT. Almost every student struggles to complete this game within the time constraint, so do not be discouraged if you had trouble with this game. Instead, study each rule and its implications so that the next time the test makers attempt to use these ideas to create difficulty, you will be prepared.

December 2010 Game #3: Questions 14-18

This is an Advanced Linear: Unbalanced: Overfunded, Numerical Distribution game.

This is arguably the toughest game on this test. The game scenario specifies that five talks—F, G, H, I, and L—are held *in successive order*. Thus, these five talks should be the base of the game. Four employees each then attend two of the talks, leading to the following Linear setup:

Q Q R R S S T T [8]

___ ___ ___ ___ ___
F G H I L

With each employee attending two talks, there are eight variables to be placed (which are represented by doubling Q, R, S, and T in the variable list). These eight variables must be placed into the five talks, with the stipulation that no talk can be attended by more than two employees. Thus, we have the classic elements for a Numerical Distribution:

8 employees ⟶ 5 talks

Maximum 2 per talk; No minimum per talk

Using this information, two employees-to-talks distributions are possible:

2-2-2-2-0

and

2-2-2-1-1

In the 2-2-2-2-0 distribution, four of the talks are attended by two employees each, and one talk is not attended by any employee.

In the 2-2-2-1-1 distribution, three of the talks are attended by two employees each, and two talks are attended by exactly one employee each.

The drawback to these distributions is that our Linear scenario is somewhat fluid; that is, a talk can have 0, 1, or 2 attendees depending on the distribution, but there is no way to fix the number of attendees for each talk at this point. Let's examine the rules and hope there is some information that fixes some of the attendees or talks.

The first rule establishes Not Laws for Q on F and H:

Q Q R R S S T T[8]

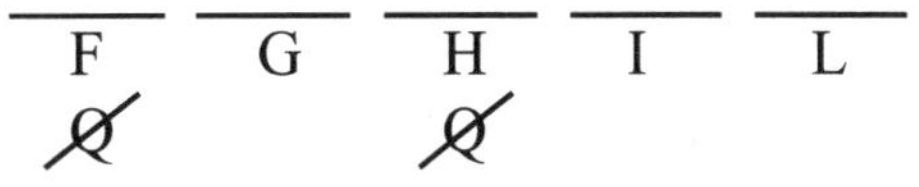

Accordingly, Q must attend two of G, I, and L.

The second rule establishes two more Not Laws, this time for R on G and H:

Q Q R R S S T T[8]

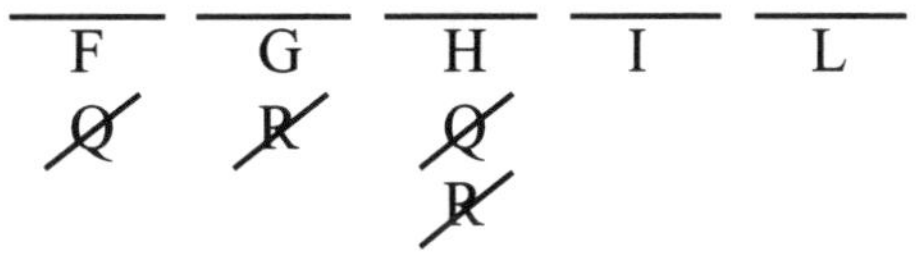

Note that H is particularly restricted at this point, with only S or T as possible attendees. This is not shown as a dual-option because H can have zero attendees. Interestingly (and likely not coincidentally), the next rule establishes that S and T do not attend the same talk:

This is an intriguing rule, because with only five available talks (depending on the distribution), the placement of either S or T has a significant impact on the other variable. For example, in the 2-2-2-2-0 distribution, if you know which two talks S attends, you then know T must attend the other two talks that have attendees.

However, this rule is most interesting when considered in reference to H. Because only S and T can attend H, and S and T cannot both attend the same talk, we can determine that H either has no attendees or that H has exactly one attendee (S or T). That's a particularly useful inference, because

H can be used to determine the proper distribution:

> If the 2-2-2-2-0 distribution is in effect, then H must be the talk with zero attendees. Remember, H can have at most one attendee (S or T), so if another talk were to have no attendees, then H would have to have two attendees. But, since H can never have two attendees, we can infer that no other talk can have zero attendees (and thus, globally, all of the other talks must have at least one attendee). As only H can be the talk with no attendees, in the 2-2-2-2-0 distribution then the other four talks have exactly two attendees each, leading to the following distribution: 2_F-2_G-2_I-2_L-0_H.
>
> If S or T attends H, then the 2-2-2-1-1 distribution applies. Consequently, F, G, H, I, and L all have at least one attendee, and three of F, G, I, and L have two attendees: 2-2-2-1-1_H.

The last two rules are similar in form: both are conditional and each establishes that the first talk attended by a certain employee is also attended by another specific employee (but not necessarily that employees first talk):

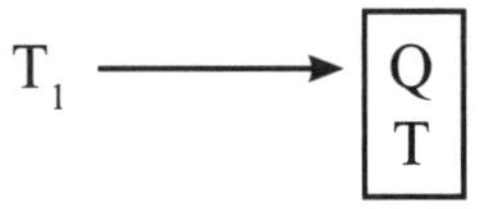

The fourth rule can be combined with the first rule to produce a useful inference: T cannot attend F. Because Q cannot attend F, if T were to attend F there is no way to satisfy the fourth rule. Thus, T cannot attend F, which can be shown as a T Not Law on F:

QQ RR SS TT [8]

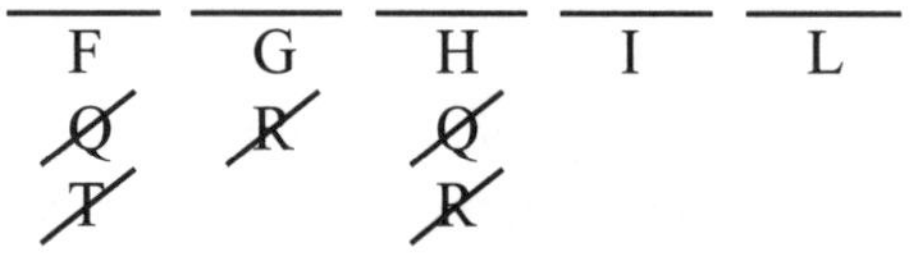

While this is the first inference that follows from these two rules, there are two other powerful inferences that follow from combining these rules with other rules. The two most restricted talks are F and H. H was already discussed above, so the next logical point of examination is F.

As established in the discussion of the distributions above, F (and G, I, and L) must always have at least one attendee. Because Q and T cannot attend F, only R and S are available to attend S. But, when the final rule is considered, a powerful inference results: S must always attend F. Here's why: if R attends F, then from the final rule S must also attend F. But, if R does not attend F, then only S remains to attend F, and because F must always have at least one attendee, S must then attend F. In either case, S attends F, and we can add that to our diagram:

Q Q R R ~~S~~ S T T [8]

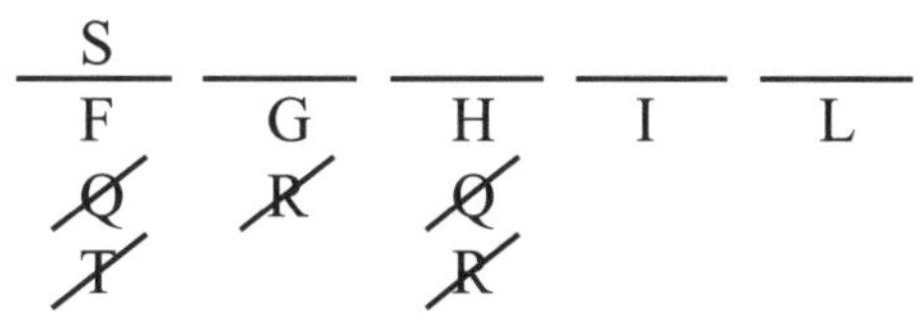

With F and H both discussed, G is the only remaining restricted talk that has not yet been examined. Interestingly, the inference involving G is even trickier than the inference involving F.

Because R cannot attend G, only Q, S and T are available to attend G. Of course, from the third rule, S and T cannot attend the same talk, so there are only three options for employees to attend G:

1. Q and S

   Q and S can both attend G under the 2-2-2-2-0 distribution: if S and R attend F, H is empty, and Q and T attend I (T attends L as well).

2. Q and T

   If the first talk that T attends is G, then from the fourth rule Q must also attend G.

3. Q alone

   Under the 2-2-2-1-1 distribution, Q can attend G alone if R and S attend F, S attends H, and Q and T attend I.

S cannot attend G alone because then S would attend both F and G, and from the fourth rule T would have to attend one of those, which would have to be G. T cannot attend G alone due to the actions of the fourth rule as well. Thus, in each of the three possible scenarios, Q must attend G. This inference can be added to the diagram, leading to the final diagram for the game (the numbers above each talk represent the numerical possibilities):

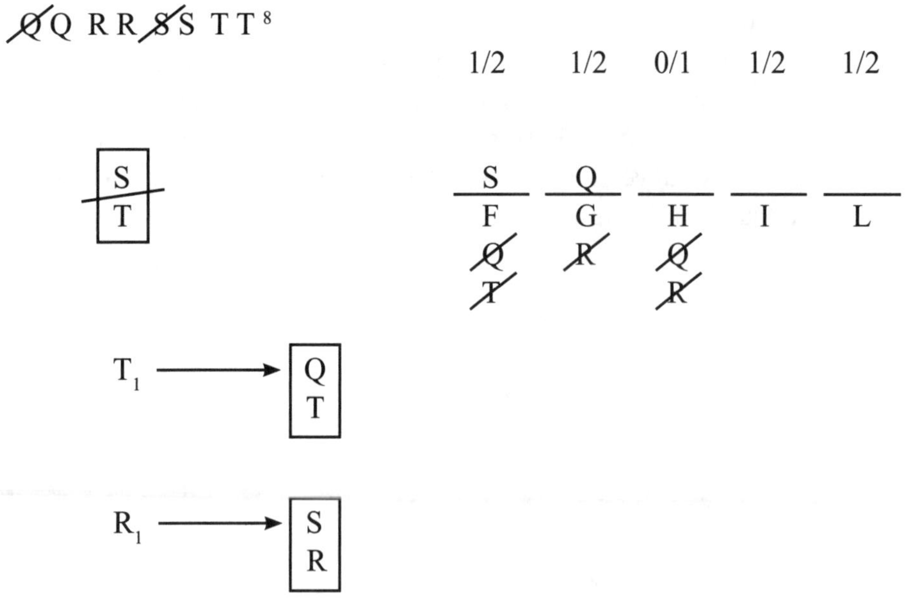

2_F-2_G-2_I-2_L-0_H

2-2-2-1-1_H

There is also a case to be made for creating two templates (one for each distribution), but the information in the final diagram is sufficient to attack the questions, especially if you get the inferences that H is the only talk that can have no attendees, and that S attends F, and Q attends G (and regrettably, these are all tough inferences, and it is very hard to get any one of them, let alone all three).

Question #14: Global, Could Be True, List. The correct answer choice is (C)

As with all complete List questions, simply apply the rules to the answer choices.

Answer choice (A): This answer choice is incorrect because S and T both attend L, which is a violation of the third rule.

Answer choice (B): This answer choice is incorrect because R attends H, a violation of the second rule.

Answer choice (C): This is the correct answer choice.

Answer choice (D): This answer choice is incorrect because Q does not attend the first talk that T attends, a violation of the fourth rule.

Answer choice (E): This answer choice is incorrect because S does not attend the first talk that R attends, a violation of the fifth rule.

Question #15: Local, Must Be True. The correct answer choice is (A)

If no employee attends H, then the 2-2-2-2-0 distribution is in effect, and each of the other talks are attended by exactly two people.

In this scenario, F must have two attendees, and the only two employees that can possibly attend F are R and S. Accordingly, answer choice (A) is correct.

Question #16: Global, Could Be True, List. The correct answer choice is (A)

This questions asks for a list of the talks that R and S could attend together. In the correct answer to question #14, which was (C), R and S both attended F. Thus, without further consideration, answer choices (C) and (E) can be eliminated because neither contains F. Remember—always use prior work that you are confident is correct (and with a List question you should be very confident)!

From our discussion of G, we have determined that Q must attend G. As no talk can have more than two attendees, R and S cannot both attend G. Thus, answer choice (B) can be eliminated.

Only answer choices (A) and (D) remain in contention, and the difference between the two answer choices is that (A) contains I whereas (D) does not. Thus, if you can determine whether it is possible for R and S to attend I together (or not), you will be able to determine the correct answer. This simple hypothetical proves that R and S can attend I together:

Q Q R R S S T T ^{8}

R	T		R	T
S	Q		S	Q
F	G	H	I	L

Consequently, answer choice (A) is correct.

Question #17: Local, Not Necessarily True, FTT. The correct answer choice is (D)

The question stem indicates that Q is the only employee to attend L. This places the game into the 2-2-2-1-1 distribution, and the local condition can be added to the base diagram as follows:

~~Q~~ ~~Q~~ R R ~~S~~ S T T ^{8}

				1
S	Q			Q
F	G	H	I	L

Of course, H can only have 0 or 1 attendees, and so H is the other talk with just one attendee (which must be S or T), and F, G, and I each have two attendees:

~~Q~~~~Q~~ R R ~~S~~S T T ^{8}

2	2	1	2	1
___	___		___	
S	Q	S/T	___	Q
F	G	H	I	L

With Q attending both G and L, Q cannot attend any other talks. When the fourth rule is considered, T's first talk must be either G or L. Since T's first talk can't be the last talk at the conference (because T must attend two talks), we can infer that T attends G:

~~Q~~~~Q~~ R R ~~S~~S ~~T~~T ^{8}

2	2	1	2	1
___	T		___	
S	Q	S/T	___	Q
F	G	H	I	L

This could also be inferred by recognizing that the only candidates to attend G are Q, S, and T, and because S is already attending two other talks, Q and T are the only two employees that can attend G in this scenario.

In addition, as established during the game setup, the only employees that can attend F are R and S. Thus, because F must have two attendees, R and S both attend F in this question:

~~Q~~~~Q~~~~R~~R ~~S~~S ~~T~~T ^{8}

2	2	1	2	1
R	T		___	
S	Q	S/T	___	Q
F	G	H	I	L

At this point, the attendees of F, G, and L are fixed, leaving only H and I still unresolved. H must be attended by S or T, but there is no way to determine which one attends. The remainder of S/T attends I, along with R, who has not yet been assigned to a second talk. This leads to the final diagram for this question:

Q Q R R S S T T [8]

	F	G	H	I	L
	2	2	1	2	1
	R	T		S/T	
	S	Q	S/T	R	Q

The only uncertainty involves S and T, and so you should immediately examine the answer choices that contain S or T. Because S can attend I instead of H, answer choice (D) is not necessarily true and is therefore correct.

Question #18: Local, Not Necessarily True, FTT. The correct answer choice is (E)

This question is similar to question #17, with the exception that R is now the only employee to attend I.

~~Q~~Q ~~R~~R ~~S~~S T T [8]

	F	G	H	I	L
				1	
	S	Q		R	

Again the 2-2-2-1-1 distribution applies, and the inference pattern follows a somewhat similar route to question #17.

H can only have 0 or 1 attendees, and so H is the other talk with just one attendee (which must be S or T), and F, G, and I each have two attendees:

~~Q~~Q ~~R~~R ~~S~~S T T [8]

	F	G	H	I	L
	2	2	1	1	2
	___	___			___
	S	Q	S/T	R	___

F, G, and L each have two attendees, and thus R and S must attend F (they are the only two possible candidates):

~~Q~~Q ~~R~~~~R~~ ~~S~~S T T ^{8}

2	2	1	1	2
R	___			___
S	Q	S/T	R	___
F	G	H	I	L

If G has two attendees, then it must be either Q and S or Q and T. If it were Q and S, then S would attend both F and G, leaving T to attend H. But, this causes a violation of the fourth rule because there is no room for Q to attend H as well. Thus, Q and S cannot attend G in this question, and instead Q and T must be the attendees at G:

~~Q~~Q ~~R~~~~R~~ ~~S~~S ~~T~~T ^{8}

2	2	1	1	2
R	T			___
S	Q	S/T	R	___
F	G	H	I	L

At this point, the attendees of F, G, and I are fixed, leaving only H and L still unresolved. H must be attended by S or T, but there is no way to determine which one attends. The remainder of S/T attends L, along with Q, who has not yet been assigned to a second talk. This leads to the final diagram for this question:

Q Q R R S S T T ^{8}

2	2	1	1	2
R	T			S/T
S	Q	S/T	R	Q
F	G	H	I	L

The only uncertainty involves S and T, and so, as in the last question you should immediately examine the answer choices that contain S or T (again, as in the prior question, these answers are (C), (D), and (E). This is not surprising because the test makers want you to have to work through more answer choices as you approach the end of a game). Because T can attend L instead of H, answer choice (E) is not necessarily true and is therefore correct.

Overall, this is not a fun game. The three key inferences are each difficult to draw, and without them the game is exceptionally difficult. When combined with the second game, the two games form one of the toughest game tandems in LSAT history.

December 2010 Game #4: Questions 19-23

This is a Basic Linear: Balanced game.

After the above average difficulty of the first game, and the extremely high level of difficulty in the second and third games, one would expect that the fourth game would be extremely easy. While this is somewhat true, this game is not as easy as would be expected based on the difficulty of the first three games. This, in part, was one reason the curve for this test was so generous.

The game scenario indicates that six witnesses will testify in a trial in successive order, leading to the following Basic Linear setup:

M R S T U W ^{6}

___ ___ ___ ___ ___ ___
1 2 3 4 5 6

The first rule establishes that S testifies immediately before T or U. This can be diagrammed in one of two ways:

1. [S T/U]

2. [ST]
or
[SU]

The choice of representation is yours; either conveys the meaning of the rule correctly. For our purposes, we will use the first representation as it takes slightly less time to draw. Regardless of the representation that you choose, S can never testify last, and so an S Not Law can be placed under the sixth position:

M R S T U W ^{6}

___ ___ ___ ___ ___ ___
1 2 3 4 5 6
$\not{S}$ (under 6)

Note that you cannot draw any Not Laws for T and U from this rule because only one must be immediately behind S, leaving the other to move freely.

The second rule establishes a double-branched vertical sequence:

```
        R
U > - - - -
        W
```

This rule creates four more Not Laws: U cannot testify fifth or sixth, and R and W cannot testify first. These can be added to our diagram:

M R S T U W [6]

1	2	3	4	5	6
~~R~~				~~U~~	~~S~~
~~W~~					~~U~~

The third rule is somewhat similar to the first rule, and can also be diagrammed in two different ways:

1. [T/W M]

2. [TM]
or
[WM]

From this rule we can determine that M can never be first, which is best shown as another Not Law:

M R S T U W [6]

1	2	3	4	5	6
~~R~~				~~U~~	~~S~~
~~W~~					~~U~~
~~M~~					

At this point, the most restricted space is the first one, and only three witnesses could testify first, a fact best shown with a triple-option. Note that, perhaps not coincidentally, these are the three variables affected by the first rule. Consequently, any time S does not testify first, one of T and U will testify immediately after S, and the other will testify first (and U is affected by the second rule, and T is affected by the third rule, so the options are even more limited).

Adding the triple-option to the diagram leads to the final setup for the game:

MRSTUW [6]

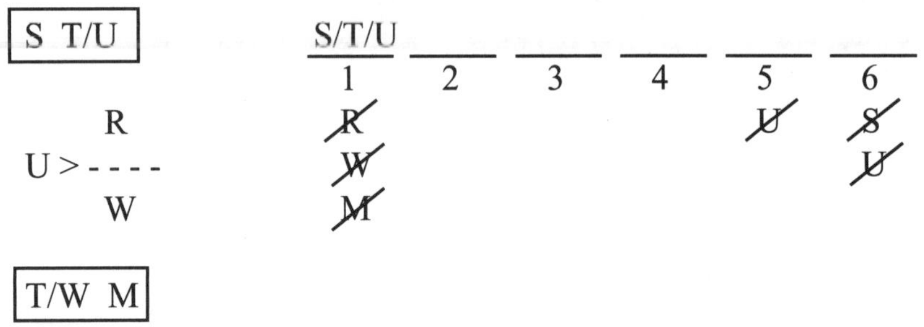

One aspect to note is that the first and second rules are connected through U, and that the second and third rules are connected through W. Each rule is relatively "loose," but the connection of rules must be tracked throughout the game.

Question #19: Global, Could Be True, List. The correct answer choice is (B)

As with all complete List questions, simply apply the rules to the answer choices.

Answer choice (A): This answer choice is incorrect because R testifies earlier than U, which is a violation of the second rule.

Answer choice (B): This is the correct answer choice.

Answer choice (C): This answer choice is incorrect because neither T nor W testifies immediately before W, a violation of the third rule.

Answer choice (D): This answer choice is incorrect because neither T nor U testifies immediately after S, a violation of the first rule.

Answer choice (E): This answer choice is incorrect because R and W testify earlier than U, which is a violation of the second rule.

Question #20: Local, Could Be True. The correct answer choice is (E)

The question stem establishes that T testifies first:

M R S T U W [6]

T					
1	2	3	4	5	6

With T testifying first, U must testify immediately after S in order to conform to the first rule:

[SU]

Of course, from the second rule, U must also testify earlier than R and W:

R
[SU] > - - - -
W

With this sequence in place, only two basic scenarios are possible, each based on complying with the third rule:

M R S T U W [6]

#2: WM block	T	S	U	(R / [WM])		
#1: TM block	T	M	S	U	R/W	W/R
	1	2	3	4	5	6

Accordingly, answer choice (E) is correct.

Question #21: Local, Must Be True. The correct answer choice is (A)

If S testifies fifth, then T must testify sixth in order to conform to the first rule (U cannot testify sixth because of the actions of the second rule). Because only S, T, and U can testify first, and S and T already testify fifth and sixth, U must then testify first. Thus, answer choice (A) is correct.

Question #22: Global, Cannot Be True, List. The correct answer choice is (A)

This is an interesting question because our final diagram contained no Not Laws on either the third or fourth positions. The first step, then, is to refer to prior work in order to eliminate answers. Any combination of variables that can successfully be placed third and fourth can be used to eliminate one of the incorrect answers (this is a Cannot Be True question, so each incorrect answer Could Be True; thus, if a combination is shown to be possible, that answer choice can be eliminated).

Question #19 shows that U and R can testify third and fourth, but that combination does not appear as one of the answers.

Question #20 shows that S and U (option #1), U and R (option #2), and U and W (option #2) can each testify third and fourth, which eliminates answer choices (C) and (E).

Of the three remaining answer choices—(A), (B), and (D)—answer choice (A) is the most promising. Why? Let's examine the surface merits of each, by discussing both of the variables in each answer:

Answer choice (A): The first variable (M) is involved in the third rule, and forces one of two variables (T or W) to be second. This is extremely restrictive.

The second variable (T) is involved in the first and third rules, and from the first rule is one of the options to follow another variable in a block. When T is behind M, T cannot be behind S, and so the first rule then dictates that U must testify after S. From the third rule only T or W can testify immediately before M, so when T is behind M, W must testify immediately before M, or second. Thus, the placement of these two variables leads to great restrictions, possibly great enough to lead to an impossible situation.

Answer choice (B): The first variable (R) is involved in the second rule, and forces U to be first or second. This is restrictive, but not as restrictive as the first variable in answer choice (A)

The second variable (S), is involved in the first rule, but that variable is placed in such a position that it can still meet the condition of the first rule without restriction. This is also less restrictive than the second variable in answer choice (A).

Answer choice (D): The first variable (T) is from a block rule, but it is placed in such a position that it can still meet the condition of the first rule without restriction.

The second variable (R) is involved in the sequence, and while this forces U to testify first or second, it is not as restrictive as the second variable placement in (A).

So, if we were using hypotheticals to solve this question, answer choice (A) would be the best starting point. Some might say that you would naturally start at (A) anyway, but that is beside the point. In this question they happen to be the same, but in another question it might be (D) that is the best starting point. Having that information would then save a considerable amount of time in making hypotheticals. Let's now look at answer choice (A) and see what occurs when M testifies third and T testifies fourth:

M R S T U W [6]

		M	T		
1	2	3	4	5	6

As mentioned previously, this scenario forces W to be second, and also creates an SU block:

M R S T U W [6]

SU

	W	M	T		
1	2	3	4	5	6

At this point, the only placement option for the SU block is fifth and sixth, which is impossible due to the requirements of the second rule. Thus, M and T cannot testify third and fourth because that leads to an impossible outcome, and therefore answer choice (A) cannot be true and is correct.

Question #23: Global, Cannot Be True, List. The correct answer choice is (D)

This question is similar to question #23, but instead asks for the variables that cannot be first and second, respectively. The first step is to quickly check the R, W, and M Not Laws on the first position. Regrettably, this reveals no violation. Second, check prior hypotheticals to eliminate the answer choices that could be true and are therefore incorrect. The work in question #20 eliminates answer choice (B), and the work in question #21 helps eliminate answer choice (E).

The three remaining answer choices all feature a combination of variables from the group S, T, and U. Given that all three are featured in the first rule, this is surely notable! Let's examine each:

Answer choice (A): This arrangement conforms to the rule perfectly, and allows U, also a critical variable due to its role in the second rule, to testify relatively early on. Thus, this answer does not appear to create any issues.

Answer choice (C): Placing T and S first and second, respectively, forces U to testify third in accordance with the second rule. By itself this creates no issues, and allow for ample to room to satisfy the second and third rules.

Answer choice (D): This is the correct answer choice. If U and T are first and second, then neither can testify immediately after S. As this violates the first rule, this answer choice cannot be true and must therefore be correct.

Chapter Six: The December 2010 LSAT Deconstructed

The explanations below are presented in the same order that the questions are given on the exam. Please keep in mind that all explanations draw on methods discussed in *The PowerScore LSAT Logical Reasoning Bible*. Please refer to that text if you desire a more detailed discussion of a particular concept or approach. If you encounter any unknown terms, a glossary is provided at the end of the book.

December 2010 Section 4: Logical Reasoning

Overview: This was a relatively difficult Logical Reasoning section, with a high percentage of Second Family questions. As would be expected, the questions were generally more challenging toward the latter half of the section, which included three of the five Strengthen questions, two challenging Justify the Conclusion questions (#16 and #18), and a tricky Parallel Reasoning question (#25). Conditional reasoning dominated this section, with roughly one third of all questions containing conditional reasoning. Some of these questions required the ability to manipulate complex conditional relationships, and this compounded the overall difficulty of the section. There was also a high incidence of stimuli containing causal reasoning of various difficulty levels.

Question #1: Main Point, CE. The correct answer choice is (C)

The argument opens with a marine biologist stating that scientists have long wondered why the fish around coral reefs are so colorful. One possible explanation, the biologist observes, is that the coral reefs themselves may be quite colorful, thus providing the fish with a suitable environment for camouflage. In the last half of the stimulus, the biologist rejects this hypothesis by asserting that "this suggestion" (i.e. that colorful fish are camouflaged by the coral reefs) is mistaken. The biologist's conclusion is based upon the premise that since most corals are relatively dull browns and greens, a coral reef stripped of its fish would be monochromatic, i.e. not colorful.

Your ability to quickly identify the correct answer to a Main Point question is directly tied to your understanding of the structure of the argument and its conclusion. Since the correct answer is often simply a paraphrase of the conclusion, test makers are prone to hiding the conclusion by introducing competing viewpoints and/or subsidiary conclusions in order to increase the level of difficulty of the question. The argument/counterargument structure can thus be summarized as follows:

Argument ("one suggestion"):

Premise 1:	Many animal species use camouflage to avoid predators
Premise 2:	Coral reefs are colorful
Conclusion:	The fish are camouflaged by the reefs

Because this viewpoint attempts to explain a particular phenomenon (colorful fish round the reefs), the conclusion contains the following causal reasoning structure:

Cause		Effect
Camouflage	⟶	Colorful fish

Counterargument ("marine biologist"):

Premise 1:	Most corals are relatively dull browns and greens
Sub. Conclusion:	A reef stripped of its fish is monochromatic
Main Conclusion:	The hypothesis that the fish are colorful because they are camouflaged by the reefs is mistaken.

The author's strategy for attacking the causal argument is based on the assertion that the effect occurs (colorful fish) without the cause (colorful reefs). This is a common way to attack causal arguments on the LSAT.

The key here is to avoid getting distracted by the abundance of detail and focus instead on the key elements that point to the marine biologist's main conclusion. Note, for instance, that whenever the stimulus begins by describing one possible explanation for a given phenomenon, the author's conclusion will most likely counter it. Also, Main Point questions are especially likely to have their conclusions "hidden" somewhere in the middle of the stimulus, without a clear conclusion indicator. In fact, the conclusion indicator "therefore" (line 4) is used in a somewhat misleading way to indicate not the author's main conclusion, but rather the opposing viewpoint.

Answer choice (A): The hypothesis that fish are camouflaged by the bright colors of the coral reefs is not the main conclusion of the argument, but rather the opposing viewpoint that the author claims is mistaken. Answers containing opposing viewpoints are frequent decoys in Main Point questions.

Answer choice (B): Even though many animal species use camouflage to avoid predators, this is a premise for the opposing viewpoint that the author asserts is mistaken.

Answer choice (C): This is the correct answer choice, as it matches our prephrase of the conclusion.

Answer choice (D): While a reef stripped of its fish is indeed monochromatic, this is a premise used in support of the conclusion that camouflage cannot explain the bright colors of the fish. Factual evidence is rarely the main point of the argument, because such evidence is almost always used in support of another idea.

Answer choice (E): Although the author did observe that the corals in coral reefs are mostly dull hues of brown and green, this is a premise used to explain why a reef stripped of its fish is monochromatic, and therefore unable to provide camouflage for the colorful fish. Do not fall into the trap of assuming that the last sentence of the stimulus will always contain the conclusion: oftentimes, the conclusion is hidden somewhere else the argument, especially in Main Point questions.

Question #2: Strengthen—Principle. The correct answer choice is (D)

The argument structure can be analyzed as follows:

Premise:	To discover what percentage of teenagers believe in telekinesis—the psychic ability to move objects without physically touching them—a recent survey asked a representative sample of teenagers whether they agreed with the following statement: "A person's thoughts can influence the movement of physical objects."
Premise:	But because this statement is particularly ambiguous and is amenable to a naturalistic, uncontroversial interpretation,
Conclusion:	the survey's responses are also ambiguous.

In summary, the author claims that a survey seeking to discover what percentage of teenagers believe in telekinesis uses an ambiguously phrased question, and, on that basis, the author concludes that the survey's responses will also be ambiguous. Unfortunately, we have no evidence suggesting that an ambiguously worded question is likely to produce an ambiguous response. Just because the statement is amenable to a naturalistic, uncontroversial interpretation does not necessarily mean that any students would actually interpret it in such way, let alone imply that their responses would be as ambiguous as the question itself.

Because the question stem asks us to identify a general proposition to which the stimulus conforms, this is a Strengthen-PR question (unlike a question stem asking us to identify a proposition that conforms to the stimulus, which would be a Must-PR question). It is also worth noting that the phrase "general proposition" is often used in place of "principle." Our goal, therefore, is to take a broad, general proposition that, when applied to the situation in the stimulus, helps support the conclusion that the survey's responses are likely to be ambiguous.

Answer choice (A): The issue with the statement regarding telekinesis is not that it is uncontroversial, but that it is ambiguous. The uncontroversial interpretation of the statement is only a result of its allegedly ambiguous meaning. Furthermore, the author never suggested that this statement was downright useless—she merely expressed a reservation concerning the responses generated by a survey that contains ambiguous statements. This answer choice does not help prove the conclusion and is therefore incorrect.

Answer choice (B): The problem with this answer is that it does not help strengthen the conclusion that the survey's responses are ambiguous. Even if every statement is amenable to multiple interpretations, this does not automatically mean that survey responses to that question are ambiguous.

Answer choice (C): This is the most frequently selected incorrect answer choice, as it relates the language of a survey's questions to the nature of its responses. However, answer choice (C) is a Mistaken Negation of the correct answer. Applying this principle fails to strengthen the argument since it applies to surveys whose questions *are* well phrased, not surveys whose questions are not.

Just because the responses to well phrased questions are unambiguous does not prove that the responses to poorly phrased questions are ambiguous.

Answer choice (D): This is the correct answer choice. When combined with the premise that the statement regarding telekinesis is ambiguous, this principle provides overwhelming support for the conclusion that the responses generated by that question are also ambiguous.

Note the general nature of the language used in this principle. Although it relates the phrasing of the questions to the survey's outcome, this principle does not address the topic of psychic ability or uncontroversial interpretations, nor does it specifically examine the impact of "ambiguous statements" on a survey's responses. Instead, the principle focuses on "poorly phrased questions." However, because ambiguous statements can be subsumed within the category of "poorly phrased statements," the specific situation described in the stimulus still falls under the purview of this principle. Such generalities are quite common of Strengthen-PR answer choices.

Also note that even if you disagree with this principle, you cannot eliminate answer choice (D) on that basis alone. Remember, in Strengthen questions, the question stem implies that the answers should be taken as true.

Answer choice (E): The author's argument is not focused on statements about psychic phenomena in general, but rather on the ambiguous wording of certain statements regarding psychic phenomena. If statements about psychic phenomena can always be given naturalistic interpretations, then any survey seeking to determine our beliefs in psychic phenomena will be inherently biased in favor of naturalistic explanations. Because adopting this principle is inconsistent with the author's reasoning, this answer choice cannot strengthen the conclusion and is therefore incorrect.

Question #3: Strengthen, CE. The correct answer choice is (A)

The conclusion of the argument suggests that having a perfect pitch is a consequence of genetic factors:

Premise:	A person who has perfect pitch has a higher chance of being related to someone else who has it than a person without perfect pitch
Conclusion:	Having a perfect pitch is a consequence of genetic factors

The relationship between premise and conclusion is a causal one, which can be diagrammed as:

GF = genetic factors
PF = perfect pitch

<u>C</u> <u>E</u>

GF ⟶ PF

As with all causal arguments, you must critically evaluate the causality described in the conclusion. The conclusion, which is easy to spot due to the conclusion indicator "this shows that," is based on a study that observed a correlation between having perfect pitch and having a relative who also has perfect pitch. Correlations between two variables do not automatically imply that one causes the other, as they may be coincidental effects of another cause, among other reasons. For instance, what if people who have relatives with perfect pitch are more likely to attend concerts, study the piano, or receive musical training? To strengthen the cause and effect relationship, look for answers that eliminate such alternate causes and show that nothing else but genetics can explain why those who have perfect pitch tend to be related to someone else who has it.

Answer choice (A): This is the correct answer choice, as it strengthens the argument by eliminating an alternate cause for the stated effect. If people who have relatives with perfect pitch are no more likely to receive superior musical training, their perfect pitch cannot be the result of such training. Note that this answer choice does not prove the cause and effect relationship—it is still possible that other causes could account for the stated effect. In Strengthen questions, your choice should be based upon a comparative analysis between the five answer choices, and the correct answer choice does not have to prove the conclusion 100% to be correct.

Answer choice (B): Whether the *researchers* conducting the study had perfect pitch is irrelevant to our evaluation of the study's conclusion. This answer choice is incorrect.

Answer choice (C): Discussing the implications of the stated effect (perfect pitch) is a digression that neither strengthens nor weakens the causal argument.

Answer choice (D): This Opposite answer hurts the argument by suggesting that children whose parents have perfect pitch receive more musical training, and may develop perfect pitch as a result of such training. Because alternate causes weaken the argument, this type of wrong answer choice appears frequently in Strengthen questions.

Answer choice (E): If anything, this answer may hurt the argument by showing that having perfect pitch is also correlated with (and may thus be the result of) musical training. However, because we do not know if such training is the result of having relatives who have perfect pitch, this answer does not contribute to the causal explanation of the correlation cited by the study.

Question #4: Method of Reasoning—AP, CE. The correct answer choice is (C)

The argument is structured as follows:

Premise:	Paleontologists recently excavated two corresponding sets of dinosaur tracks, one left by a large grazing dinosaur and the other by a smaller predatory dinosaur.
Premise:	The two sets of tracks make abrupt turns repeatedly in tandem.
Sub. Conclusion:	The predator was following the grazing dinosaur and had matched its stride.
Premise (analogy):	Modern predatory mammals, such as lions, match the stride of prey they are chasing immediately before they strike those prey.
Conclusion:	The predatory dinosaur was chasing the grazing dinosaur and attacked immediately afterwards.

Like many Method—AP arguments, the conclusion is in the final sentence of the stimulus, and in this case is introduced by the conclusion indicator "this suggests that." Because most test-takers expect the conclusion to appear there, they will probably not ask you to identify it—that would be a relatively simple task. Instead, the statement referenced in question stem ("the predatory dinosaur was following the grazing dinosaur and had matched its stride") is a premise used to support the main conclusion, though its relationship to the rest of the argument merits further analysis.

Because the factual findings of studies and investigations usually function as evidence supporting the conclusion, the fact that the two sets of dinosaur tracks make abrupt turns serves the role of a pure premise. On the basis of that observation, the author concludes ("suggesting that" is a conclusion indicator) that the predator was following the grazing dinosaur and had matched its stride. The next sentence, however, clarifies the importance of this finding. Because modern predatory mammals also match the stride of prey they are chasing immediately before they strike, the author then concludes that the same situation occurred between the two dinosaurs in question (essentially, the author assumes that the cause of the similar tracks is the similar predatory behavior).

Structurally, the statement referenced in the question stem is both a premise and a conclusion: it is supported by the description of the dinosaur tracks, but it also provides the basis for the analogy that supports the main conclusion of the argument. Because the argument structure in Method—AP questions tends to be more complex than in the typical argument, it is critical to identify each argument part correctly and understand how they relate to each other before attacking the answer choices.

Answer choice (A): This answer can be immediately eliminated, since this statement *does* help establish the overall conclusion of the argument, and not simply the scientific importance of that conclusion. In fact, it is not entirely clear what the scientific importance of the conclusion is.

Answer choice (B): Given that stimulus does not contain an argument/counterargument structure, there is no evidence that one hypothesis is being rejected in favor of another hypothesis.

Answer choice (C): This is the correct answer choice. The statement referenced in the question stem establishes the basis for the analogy between dinosaurs and modern predators, which supports the overall conclusion of the argument.

Answer choice (D): There is no evidence of any possible objection to the argument's conclusion (such as an alternate cause for the pattern of dinosaur tracks). Had the author suggested that, for instance, predatory dinosaurs do not normally follow large grazing dinosaurs unless they were planning to attack them, this would fit the description in this answer choice.

Answer choice (E): We know this answer is incorrect because it claims the statement is the main conclusion, when it was in fact a sub-conclusion.

Question #5: Weaken, CE. The correct answer choice is (B)

Since the key to weakening an LSAT argument is to focus on the conclusion, it is essential to break down the argument, which is structured as follows:

Premise:	Over the past 25 years, the incidence of skin cancer caused by exposure to the sun has continued to grow.
Premise:	The growing incidence of skin cancer has occurred in spite of an increasingly widespread use of sunscreens.
Conclusion:	Using sunscreen is unlikely to reduce a person's risk of developing such skin cancer.

The conclusion of the argument is the final sentence, which contains the conclusion indicator "this shows that." By suggesting that sunscreen products are unlikely to reduce the risk of developing skin cancer, the author assumes that there is no causal relationship between sunscreen use and reducing cancer risk:

↑SU = increased sunscreen use

↓CR = decreased cancer risk

C   E

↑SU —+→ ↓CR

To weaken this argument, you need to show that a causal link does exist, i.e. that using sunscreen may still reduce a person's risk of developing skin cancer, despite the growing incidence of skin

cancer over the past 25 years. Almost all correct LSAT Weaken question answers leave the premises intact and focus instead on the conclusion of the argument. Thus, in prephrasing an answer, attempting to attack the facts concerning the increase in skin cancer or the increased use of sunscreen is unlikely to be fruitful. Instead, look to undermine the statement in the conclusion.
Because personalizing an argument can often yield a stronger prephrase, imagine how you would respond if you were, say, a dermatologist who spent her entire career advising patients to use sunscreen in order to protect themselves against skin cancer. What if people tend to spend a larger amount of time in the sun today than they did 25 years ago? In that case, it is possible that the incidence of skin cancer would have been even greater without the use of sunscreens. Or perhaps the effects of sun damage are cumulative and take a long time to develop into skin cancer. Given that the widespread use of sunscreens is a relatively recent phenomenon, we would not be able to observe a decrease in the cancer rates until much later, even if sunscreen do help reduce the risk of skin cancer later in life.

The key to prephrasing a good answer, especially to Weaken questions, is to personalize the argument and understand what the correct answer must *do* (not necessarily *say*). Do not get "boxed in" by your prephrase—sometimes there are multiple ways to weaken a given conclusion.

Answer choice (A): Even if most people who purchase sunscreens do not purchase the most expensive product, this does not suggest that sunscreens work, and therefore does not weaken the conclusion. If you found this answer choice attractive, you must have assumed that the effectiveness of sunscreens somehow depends on how expensive they are. Although such an assumption can potentially explain why most people do not see the benefits of using sunscreen (they do not buy the most expensive products), the stimulus contains no evidence that cost and effectiveness are associated. Therefore, this answer choice is incorrect.

Answer choice (B): This is the correct answer choice. If skin cancer generally develops among the very old as a result of sunburns experienced when very young, then the widespread use of sunscreens would not lower their own risk of developing cancer. However, sunscreen use can still prevent the very young from developing cancer later in life, but this benefit will not become apparent until much later. Consequently, the growing incidence of skin cancer in recent years cannot be interpreted as conclusive evidence that sunscreen products fail to protect against it. As a point of interest, note that because of the contradictory nature of the premises (sunscreen use increased but cancer incidence also increased), this answer choice has the feel of a Resolve the Paradox question answer choice.

Answer choice (C): If anything, this answer would serve to strengthen the argument. While the opinion of experts is often an irrelevant consideration in many arguments, in this case the argument concerns skin cancer, and dermatologists would have applicable expertise in that area. Thus, because at best this answer is irrelevant and at worst it strengthens the argument, this answer choice is incorrect.

Answer choice (D): If people who know that they are especially susceptible to skin cancer avoid spending a large amount of time in the sun, their behavior may lower their risk of developing skin cancer, regardless of whether they use sunscreen products or not. However, the fact that a particular group of people found another way to lower their risk has no impact on the effectiveness of sunscreen products, which is at the heart of this argument.

Answer choice (E): This answer choice states that those who use sunscreens most regularly are people who believe themselves to be most susceptible to skin cancer. However, it is unclear whether the use of sunscreen lowered their susceptibility to cancer. Just because the overall incidence of skin cancer has increased does not tell us whether it is evenly distributed between those who are susceptible to the disease and those who are not. In fact, if the vast majority of cancer patients were people who were susceptible to the disease (and therefore used sunscreen regularly, as this answer choice suggests), this would provide fairly strong evidence that using sunscreen is unlikely to reduce a susceptible person's risk of developing cancer. Because this would strengthen the conclusion of the argument, this answer choice is incorrect.

Question #6: Must Be True, SN. The correct answer choice is (A)

The stimulus contains a fact set. When analyzing it, you should notice the sufficient condition indicator "if" in the first sentence: you must meet *both* sufficient conditions in order to establish that the proposal will not be funded. Do not be distracted by order in which the conditions are presented—the necessary condition here appears before the two sufficient conditions, and this is a presentation trick often used by the test makers in order to test your understanding of how conditional relationships work.

The first sentence can be diagrammed as follows:

50P = 50 people per year available for hire
25% = duplicate 25% of the material covered in other departments
PF = proposal is funded

$< 50P$

and ⟶ ~~PF~~

$> 25\%$

In taking the contrapositive of a conditional statement containing two sufficient conditions, "and" becomes "or" and vice versa:

$\geq 50P$

PF ⟶ or

$\leq 25\%$

Note also that instead of simply negating each of the sufficient conditions, we automatically translated them into their functional meaning (for example, "not less than 50 people" becomes "at least 50 people" or "50 or more people" when negated).

In considering the contrapositive of the initial conditional statement, for the proposal to be funded, at least one of the two necessary conditions must be met: either at least 50 people must be available for hire, or else the department must duplicate no more than 25 percent of the material covered in other departments. According to the stimulus, the proposed Area Studies Department will receive funding, and the proposal duplicates more than 25 percent of the material covered in the Anthropology Department. Therefore, because the sufficient condition occurs and one of the two possible necessary conditions does not occur, the other necessary condition must occur and at least 50 people per year must be available for hire. This prephrase immediately reveals answer choice (A) to be correct.

Answer choice (A): This is the correct answer choice. If one of the necessary conditions cannot be met (the Area Studies Department duplicates more than 25 percent of the material covered in other departments), the other condition must be met, i.e. Area Studies must have at least 50 people per year available for hire. Otherwise, the department would not be funded.

Answer choice (B): Whether Area Studies duplicates more than 25 percent of the material covered in any existing department other than Anthropology is unknown. All we know is that it duplicates more than 25 percent of the material in the Anthropology department.

Answer choice (C): It is entirely plausible that Area Studies would have been funded even if it did not duplicate more than 25 percent of the material covered in Anthropology. In fact, one of the necessary conditions a department must meet in order to receive funding is to ensure that it does not duplicate more than 25 percent of the material in other departments. Although meeting this condition does not ensure funding (this would be a Mistaken Reversal), it certainly does not preclude it.

Answer choice (D): Just because Area Studies duplicates more than 25 percent of the material in Anthropology does not mean that the reverse is also true. We can only infer this if we knew that the two departments cover an identical amount of material. However, if Area Studies covers more material than Anthropology, it is possible that Anthropology duplicates a much smaller fraction of the Area Studies material, even though Area Studies duplicates 25 percent of the Anthropology material.

Take a simpler scenario: John has 4 apples and Mary has 10. If they share one apple in common, Mary shares 25% of John's apples, whereas John shares only 10% of Mary's apples.

Answer choice (E): This Opposite answer is the logical opposite of answer choice (A). If Area Studies meets neither one of the two necessary conditions for receiving funding—it duplicates 25 percent of the material covered in another department *and* has fewer than 50 people per year available for hire, it would not receive funding. This would contradict the final sentence in the stimulus, in which the administrator explicitly states that they will fund the new department.

Question #7: Resolve the Paradox. The correct answer choice is (C)

The stimulus contains a fact set about the two bird populations—one captive and one wild—of the same species of bird. Over a period of thirty years, the average beak size of the captive birds did not change, while the average beak size of the wild birds decreased significantly. The correct answer must account for the difference in beak size between the two groups of birds. More specifically, it must explain why the average beak size of the wild birds decreased during the study period, while the captive birds' beaks did not.

Note that the stimulus does not contain a true paradox, just an odd situation that is presented without explanation. The correct answer must explain how the situation came into being while allowing both sides of the situation to be factually correct. It would be a mistake, for instance, to question the finding that the average beak size of the wild birds decreased because the decrease is presented as a fact in the stimulus. As in all Resolve questions, because you are not seeking to disprove one side of the situation, look for an answer choice that contains a possible cause of the situation.

Answer choice (A): At first glance, this may seem to be an attractive answer. After all, if the small-beaked wild birds were easier to capture and measure, that would explain why wild birds were observed as having smaller beaks. But the researcher never stated that wild birds had smaller beaks in general; rather, their size *decreased* over time. If small-beaked wild birds had been easier to capture from the beginning, this would suggest that the research was biased in favor of capturing small-beaked wild birds from the very beginning of the study period. Even if this was the case, this does not explain why the beak size decreased over time.

The key to Resolve questions is close reading. Answer choice (A) is attractive because it appears to possibly explain the difference in beak size between the two groups of birds, but it actually provides no explanation for the change in the beak size of the wild birds. Instead, it gives a reason why these birds would have been consistently observed as having smaller than average beaks, which was not the case. In short, this answer attempts to explain a difference with a similarity, which is always incorrect in a Resolve question. You must make sure that the answer you select does not deviate from the circumstances described in the stimulus.

Answer choice (B): Even if large-beaked wild birds were easier to capture and measure, why did the researchers observe a decrease in their beak size? This answer provides no explanation, and thus cannot be correct.

Answer choice (C): This is the correct answer choice. If changes in the wild birds' food supply during the study period favored the survival of small-beaked birds, then over time there would be sufficient evolutionary pressure on beak size to gradually change it. As this answer choice explains the difference in beak sizes, this answer choice is correct.

Some students might object to this answer because the situation seems unrealistic: during extended periods of drought, for instance, birds with larger beaks are favored because larger beaks are more helpful for opening hard seeds. However, remember that the question stem tells you that each answer choice should be taken as true. Since this answer choice clearly states that changes in the food supply favored the survival of small-beaked birds during the period of the study, you must accept that as true and then analyze what effect that would have.

Answer choice (D): Information about body size does not necessarily explain the difference in beak size between the two groups of birds. Consequently, this answer choice is incorrect.

Answer choice (E): There are two ways to look at this answer. In the first, if researchers observed a significant decrease in the average beak size of the wild birds, most likely they measured some bird beaks on more than one occasion. But even so, that would not provide an explanation for the researchers' findings. The second way of looking at this answer is that measuring the beak of the same bird more than once is at best a randomizing factor, and a random factor cannot explain what is clearly a pattern of decrease. Regardless, under either scenario, this answer is still incorrect.

Question #8: Must Be True. The correct answer choice is (C)

Unlike many Must Be True question stimuli, this stimulus contains an argument, which is structured as follows:

Premise: Comparative study of traditional narratives from widely separated epochs and diverse cultures reveals common themes and story types.

Conclusion: Storytelling appears to be a universal aspect of both past and present cultures.

Even though there are no clear conclusion indicators to help us identify the conclusion, the second sentence in the stimulus describes the findings of a study, which typically function as evidence (or premises) for the conclusion of the argument. Furthermore, you should notice that the first sentence contains a broad statement, the specific support for which was presented in the second sentence.

The question stem asks us to identify a statement most supported by the evidence from the study of traditional narratives. When prephrasing an answer to this question, ask yourself what did you read in the stimulus, and what conclusion can you draw from the information regarding traditional narratives? Since the author already provided us with a conclusion, the correct answer is likely to be a variation on the same theme. It is also important to know exactly what the author said, and not to generalize. Some of the incorrect answer choices will prey upon those who did not read the stimulus closely and present information that is likely to be true, but is not necessarily provable by referring to the stimulus.

Note that there is a difference between knowing what the author said, and remembering the information in the stimulus verbatim. Although many Must Be True questions do test you on the details, there is no need to remember, for instance, the specific examples of common themes or common story types. As with Reading Comprehension questions, remembering such minutiae is not as important as understanding the structure of the argument. As you attack the answer choices, you can always return to the stimulus and quickly re-read the details to confirm your perceptions. Furthermore, the question stem asks us to identify an inference based on the evidence regarding traditional narratives, which is fairly general. The correct answer will likely be a more general, conclusionary statement that is not focused on the details that comprise such evidence.

Answer choice (A): The author never suggested that storytellers borrow themes from other cultures, merely that such themes are shared across cultures and epochs. Clearly, if storytellers borrowed themes from other cultures, this would be one possible cause for such similarities. However, since many other factors can explain the findings of the study, this answer cannot be definitively proven by referring to the facts stated in the stimulus.

Answer choice (B): Just because the author understands that narrative is a universal aspect of human culture does not mean that the *storytellers* were conscious of that fact. This answer choice is attractive because it restates the conclusion of the author's argument, but contains a shift in the perspective from the author's to the storytellers'. Since such shifts appear frequently in incorrect answers to Logical Reasoning and Reading Comprehension questions, avoiding them requires careful reading of the stimulus and the answer choices.

Answer choice (C): This is the correct answer choice. Since the study of narratives revealed common themes and story types from a wide variety of cultures and epochs, clearly there are certain concerns and interests that arise in all cultures.

Note the relatively abstract, general nature of this answer. It does not specify, for instance, why such concerns and interests arise in all cultures—there can be multiple explanations for that phenomenon. Also, this answer choice does not claim that ***all*** human concerns and interests arise in all of the world's cultures. Instead, only "certain" concerns and interests do. Words such as "certain" and "some" provide a convenient way for test makers to qualify the scope of the correct Must Be True answer so as to make it provable by the facts stated in the stimulus.

Answer choice (D): The stimulus contains no evidence for inferring the relative importance of storytelling in ancient cultures versus modern cultures. Just because storytelling appears to be universal in both types of cultures does not mean that it was equally important.

Answer choice (E): No mention was made of the "best way" to understand a culture, only that cultures share certain common attributes. This Exaggerated Answer takes information from the stimulus and attempts to make a broader statement that is not supported by the stimulus. Note also that answers that use the phrase "best way" (or any synonymous phrase) are almost always incorrect on LSAT questions.

Question #9: Parallel Flaw, SN. The correct answer choice is (C)

The stimulus features conditional reasoning, which is identifiable by the use of the sufficient condition indicator "if" in the first sentence. The conditional relationship can be diagrammed as follows:

FBP = First child born prematurely
SBP = Second child born prematurely

FBP ⟶ SBP

The first clause of the second sentence indicates that the necessary condition has not occurred, as Jackie's second child was not born before its due date:

~~SBP~~$_{Jackie}$

On the basis of this information, the author concludes that it is likely that the sufficient condition did not occur, i.e. that Jackie's first child was probably not born before its due date:

~~FBP~~$_{Jackie}$

While the conclusion appears to be based on the contrapositive of the conditional relationship, there is a peculiarity in the language that reveals the flaw in the argument, and that you can use to your advantage when attacking the answer choices: the phrase "likely" appears just before the necessary condition in the first sentence, and when this event has been found not to occur, the author uses the same phrase ("likely") to qualify the conclusion.

The entire form of the argument, then, appears as follows:

Premise: FBP ⟶ SBP (likely)

Premise/Conclusion: ~~SBP~~$_{Jackie}$ ⟶ ~~FBP~~$_{Jackie}$ (likely)

Many students, when examining this argument, do not realize at first that there is a flaw present. The structure appears to be that of a contrapositive, and they simply accept that the argument is sound and move on. But, the question stem clearly notes that the argument is "questionable," so let us take a moment and see where the error occurs. As mentioned before, the use of "likely" is at the heart of the problem, and in the argument the author does not make a perfect contrapositive but rather shifts the word "likely" from the from one necessary condition to the other necessary condition (as opposed to the sufficient condition, where the "likely" should have moved during the contrapositive). Here's how the argument would have appeared *if the argument was sound*:

Premise: FBP ⟶ SBP (likely)

Premise/Conclusion: ~~SBP~~$_{Jackie}$ (likely) ⟶ ~~FBP~~$_{Jackie}$

Note how the "likely" should have moved from the necessary to the sufficient, but in the actual argument the author moved it from the necessary condition to the necessary condition (which was the conclusion).

Because your job is to parallel the argument, you must parallel the conclusion as well as the premises, making sure to "match" the certainty level of all subcomponents in the argument. The correct answer choice should contain a seeming-contrapositive argument form, and also have the same probabilistic language ("likely" or a similar term) modifying both the necessary condition and the conclusion. This knowledge allows you to quickly eliminate answer choices (D) and (E) from consideration, and focus your analysis of the conditional relationships in answer choices (A), (B), and (C).

Answer choice (A): Although this answer choice uses the same probabilistic language as the stimulus ("probably" is synonymous with "likely"), it is incorrect because the argument is in the form of Mistaken Negation:

Premise: Finish Project ⟶ Go to Fair (probably)

Premise/Conclusion: ~~Finish Project~~$_{Ben}$ ⟶ ~~Go to Fair~~$_{Ben}$ (probably)

Note that this answer choice uses the sufficient condition indicator ("people who") instead of "if." This difference is inconsequential and should not be used as grounds for eliminating the answer.

Answer choice (B): Although this answer choice also uses the same probabilistic language as the stimulus, it is incorrect because the argument is in the form of Mistaken Reversal:

Premise: Resp. Owner ⟶ Good with Kids (probably)

Premise/Conclusion: Good with Kids ⟶ Resp. Owner (probably)

As with answer choice (A), the difference between the sufficient condition indicator used in the stimulus ("if") and the answer choice ("all") is irrelevant, since they both modify the same type of condition.

Answer choice (C): This is the correct answer choice. The argument is in a contrapositive form and therefore matches the logical validity of the stimulus. It also uses the identical term "likely" in the necessary condition and a synonymous term "probably" in the conclusion:

Premise: Movie a Hit ⟶ Sequel a Hit (likely)

Premise/Conclusion: ~~Sequel a Hit~~$_{HawkII}$ ⟶ ~~Movie a Hit~~$_{HawkI}$ (probably)

Also, note that this reasoning matches precisely the abstract nature of the argument in the stimulus: if the first occurrence in a series of events has a certain characteristic, the second occurrence in that series is likely to have the same characteristic. Therefore, if the second occurrence did not have that characteristic, it is likely that the first one did not either. You should not be concerned with the fact that the characteristic in the stimulus was a negative one (premature birth), whereas the characteristic in answer choice (C) is positive (box-office hit). Remember—the topic in Parallel Reasoning questions does not matter, as your only job is to identify an argument that has a similar pattern of reasoning.

Answer choice (D): This argument is valid, but it is not in a quasi-contrapositive form. In fact, the conclusion is a Repeat of the premise:

Premise: Fail (likely) ⟶ ~~Invest~~

Premise/Conclusion: Fail_{PS} (likely) ⟶ ~~Invest~~_{PS}

Also note that the word "likely" here qualifies the sufficient condition of relationship, not the necessary condition as in the stimulus. Furthermore, the conclusion does not feature the same probabilistic language. A savvy test taker who notices this difference may choose not to even diagram this answer choice, and automatically eliminate it from consideration.

Answer choice (E): This answer choice is incorrect because the argumentation is in the form of Mistaken Reversal:

Premise: Sailing_{Tai} ⟶ Nice Weather

Premise/Conclusion: Nice Weather ⟶ Sailing_{Tai} (probably)

As with answer choices (A) and (B), the difference between the indicators used in the stimulus and the answer choice is irrelevant. In this case, the phrase "only if" indicates that having a nice weather is a necessary condition for sailing; the fact that the same indicator was not used in the stimulus does not matter.

What matters, is that the necessary condition in the premise does not feature the same probabilistic language we have come to expect. This difference, although minor, is sufficient to eliminate this answer from contention, the Mistaken Reversal error notwithstanding. Remember, all relevant elements of the argument must be paralleled, not just some of the elements. This can save you time, as you need not diagram every single answer choice in order to arrive at the correct answer.

Question #10: Flaw in the Reasoning, SN. The correct answer choice is (B)

The stimulus features conditional reasoning, which is identifiable by the use of the necessary condition indicator "only if" in the third sentence. The argument has the following structure:

LW = Liquid Water
LE = Life Evolves

Premise: LW_{Europa}

Premise: LE ——→ LW

Conclusion: LE_{Europa} (likely)

In light of the data suggesting that there are oceans of liquid water under the ice of Europa, the journalist considers it likely that some primitive life has evolved on Europa. Her rationale is that life can only evolve in the presence of liquid water. You should immediately recognize that this argumentation takes the form of a Mistaken Reversal: just because a there is strong evidence that a condition necessary for life to evolve has been met does not establish that life is likely to evolve. It is quite possible that there are other requirements for a planet to support life, such as an adequate energy source or other geophysical and geochemical criteria.

Note that even though the journalist qualifies her conclusion with the word "likely," her argument is still flawed, because satisfying a condition necessary for a certain event to occur only ensures that the event *can* occur, not that it is *likely* to occur. Because the author mistakes a necessary condition for a sufficient condition, the correct answer choice will probably use at least one of these key words (or their synonyms) to describe the error in conditional reasoning. This gives savvy test takers an advantage: if you identify a stimulus with conditional reasoning and are asked a Flaw question, quickly scan the answers and identify those that contain such key words as "sufficient," "necessary," or both. Although this approach may not eliminate all four incorrect answers, it usually helps narrow down the number of possible contenders.

Answer choice (A): At first glance, this seems to be an attractive answer, since it does focus on the conditional aspect of this argument and uses the word "necessary," which we expect to find in the correct answer. However, upon close inspection you should notice that this answer choice does not describe a Mistaken Reversal, but the contrapositive: if a condition is necessary for the evolution of life (liquid water), then life cannot evolve if this condition is not met (i.e. if there is no liquid water). This is a classic description of a contrapositive statement, and does not describe a Flaw in the reasoning.

Remember—although the word "necessary" makes this answer choice attractive, test makers often exploit what students perceive to be "shortcuts" and turn them into traps. To avoid falling into this one, you must prephrase and look for an answer describing a Mistaken Reversal. Although it would be acceptable to flag answer choice (A) as a contender, make sure to read all five answers before making your choice. Ultimately, only (A) and (B) contain the key words we are looking for ("sufficient," "necessary"), and a more careful comparison between the two reveals that (B) contains the proper description of a Mistaken Reversal, whereas (A) describes a logically valid argument.

Answer choice (B): This is the correct answer choice. By confusing a necessary condition for a sufficient one, the journalist ignores the possibility that liquid water may not be the only condition necessary for the evolution of life. If other requirements need to be met before a planet can support life, then having liquid water on Europa does little to increase the likelihood that primitive life has evolved there.

Note that there are multiple ways to describe the same flaw in conditional reasoning. Compare the following examples, all of which amount to the same description of a Mistaken Reversal:

> The author treats something that is necessary for bringing about a state of affairs as something that is sufficient to bring about a state of affairs.
>
> From the assertion that something is necessary for the evolution of life, the journalist concludes that the same thing is sufficient to ensure the evolution of life.
>
> The journalist takes for granted that if a condition is necessary for the evolution of life, satisfying that condition alone increases the likelihood that life would evolve.

Because there are so many ways to describe a conditional reasoning flaw, it is important to prephrase an answer describing a Mistaken Reversal but keep an open mind—do not let yourself get "boxed in" by the exact language of your prephrase.

Answer choice (C): The stimulus contains no evidence suggesting that life is likely to be present on Europa if, but only if, life evolved on Europa. Both the premise and the conclusion focus on the conditions necessary (or sufficient) for life to *evolve* on Europa, not whether such evolution is a necessary or a sufficient condition for life to be present there.

Answer choice (D): The journalist does not overlook the possibility that there could be unfamiliar forms of life that have evolved without the presence of liquid water. If true, this possibility would only increase the likelihood that life has evolved on Europa, with or without liquid water. Furthermore, because the journalist qualified her premise with the phrase "life ***as we know it***," the possibility that some other life forms do not depend on water is consistent with it.

Answer choice (E): This answer choice implies that the data transmitted by the spacecraft does not necessarily indicate the presence of liquid water, as other conditions could potentially account for such data. Although there may be room for other interpretations of the data, the factual premise on which the author depends strongly suggests that liquid water is present. Questioning the factual validity of any premise is rarely an appropriate strategy on the LSAT, and does not capture the main problem in this argument.

Question #11: Must Be True, SN. The correct answer choice is (B)

The stimulus contains a fact set and features conditional reasoning, which is identifiable by the use of the necessary condition indicator "unless" in the first sentence. Applying the Unless Equation, the phrase modified by "unless" becomes the necessary condition, whereas the remainder is negated and becomes the sufficient condition. However, you should notice the sufficient condition indicator "any" modifying the clause "antibiotics used against the bacteria," which needs to be factored into the relationship.

Thus, if the bacterial species does not become resistant to the antibiotics used against it, then either the antibiotics did not completely eliminate the bacterial species, or no antibiotics were used against it:

BR = Bacterial resistance
CE = Complete elimination of bacteria
AU = Antibiotic used against bacteria

Premise: ~~BR~~ → CE or ~~AU~~

Contrapositive: AU and ~~CE~~ → BR

In the contrapositive form, if any antibiotic is used against the bacterial species and that antibiotic does not completely eliminate it, the bacterial species will develop greater resistance to that antibiotic. Some students would prefer to diagram the contrapositive first, since the "unless" modifier is logically equivalent to the phrase "if not."

The second premise tells us that no single antibiotic now on the market is powerful enough to eliminate bacterial species *x*:

Premise: ~~CE~~$_x$

Therefore, we can use the contrapositive of the conditional relationship in the first premise to prephrase the conclusion that if any antibiotic is used against bacterial species *x*, the species will become more resistant to it (since the other sufficient condition has already been established):

Conclusion: AU → BR$_x$

This prephrase is tremendously helpful in attacking the answer choices and immediately proves that answer choice (B) is correct. Because stimuli containing conditional reasoning in combination with Must Be True questions frequently produce contrapositive answer choices, you should apply the contrapositive and prephrase an answer choice based on the contrapositive.

Answer choice (A): On the basis of the evidence presented in the stimulus, we cannot estimate the likelihood that an antibiotic can be developed to eliminate bacterial species *x*. Although no single antibiotic now on the market is powerful enough to eliminate bacterial species *x* completely, it is impossible to predict what can happen in the future.

Answer choice (B): This is the correct answer choice, which predictably contains the contrapositive of the first sentence of the stimulus: because no single antibiotic now on the market is powerful enough to eliminate bacterial species *x*, any antibiotic used against the bacterial species will become more resistant to it.

$$\begin{array}{l} CE_x \\ \text{and} \longrightarrow BR_x \\ AU \end{array}$$

Answer choice (C): At first glance, this may seem like an attractive answer. If no single antibiotic now on the market is powerful enough to eliminate bacterial species *x* completely, is it not likely that the only way of completely eliminating bacterial species *x* is by combining two or more antibiotics? Unfortunately, we are looking for an answer that Must Be True, not just likely to be true. There is always the possibility that there are other ways to completely eliminate bacterial species *x* (take across-the-board mandatory immunizations, for instance). Because we have no information as to whether there are other ways to eliminate the bacterial species in question, this answer choice cannot be proven by the stimulus and is therefore incorrect.

Answer choice (D): Although no single antibiotic is powerful enough to eliminate the bacterial species *x*, perhaps there are other ways to eliminate it (vaccinations, a combination of several different antibiotics, etc.). Even if those ways did not work, it would still be unreasonable to conclude that the bacterial species in question will inevitably become more virulent. The topic of virulence was never discussed in the stimulus, and therefore cannot be proven by the information in it.

Answer choice (E): This appears to be an attractive answer because we do know that a bacterial species will inevitably develop greater resistance within a few years to any antibiotics used against it, unless those antibiotics can completely eliminate it. Clearly, no antibiotic on the market can completely eliminate bacterial species *x*. However, we cannot be 100% certain that the bacteria today is more resistant to some of the antibiotics that have been used against it in the past, because we do not know when (or whether) these antibiotics were actually used. The author clearly states that it takes a few years for the bacterial species to develop greater resistance to any antibiotic that fails to completely eliminate it. Therefore, if the ineffective antibiotics were used only a few months ago, we cannot expect that the bacteria are more resistant to them today than it was before they were used.

Question #12: Main Point. The correct answer choice is (D)

The argument is structured as follows (reordered for clarity):

Premise:	It is not uncommon for a politician to criticize his or her political opponents by claiming that their exposition of their ideas is muddled and incomprehensible.
Counter-premise:	Every politician knows that political mobilization requires commonality of purpose.
Sub. Conclusion:	Political agendas promoted in a manner that cannot be understood by large numbers of people will not be realized.
Conclusion:	Such criticism is never sincere.

Your ability to quickly identify the correct answer to a Main Point question is directly tied to your understanding of the structure of the argument and its conclusion. Since the correct answer is often a simple paraphrase of the conclusion, test makers often introduce competing viewpoints, counterarguments, subsidiary conclusions, and double negatives in order to increase the level of difficulty of the question. Despite the relatively convoluted nature of this argument, there are certain clues you should use to your advantage.

First, we can simplify the first sentence by removing the double negative construction in it ("not uncommon"). Simply put, the political scientist observes that it is common for politicians to criticize their opponents for promoting ideas in an incomprehensible manner. Second, note that whenever the stimulus begins by describing someone else's position (politicians criticizing their opponents), you can be sure that the author's conclusion will ultimately counter it.

Predictably, the author asserts in the second sentence of the stimulus that such criticism is never sincere. Why? Because political mobilization requires commonality of purpose, and political agendas promoted in a manner that cannot be understood by large numbers of people will not be realized. The indicator "however" indicates the presence of a counter-argument, and a possible conclusion. Also, since the last sentence provides grounds for accepting the author's conclusion, the statements in that sentence function as premises for the main conclusion.

Thus, the main conclusion of the argument lies in the second sentence of the stimulus and can be paraphrased as follows:

> It is insincere for a politician to criticize his or her political opponents by claiming that their exposition of their ideas is muddled and incomprehensible.

This prephrase helps identify answer choice (D) as correct.

Observant test-takers would also note that the premise indicator "for" in the last sentence implies that the second clause of that sentence ("political mobilization requires commonality of purpose") supports the first ("Political agendas promoted in a manner that cannot be understood by large numbers of people will not be realized"). Therefore, the second clause of the last sentence functions as a pure premise, while the first clause serves the role of a subsidiary conclusion. Ultimately, this is irrelevant to answering the Main Point question, since both statements support the main conclusion of the argument.

Answer choice (A): This answer choice is incorrect because the author never argued that the people who promote political agendas in an incomprehensible manner are insincere. Rather, the author regards as insincere those who *criticize their political opponents* for promoting political agendas in an incomprehensible manner.

Answer choice (B): Just because author regards as insincere those who criticize their opponents for promoting ideas in an incomprehensible manner does not mean that sincere critics should never focus their criticisms on the manner in which their opponents' agenda is promoted. This statement is too broad and not supported by the information in contained in the stimulus. A sincere critic can criticize the manner in which her opponents' political agenda is promoted, as long as she does not claim that their exposition is muddled and incomprehensible.

Answer choice (C): Although the ineffectiveness of a confusingly promoted political agenda may be a reason for refraining from criticism of those who are promoting it, this is certainly not the author's main conclusion. Your initial prephrase of the conclusion should help you eliminate this answer choice rather quickly.

Answer choice (D): This is the correct answer choice, as it is simply a paraphrase of the main conclusion in the second sentence of the stimulus.

Answer choice (E): Although the author would agree with the statement that mobilizing large numbers of people requires a comprehensible political agenda, this is a premise used in support of the conclusion that politicians criticizing the incomprehensibility of their opponents' political agendas are being insincere. Do not fall into the trap of assuming that the last sentence of the stimulus will always contain the conclusion: oftentimes, the conclusion is hidden somewhere else the argument, especially in Main Point questions.

Question #13: Flaw in the Reasoning, CE. The correct answer choice is (C)

The argument is structured as follows:

Premise: Many symptoms of mental illnesses are affected by organic factors such as a deficiency in a compound in the brain.

OF = Organic factors
SMI = Symptoms of mental illness

C		E
OF	⟶	SMI

Premise: The symptoms of mental illness vary among different countries.

Conclusion: The organic factors that affect symptoms of mental illnesses are not distributed evenly around the globe.

The relationship between the second premise and the conclusion is also causal, which can be diagrammed as:

SMI_V = Variation of symptoms of mental illness
OF_V = Variation of organic factors

C		E
OF_V	⟶	SMI_V

The conclusion, which is easy to spot due to the conclusion indicator "this variation establishes that," is based on the finding that the incidence of symptoms in people with mental illness varies among different countries. Because organic factors can affect the symptoms of mental illness, the author attributes the variation in symptoms to an uneven distribution (i.e. variation) of organic factors around the globe. Literally, the author believes that different symptoms in different places are the result of what organic factors are present, and the variation in those symptoms shows that the organic factors are not distributed evenly.

Arguments that draw causal conclusions are inherently flawed because there may be another explanation for the stated causal relationship. Take depression, for instance. If doctors treat depression differently in the U.S. than in Japan, then it is quite possible that depression would manifest itself differently in the U.S. than it would in Japan, because some treatments may be better able to control certain symptoms better than others. Cultural factors may also play a role in how the symptoms of depression are being reported. Because the author assumes that there is only one cause for the variation in the incidence of symptoms in people with mental illness, you should attack the answers looking for a description of this error.

Remember—the key to determining the error of reasoning is to focus on the connection between the premises and the conclusion, not on whether the premises are factually true. In this instance, it would have been counterproductive to doubt whether organic factors can indeed affect the symptoms of mental illness, since the causal relationship between the two functions as a premise and should not be questioned. Instead, focus on how the premises were used to support the conclusion.

Answer choice (A): Although the author does not specify exactly how many different mental illnesses are being discussed, this is not a flaw. An author is not required to specify every single fact or statement within in an argument. The conclusion would be equally strong regardless of how many mental illnesses are being discussed.

Answer choice (B): This is an attractive answer at first glance because some students see the nutritional element as an alternative explanation for the variation in symptoms. Even if nutrition contributed to deficiencies in compounds in the brain and nutritional factors varied from culture to culture, this would most likely be an effect of the uneven distribution of organic factors (foods eaten vary from culture to culture, and are often largely based on what is available locally or regionally). As this answer describes another effect of the cause, this answer does not describe a flaw in the argument. Note that, even if you dispute that this is an effect of the cause, this answer would still not describe an error in the argument or show that organic factors are not responsible for the variation in symptoms.

Answer choice (C): This is the correct answer choice. If cultural factors significantly affect how mental illnesses manifest themselves in symptoms, this would provide an alternate cause for the observed variation among different countries in the incidence of symptoms in people with mental illness. The possibility that an alternate cause can explain the given effect challenges the implicit assumption that there is only one cause for that effect, thereby making the reasoning vulnerable to criticism.

Note that the idea in answer choice (C) could have been phrased in many different ways:

> "takes for granted that cultural factors do not significantly affect how mental illnesses manifest themselves in symptoms"
>
> "presumes, without justification, that no other factors can significantly affect the manifestation of mental illnesses"
>
> "ignores the possibility that some other factor can affect the incidence of symptoms in people with mental illnesses"
>
> "fails to exclude an alternative explanation for the observed effect"

As always, it is important to identify the logical flaw in causal reasoning, but do not assume that there is only one way to describe that flaw. Be flexible with your prephrase.

Answer choice (D): At first, this may seem like an attractive answer choice, since it describes a possible unwarranted assumption. However, the author never implied that *any* change in brain chemistry would manifest itself as a change in mental condition. If she made that assumption, its logical opposite would have to weaken the conclusion. It does not. Even if some changes in brain chemistry did not manifest themselves as changes in mental condition, this would be consistent with both the premise and the conclusion of the argument. After all, the premise stated that many symptoms of mental illnesses are affected by *deficiencies* in a compound in the brain, not general changes in brain chemistry.

Since the statement described in answer choice (D) is not necessary for the conclusion of the argument to be logically valid, it is not an assumption.

Answer choice (E): The author never discussed whether the causes of mental phenomena are only physical phenomena; the scope of the argument was limited to the causal relationship between organic factors and symptoms of mental illnesses. Furthermore, it would be relatively easy to check if the author made this assumption by examining whether its logical opposite weakens the conclusion. It does not. Even if mental phenomena were not simply manifestations of physical phenomena, this would be consistent with the conclusion that the variation of symptoms of mental illness is due to a variation in the organic factors that affect them.

Question #14: Weaken, CE. The correct answer choice is (E)

The politician uses an analogy to support his conclusion: because the privatization of the telecommunications industry benefited consumers by allowing competition among a variety of telephone companies, the politician concludes that same benefit will result from the privatization of national parks. For the benefits of privatization to be analogous in this respect, it is necessary that national parks and the telecommunications industry be fundamentally similar. However, if they were not, then the author would be guilty of a False Analogy.

The argument is structured as follows:

PT = Privatization of the telecommunications industry
PP = Privatization of national parks
CC = Competition among companies
BC = Benefit consumers

	C	E/C	E
Premise:	PT ⟶	CC ⟶	BC
	C	E	
Conclusion:	PP ⟶	BC	

Given that the question stem asks us to weaken the argument, you should attack the answers by looking for a statement that, if true, would show that national parks and the telecommunications industry are different in a way that undermines the credibility of the author's conclusion. More specifically, you should notice that the premise regarding the telecommunications industry relies on a crucial link between privatization and consumer benefit: the increased competition among companies, which forced down prices and improved services. Since there is no evidence that privatizing national parks would result in the same increased competition, this may prove detrimental to the strength of the analogy used to support the conclusion.

Remember—in an argument by analogy, the author uses the presumption of similarity between two things to argue that they probably have additional traits in common. Analogies are often used to clarify the relationship between the items or reveal a fundamental truth about one of the items. When used properly, an analogy can be a powerful tool of argumentation. However, if the author treats as similar two cases that are different in a critical respect, then the analogy is false and the conclusion is questionable. If you see an analogy in the stimulus followed by a Weaken question stem, focus on undermining the strength of the analogy.

Answer choice (A): Since the conclusion is confined to the probable benefit of privatization to *park visitors*, it is irrelevant whether such course of action is politically expedient. This is a classic Shell Game answer, used to attack a conclusion that is similar to, but slightly different from, the one presented in the stimulus. Had the author concluded, "it is feasible to privatize national parks," answer choice (A) would have been more attractive.

Savvy test takers would disregard answer choice (A) simply because it does not address the dubious analogy used in the stimulus.

Answer choice (B): Although this answer choice presents a downside to the privatization of the telecommunications industry, such privatization clearly affected only its employees and the industry in general, not its customers who ultimately benefited from the lower prices. Therefore, even if the privatization of national parks led to a similar increase in unemployment of park rangers and other service personnel, this would not necessarily affect the prices or the quality of services provided to park visitors.

Answer choice (C): Hopefully, you were able to eliminate this answer choice quickly. Even if park visitors were unaware of any proposals to privatize the management of parks, this does not mean that they won't benefit from such proposals.

Answer choice (D): At first glance, this may seem like an attractive answer, given the attempted attack on the analogy between national parks and the telecommunications industry. However, this attack is pointless because it focuses on an irrelevant distinction between the two.

Even if privatizing the national parks would benefit a much smaller number of consumers to a much smaller extent than did the privatization of the telecommunications industry, it is still possible that the privatization of parks benefits most (if not all) park visitors. This is because it is entirely plausible that the number of park visitors is much smaller than the number of, say, cell phone users, which would explain why a lot fewer people would benefit from privatized national parks. Furthermore, just because the extent of the benefit to park visitors is smaller when compared to the benefit to cell phone users does not mean that the benefit is not real or valuable. As long as the benefits of privatization outweigh the costs to park visitors, the proposal to privatize the national parks has merit.

Answer choice (E): This is the correct answer choice. If privatizing the national parks produces much less competition between different companies than did privatizing the telecommunications industry, then it is unreasonable to expect that park visitors would benefit from the proposal to privatize the parks. After all, the reason why privatization of the telecommunications industry benefited consumers is that it allowed competition among a variety of telephone companies to improve service and force down prices. If the intermediate effect of increased competition does not occur as a result of privatizing the national parks, then the causal chain is interrupted and the analogy between the two falls apart.

Question #15: Strengthen—Principle. The correct answer choice is (D)

According to the author, jewel collectors do not buy diamonds unless they are guaranteed to be genuine. Applying the Unless Equation, the phrase modified by "unless" becomes the necessary condition, whereas the remainder is negated and becomes the sufficient condition:

BD = Buy Diamonds
GG = Guaranteed Genuine

<u>S</u>   <u>N</u>

BD ——→ GG

The author seems to find this convention perplexing. If the naked eye cannot distinguish the real diamond from the counterfeit, she argues, the counterfeit would give just as much aesthetic pleasure as the real diamond. Because of this, the author concludes that both jewels should be deemed of equal value.

The author's argument is structured as follows:

Premise:	The naked eye cannot distinguish a real diamond from a counterfeit.
Sub. Conclusion:	A counterfeit provides the same degree of aesthetic pleasure as a real diamond.
Conclusion:	Both jewels should be deemed of equal value.

Note that the question stem is a Strengthen—PR, not a Justify—PR because of the presence of the word "most," which weakens the force required of the correct answer. In Strengthen—PR questions, the correct answer choice provides a broad premise that, when applied to the specific situation in the stimulus, helps support the conclusion. In this problem, you must select a principle that helps prove that a counterfeit should be deemed of equal value to a real diamond because they provide the same aesthetic value. Answer choice (D) contains the statement that is closest to this prephrase, and answer choice (D) is correct.

As a general rule, when prephrasing a principle that can be used to draw the conclusion, look for any logical gaps or deficiencies in the argument that need to be fixed. Also, make sure to distinguish between opposing viewpoints and identify a principle that would support the author's position, not that of an opponent. Lastly, since a principle is usually a broad rule that specifies what actions or judgments are correct in certain situations, the correct answers often contain words such as "should," "must," and "ought to."

Answer choice (A): Since the author argues that a counterfeit provides just as much aesthetic pleasure as a real diamond, it is unclear which jewel would provide the ***most*** aesthetic pleasure. Because this principle cannot specify what course of action would be preferable in this situation, this answer choice is incorrect.

Answer choice (B): The author's conclusion revolves around the link between aesthetic pleasure and actual value. If the market value of a jewel were also a relevant consideration, this would only hurt the author's conclusion that a counterfeit should be deemed equal in value to a real diamond. If you found this answer choice attractive, you were mistakenly looking for a principle that justifies the jewel collectors' position.

Answer choice (C): Because this principle implies that the aesthetic pleasure received from a diamond is inherently *subjective*, it is inconsistent with the author's argument, which assumes that the degree of aesthetic pleasure provided can be used as an *objective* criterion of value. Moreover, because this principle leaves unclear how to measure the value of a diamond.

Be careful not to select an answer just because you would agree with the general proposition in it. Since the nature of the question forces you to identify the answer that best justifies the *author's position*, your personal views should have no role when selecting an answer choice.

Answer choice (D): This is the correct answer choice. If the value of a jewel should derive solely from the aesthetic pleasure it provides, and both jewels offer an equal degree of aesthetic pleasure, then they must be deemed of equal value. This principle connects the discrepancy between aesthetic pleasure and value, it helps justify the author's conclusion.

Answer choice (E): Applying the Unless Equation, this principle can be diagrammed as follows:

BC = Buy counterfeit jewels
D = Distinguish counterfeit jewels from real ones

S	N
BC ——→	D

This answer focuses on the practices of jewel collectors and has little to do with the author's conclusion. Since the author argues that real diamonds and counterfeits should be deemed of equal value, this answer choice does not apply to the scenario in the stimulus.

Question #16: Justify the Conclusion, FL, #%. The correct answer choice is (B)

This question tests your ability to translate relationships into symbols and then make inferences from those symbolized relationships. Although some of them are conditional, as indicated by the sufficient condition "all" in the first and third sentences, others belong to a branch of logic called Symbolic, or "Formal," Logic. The latter usually involves terms such as "some," "most," and "all."

The structure of the argument can be diagrammed as follows:

Premise: All etching tools are either pin-tipped or bladed.

Premise: Some bladed etching tools are used for engraving.

Premise: Some bladed etching tools are not used for engraving.

Premise: All pin-tipped etching tools are used for engraving.

Conclusion: There are more etching tools that are used for engraving than there are etching tools that are not used for engraving

To gain a better understanding of the relationship between the premises and the conclusion in this argument, diagram the relationships in the first three sentences as follows:

ET = Etching tools
PIN = Pin-tipped etching tools
BLA = Bladed etching tools
ENG = Etching tools used for engraving

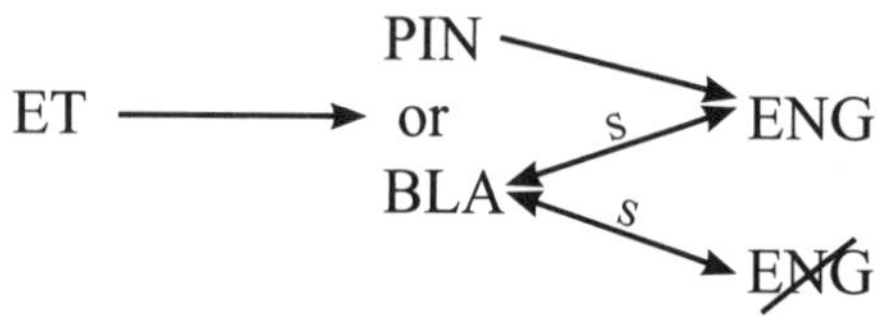

The author then uses this evidence to conclude that there are more tools that are used for engraving than there are tools that are not used for engraving:

ENG > ~~ENG~~

The question stem asks us to identify a statement that, if assumed, would enable to the conclusion to be properly drawn. Despite the word "assumed" here, this is a Justify rather than an Assumption question stem, because our job is not to identify a statement that is necessary for the conclusion to be true, but to prove the conclusion by adding a piece of information to the premises. The sufficient condition indicator ("if") in the question stem is a reminder that you must select an answer that is *sufficient* to prove the conclusion by using the Justify Formula:

Premises + Answer choice = Conclusion

Also note that, unlike a typical Strengthen question stem in which the word "most" would weaken the force required of the correct answer, this question stem does not lessen the degree of justification required. Remember—because justifying a conclusion is such a specific task, the logic behind the question must allow for airtight provability. This makes most Justify stimuli contain either Conditional Reasoning or numbers and percentages. In this case, the stimulus contains both.

A quick glance at the argument reveals a gap between the premises and conclusion—just because all pin-tipped etching tools and some bladed etching tools are used for engraving does not necessarily mean that the total number of tools used for engraving is greater than the total number of tools not used for engraving. Imagine the following scenario:

ET = 100

PIN = 10, all used for engraving.

BLA = 90, of which 20 are used for engraving, and 70 are not used for engraving

Although our scenario is consistent with the premises of the argument, there would be a total of 30 tools used for engraving and 70 tools that are not used for engraving, in direct contradiction to the conclusion. There are two reasons making this possible: (1) since we do not know the ratio of pin-tipped to bladed tools, it is perfectly plausible that there are more bladed etching tools than pin-tipped etching tools; and (2) although the stimulus does indicate that some bladed tools are used for engraving, it is quite plausible that most are not. If so, then the number of etching tools not used for engraving could easily surpass the number of etching tools that are used for engraving.

To justify the conclusion, you must look for an answer establishing that the ratio of pin-tipped to bladed etching tools is at least equal. If so, given that all pin-tipped and at least some bladed tools are used for engraving, the total number of etching tools used for engraving will always be greater than the number of etching tools not used for engraving.

This prephrase is consistent with answer choice (B), which is the correct answer.

Answer choice (A): This answer choice is tantamount to a Mistaken Reversal of a premise, and can be diagrammed as follows:

ENG ⟶ ET

Even if all the tools used for engraving were etching tools, that would not prove the conclusion. It is still quite possible that the total number of engraving tools is quite small, so that even if all of them are etching tools, only a small proportion of the tools are actually used for engraving.

Answer choice (B): This is the correct answer choice. If there the number of pin-tipped etching tools equals the number of bladed etching tools, then the number of etching tools used for engraving would always be greater than those not used for engraving. This is because all pin-tipped etching tools, plus some bladed tools, are used for engraving:

Premise:	PIN ⟶ ENG
Premise:	BLA ⟵s⟶ ENG
Justify:	PIN = BLA
Conclusion:	ENG > ~~ENG~~

Since this answer choice adds a piece of information to the premises that is sufficient to prove conclusion, it is the correct Justify answer.

Answer choice (C): Just because no etching tool is both pin-tipped and bladed does not mean that there are as many pin-tipped etching tools as there are bladed etching tools. Since this answer choice does not indicate the ratio between pin-tipped and bladed etching tools, it is incorrect.

Answer choice (D): This answer choice may weaken the argument by implying that most bladed etching tools are not used for engraving (though some are). If this were true, it becomes even more likely that the number of etching tools used for engraving is no greater than the number of etching tools not used for engraving. Of course, we still do not know the proportion of pin-tipped to bladed etching tools. As a general rule, avoid answers to Justify questions that contain words such as "some," "most," or "majority of." They are unlikely to provide you with the 100% degree of support required by the question stem.

Answer choice (E): This answer choice implies the following conditional relationship between engraving tools and bladed tools:

~~ENG~~ ⟶ BLA

This does not prove the conclusion because there could be many more bladed etching tools than pin-tipped etching tools. Imagine the following scenario:

Pin-tipped tools = 10, all of which are used for engraving

Bladed tools used for engraving = 10

Tools not used for engraving = 30 (all are bladed)

In this scenario, the total number of tools used for engraving would be 20, whereas the total number of tools not used for engraving would be 30. Therefore, answer choice (E) does not prove the conclusion, and is incorrect.

Question #17: Resolve the ParadoxX. The correct answer choice is (D)

The stimulus describes two studies that produced discrepant findings about the health benefits of consuming beta-carotene. In the 24-year study, the subjects with a high intake of beta-carotene-rich foods were much less likely to die from cancer or heart disease than were those with a low intake of such foods. On the other hand, a separate study observed no positive or negative effect on the health of subjects taking beta-carotene supplements for 12 years.

Before attacking the answers, try to explain the discrepancy in your own words. One way to do it would be to look for critical differences between the studies. After all, since the stimulus contains a paradox where two items are different, an answer choice implying that they are similar will not explain the paradox. The most obvious difference between the studies is that one of them observed subjects over the course of 24 years, whereas the other was completed in only 12 years. This might explain why the health benefits of beta-carotene were not apparent in the shorter study. Also, the 24-year study followed subjects whose diet contained beta-carotene-rich ***foods***, whereas the subjects in the 12-year study only took *supplements*. If beta-carotene supplements are not as powerful or well-absorbed as foods rich in beta-carotene, this would explain why the subjects in the 12-year study showed no health benefits.

The stimulus is followed by a ResolveX question, which means that among the five answer choices, the four incorrect answer choices will provide a resolution to the paradox, and the one correct choice will not provide a resolution.

Answer choice (A): If the human body processes the beta-carotene present in foods much more efficiently than it does beta-carotene supplements, the subjects in the 24-year study who consumed foods rich in beta-carotene would be more likely to benefit from it than the subjects who took beta-carotene supplements in the other study. Because this answer choice resolves the apparent discrepancy between the two studies, it is incorrect.

Answer choice (B): If beta-carotene must be taken for longer than 12 years to have any cancer-preventive effects, this would explain why the subjects in the 12-year study showed no health benefits. Had they been observed for a longer period of time, the cancer-preventative effects might have been more easily apparent. Because this answer choice resolves the apparent discrepancy between the two studies, it is incorrect.

Answer choice (C): If foods rich in beta-carotene also tend to contain other nutrients that assist in the human body's absorption of beta-carotene, this would explain why the group who consumed such foods showed certain health benefits that the other group did not. Because this answer choice resolves the apparent discrepancy between the two studies, it is incorrect.

Answer choice (D): This is the correct answer choice. If the 12-year study randomized the subjects into two equal groups, one of which was given a placebo and the other—a beta-carotene supplement, this would only explain why half of the subjects in that study would have had no positive or negative effect on their health (they received the placebo). However, it is unclear why the other half showed no benefit either. Because this answer choice does not explain the apparent discrepancy between the two studies, it is the correct answer.

Answer choice (E): At first glance, this may seem like an attractive answer, since it is not immediately apparent how it would resolve the paradox. To understand that, recall that any answer describing a difference in the way in which the two studies are conducted could potentially explain the discrepancy in their results. If, in the 24-year study, the percentage of subjects with a high intake of beta-carotene-rich foods who smoked cigarettes was much smaller than the percentage of subjects with a low intake of beta-carotene-rich foods who smoked, this means that the smokers were more likely to consume foods that are low in beta-carotene. Since the higher risk of cancer among the subjects with a low intake of beta-carotene-rich foods could easily be due to their smoking habits, this would compromise the validity of the 24-year study and explain the discrepancy in the results between the two studies.

Remember—for a study or a survey to provide a reliable basis for a given conclusion, it needs to account for other possible causes that can explain the conclusion. This is usually done by control groups or by careful screening of potential biases that can compromise the validity of the study.

Question #18: Justify the Conclusion, SN. The correct answer choice is (D)

This is a very challenging question, and possibly one of the most difficult logical reasoning questions on the test, in part because of the convoluted conditional approach taken by the author.

The stimulus begins with the author's conclusion that we will not be able to determine the presence of sentient beings outside our solar system unless some of them are at least as smart as humans. Although the stimulus begins with the familiar term "if," the first sentence could be more simply restructured as follows:

> We will not be able to determine the existence of other sentient beings (even if they *do* actually exist) unless some of them are at least as intelligent as humans.

We can diagram this statement by applying the Unless Equation: the phrase modified by "unless" becomes the necessary condition, whereas the remainder is negated and becomes the sufficient condition. Thus, the first sentence can be diagrammed as follows:

Determine Exist = determine the existence of sentient begins outside our solar system
As Intelligent = some of the sentient beings are at least as intelligent as humans

	S		N
Conclusion:	Determine Exist	⟶	As Intelligent

Even though there are no conclusion indicators to help us identify the conclusion, note that the second sentence contains two premises that support the observation in the first sentence: first, we will not be able to send spacecraft outside our solar system in the near future, and second, any sentient being able to communicate with us would need to be at least as intelligent as we are.

Send Spacecraft	=	Send spacecraft outside our solar system in the near future
SB Communicate	=	Sentient beings able to communicate with us

Premise (1): ~~Send Spacecraft~~

Premise (2): SB Communicate ⟶ As Intelligent

In other words, if we want to determine whether sentient beings exist outside our solar system, one approach might be to send a spacecraft. Without spacecraft as an option, however, the author asserts that we would have to rely on these beings' ability to communicate with us. This, in turn, would require that such sentient beings be at least as intelligent as humans. The relationship between premises and conclusion is implicitly conditional, and, when re-worded, can be diagrammed as follows:

Premise: Determine Exist ⟶ Send Spacecraft or SB Communicate ⟶ As Intelligent

Premise: ~~Send Spacecraft~~

Conclusion: Determine Exist ⟶ As Intelligent

The question stem asks us to identify a statement that, if assumed, would enable to the conclusion to be properly drawn. Despite the word "assumed" in the stem, this is a Justify question because our job is not to identify a statement upon which the argument depends, but rather to *prove* the conclusion by adding a piece of information to the premises. The sufficient condition indicator ("if") in the question stem is a reminder that you must select an answer that is *sufficient* to prove the conclusion by using the Justify Formula:

Premises + Answer choice = Conclusion

As with most Justify questions, there is a logical gap between the premises and the conclusion. To prove the conclusion, we must establish that there are *only two ways* to determine the existence of sentient begins outside our solar system: either we send a spacecraft outside our solar system, or the sentient themselves must be able to communicate with us. That way, if one of the two options is ruled out, the only other way to determine the existence of sentient beings would be to pursue the other option:

Justify Formula: ~~Send Spacecraft~~ ⟶ SB Communicate

Note that the relationship between the two options contains a negative sufficient condition—if one cannot occur, the other must occur. The contrapositive would serve the same function: if the sentient beings cannot communicate with us, then the only other option for determining their existence would be to send a spacecraft to its planet:

Justify (Contrap.): ~~SB Communicate~~ ⟶ Send Spacecraft

Since the contrapositive is logically identical to our prephrase, answer choice (D) is correct.

Another way to approach this Justify question would be as follows:

(1) Elements that appear in the premises but not the conclusion usually appear in the correct answer. Although these premise elements do not have to appear in the correct answer, they often do because they represent a convenient linking point. In this argument, "Send Spacecraft" appears in the premises but not in the conclusion. Therefore, it is highly likely that it would appear in the correct answer. Its absence from answer choices (A), (B), and (E) helps eliminate them.

(2) Elements that are common to the conclusion and at least one premise normally do not appear in the correct answer, because there is a bridge already established that justifies the presence of that element in the conclusion. Here, the element of "Determine Exist" is common to both the premises and the conclusion and need not be present in the correct answer. Its presence in answer choices (B), (C), and (E) helps eliminate them.

Applying these two rules of solving Justify questions mechanistically leaves answer choice (D) as the only possible contender.

Answer choice (A): Because the conclusion focuses on whether sentient beings exist *outside* our solar system, the fact that they do not exist on planets *inside* our solar system is irrelevant. Even if there were no sentient beings on planets in our solar system, that alone does not prove that there are only two ways of determining their existence.

A savvy test taker would eliminate this answer choice immediately because it does not contain the element of "Send Spacecraft." Since this element appears in the premises but not in the conclusion, we would expect it to appear in the correct answer.

Answer choice (B): Even if the sentient beings would want to communicate with us, that does not prove that we would have to rely on their ability to communicate with us. Because the possibility remains that there is a third way to determine their existence, the conclusion is not fully justified.

To some test takers, this may seem like an assumption answer (which would still make it incorrect, as we are not answering an Assumption question). However, applying the Assumption Negation technique reveals that this is not an assumption: even if the sentient beings did not want to communicate with us, that would not weaken the conclusion that determining their existence requires that these beings be at least as intelligent as we are. Granted, if they refused to communicate with us, our job of determining their existence would be made considerably more difficult, but this is irrelevant to the conclusion of the argument. Therefore, answer choice (B) is neither sufficient, nor necessary, for the conclusion to be true.

Answer choice (C): Since the author already established that sending a spacecraft to planets outside our solar system is impossible in the near future, this answer choice merely restates a premise in the argument. If you found this answer choice attractive, you probably mistook the Justify question stem for a Must Be True question stem.

Answer choice (D): This is the correct answer choice, as it is the contrapositive of the Justify

Formula:

Justify Formula:	~~Send Spacecraft~~	⟶	SB Communicate
Justify (Contrap.):	~~SB Communicate~~	⟶	Send Spacecraft

In other words, without the option of sending a spacecraft outside out solar system, the only other way to determine the existence of sentient beings is for them to communicate with us. Since their ability to communicate with us requires intelligence, it logically follows that determining the existence of sentient beings outside our solar system requires that such beings be at least as intelligent as humans.

Note that the Justify Formula could have been phrased in a number of ways:

> If we cannot send a spacecraft outside our solar system in an effort to determine the existence of sentient beings, we must rely on these beings' ability to communicate with us.
>
> To determine if there are sentient beings on other planets outside our solar system, we must either send a spacecraft there, or the sentient beings themselves must be able to communicate with us.

Answer choice (E): This is a Mistaken Reversal of the second premise in the argument. The author asserts that the sentient beings' ability to communicate with us depends on their intelligence. If the reverse were also true (i.e. that any sentient being that is at least as intelligent as humans would be capable of communicating with us), this would not prove the conclusion. The possibility remains that there is a third way to determine the existence of sentient beings outside our solar system.

A smart test taker would eliminate this answer choice immediately because it does not contain the element of "Send Spacecraft." Since this element appeared in the premises but not in the conclusion, we would expect it to appear in the correct answer.

Question #19: Flaw in the Reasoning, CE. The correct answer choice is (B)

The stimulus indicates that medical researchers examined a group of people who never experienced back pain. Surprisingly, half of them had bulging or slipped disks in their spines, conditions often blamed for serious back pain. When confronted with this apparent discrepancy, the doctor concluded that bulging or slipped disks could not cause serious back pain.

The argument, when reordered, is structured as follows:

Premise: Bulging or slipped disks are often blamed for serious back pain.

C E

Slipped disks ⟶ Back pain

Counter-premise: Some people who have bulging or slipped disks do not experience serious back pain.

Conclusion: Bulging or slipped disks could not cause serious back pain.

C E

Slipped disks ⟶ ~~Back~~ pain

Because this is a Flaw question, it is important to examine closely the relationship between premises and conclusion in order to understand the logical flaw before proceeding to the answer choices. At first glance, the conclusion seems somewhat reasonable. After all, the study establishes that there are instances in which the cause occurs (slipped disks) without the effect (back pain), which is a common way to weaken arguments based on causal reasoning. However, the introduction of evidence against a position only weakens the position; it does not necessarily prove the position false. It is still possible that slipped disks do occasionally cause back pain, just not always.

It is worth noting that the study disproves the conditional relationship between slipped disks and back pain ("if pain, then slipped or bulging disk"), not the causal relationship between the two ("slipped or bulging disk causes pain"). If we find evidence suggesting that the sufficient condition can occur without the necessary condition (slipped disks occur in the absence of back pain), we can conclude that having a slipped disk is not a sufficient condition for back pain. However, this does not disprove the hypothesis that one *causes* the other. Had the conclusion been phrased in a less definitive way ("these conditions do not *necessarily* lead to serious back pain"), the argument would have been valid.

Answer choice (A): This answer choice describes the possibility that having a slipped disk need not be present in order for someone to experience back pain, but may be sufficient to cause back pain. There is no evidence, however, that having a slipped disk is a sufficient condition for back pain. In fact, the study shows instances in which a slipped disk did not cause back pain, suggesting that a slipped disk is not a sufficient condition for back pain. Because this answer choice fails the Fact Test, it is incorrect.

Answer choice (B): This is the correct answer choice. Even though a slipped disk is not in itself sufficient to cause back pain, it may nonetheless be partly responsible for back pain in some instances. This answer choice correctly points out that having a slipped disk is not a sufficient condition for back pain (if it were, then all instances of slipped disk would lead to back pain, which is not the case). In that sense, the author undermined the idea that slipped disks always cause back pain. However, because a slipped disk can still occasionally cause back pain, the causal link between the two is still possible.

Note that there are multiple ways to describe the same error in the use of evidence. Compare the following examples, all of which describe to the same error:

> The author fails to consider the possibility that even though slipped disks do not always cause back, they sometimes can.
>
> The author confuses undermining an argument in support of a given conclusion with showing that the conclusion itself is false.
>
> The author takes for granted that just because slipped disks do not always cause back pain, they never do.
>
> The author presumes, without justification, that just because a certain factor is not in itself sufficient to produce a certain effect, it is never responsible for that effect.

Because there are many ways to describe a Flaw in the reasoning, it is important to prephrase an answer describing the error you notice, but keep an open mind.

Answer choice (C): This answer choice fails the Fact Test because the study does not describe an effect (back pain) that occurs in the absence of a particular phenomenon (slipped disk). Rather, it describes a phenomenon (slipped disk) that occurs in the absence of a particular effect (back pain).

Answer choice (D): This answer choice describes an Overgeneralization. It fails the Fact Test, because the author never suggested that half of the entire population without back pain have slipped disks. Do not be misled by the attractive language used in this answer choice. Just because it is easier to associate the wording of the answer with the description of the study ("half a given sample of the population") does not mean that the answer is correct.

Answer choice (E): This answer choice describes the possibility that even though slipped disks do not cause back pain, they are more likely to be present when the pain occurs than when the pain does not occur. However, the correlation between the slipped disks and back pain would not by itself weaken the author's conclusion, as it is still possible that slipped disks do not cause back pain even though the two are correlated. In fact, since this answer choice concedes that slipped disks do not cause back pain, it describes a possibility that is consistent with the author's argument.

Question #20: Strengthen—Principle. The correct answer choice is (E)

In this stimulus, the author attacks the manufacturer of substance T, which caused many factory workers to become ill. Although the manufacturer was unaware of the health risks posed by substance T at the time, the author argues that such ignorance does not absolve the manufacturer of responsibility, because the harm was preventable.

The second half of the stimulus contains the author's argument against the manufacturer:

Premise:	Had the manufacturer of substance T investigated its safety before allowing workers to be exposed to it, many of their illnesses would have been prevented.
Conclusion:	Earlier ignorance of the connection between substance T and the workers' illnesses does not absolve T's manufacturer of all responsibility.

Note that the question stem is a Strengthen—PR, not a Justify—PR because of the presence of the word "most" in the question stem, which weakens the force required of the correct answer. In a Strengthen—PR question, the correct answer will provide a premise that, when applied to the specific situation in the stimulus, helps support the conclusion. Since a principle is by definition a broad rule (usually conditional in nature), the presence of the Principle indicator serves to broaden the scope of the question, which requires a more abstract understanding of the underlying relationships in the argument.

In this problem, you must select a principle that helps prove that substance T's manufacturer should be held responsible for the harmful effects of that substance, since the effects were preventable. Because the manufacturer's ignorance of the problem is deemed irrelevant, the principle need not address that issue. In short, we are looking for a broad rule that takes a conditional form similar to the following:

S		N
Preventable	⟶	Responsible

Answer choice (E) contains the statement that is closest to this prephrase, and answer choice (E) is correct.

Answer choice (A): The author is not concerned with the type of compensation, if any, owed to the workers who were harmed by substance T—the focus is on whether the manufacturer of substance T should be held responsible for the preventable detrimental effects of that substance.

Answer choice (B): There are two problems with this answer. First, it does not mention the element of "harm," even though the author clearly holds the manufacturer of substance T responsible for the *harmful* consequences of handling substance T (not just for any preventable consequences). Second, and perhaps most importantly, this answer choice is the Mistaken Reversal of the principle we are looking for:

S N

Responsible ⟶ Preventable

Our objective is not to limit responsibility only to the preventable consequences of a particular action, but to ensure that, if such consequences are preventable (and harmful), the manufacturer is held responsible for them.

Answer choice (C): One major problem with this answer choice is the phrase "risks of which they were aware." Since the manufacturer was *not* aware of the health risks posed by substance T, this principle cannot help justify the author's conclusion.

Answer choice (D): This is an Opposite answer because whether or not an action's consequences were preventable is not irrelevant to the author's conclusion. On the contrary—it is the central premise in the argument. If you found this answer choice attractive, you were mistakenly looking for a principle that justifies the manufacturer's position. When approaching Strengthen—PR questions, make sure to distinguish between opposing viewpoints and identify a principle that would support the author's position, not that of an opponent.

Answer choice (E): This is the correct answer choice. If manufacturers are to be held responsible for the consequences of any of their actions that harm innocent people if those consequences were preventable, then the manufacturer of substance T should be held responsible. Substance T did harm innocent people (the factory workers), and the harm was preventable by investigation of its safety.

Question #21: Method of Reasoning, SN. The correct answer choice is (A)

The author concludes that the contract will almost certainly be awarded to Phoenix, because it has decided not to award it to the only alternative contender, Cartwright. The relationship between the premises and the conclusion is conditional and can be diagrammed as follows:

GC = Government Contract
PC = Phoenix Contracting
CC = Cartwright Company

	S		N
			PC
Premise:	GC	⟶	or
			CC
Premise:	~~CC~~		
Conclusion:	GC	⟶	PC

The conclusion is easy to spot thanks to the conclusion indicator "therefore" in the last sentence. Note a peculiarity in the language that you can use to your advantage when attacking the answer choices: the phrase "almost certainly" appears just before the necessary condition in the first sentence, and a similar phrase ("virtually certain") is used to qualify the conclusion. This makes sense, because both phrases convey a high likelihood of something happening, but make the conditional relationship less than absolute. So when one of two highly probable events ruled out, it is reasonable to conclude that the other event is "virtually certain" to occur.

The Method question stem requires you to select an answer choice that best describes the logical organization of the argument. This is simply an abstract Must Be True question, in which you can use the information in the stimulus to prove the correct answer choice. Because the argument will be described in abstract terms, knowing the details of the stimulus is not nearly as important as understanding the structure of the argument. The correct answer will probably not mention awarding government contracts or building a new highway. Instead, it will describe an argument in which a particular event is deemed highly likely to occur, because the only probable alternative cannot occur. This prephrase reveals Answer choice (A) to be correct.

Answer choice (A): This is the correct answer choice. The author concludes that it is extremely likely ("virtually certain") that an event will occur ("Phoenix will be awarded the contract") by ruling out the only probable alternative ("the government has decided not to award the contract to Cartwright").

Note that since there are many variations on the way an argument can be described, you may have prephrased an answer that uses different language. For instance:

The argument proceeds by inferring, from a claim that one of two possible events will not occur, that the other event is highly likely to occur.

The argument proceeds by predicting that a future event is likely to occur because the only viable alternative cannot occur.

The argument proceeds by inferring that one of two events is virtually inevitable by refuting the possibility of an alternative event.

In Method questions in particular, it is important to make a general, abstract prephrase of what occurred in the argument and then look for an answer choice that paraphrases it.

Answer choice (B): This is a Reverse answer. This answer choice would be attractive if you misunderstood the relationship between the premises and the conclusion. The author does not infer, from a claim that one of two possible events *will* occur, that the other event *will not* occur. On the contrary—she infers, from a claim that one of two possible events *will not* occur, that the other event *will* occur.

Answer choice (C): This is an Opposite answer. The author does not refute that awarding the contract to Phoenix is inevitable by establishing the possibility of awarding it to Cartwright. On the contrary—she establishes that the contract will be awarded to Phoenix by refuting the possibility of awarding it to Cartwright.

Answer choice (D): This is a classic half-right, half-wrong answer choice. Even though the author does predict a future event, her prediction is not based on an established pattern of past events. Because the second half of this answer choice fails the Fact Test, it is incorrect.

Answer choice (E): This is another half-right, half-wrong answer choice. Although the author does infer a claim about the probability of awarding the contract to Phoenix, her conclusion is not based on a general statistic statement (such as, "Phoenix is awarded more contracts per year than any other company"). Because the second half of this answer choice fails the Fact Test, it is incorrect.

Question #22: Strengthen, CE. The correct answer choice is (E)

The researchers' argument is structured as follows:

Premise: Children in large families—particularly the younger siblings—generally have fewer allergies than children in small families do.

Conclusion: Exposure to germs during infancy makes people less likely to develop allergies.

In other words, the researchers compared the incidence of allergies in large families vs. small families, and found that the younger siblings in large families have a lower risk of developing allergies than children in small families. They conclude that it is exposure to germs during infancy that makes people less likely to develop allergies. Because the conclusion seeks to explain an observation presented in the premise, the relationship between premise and conclusion is a causal one, and can be diagrammed as follows:

Lower Allergy Risk = Younger siblings in large families have a lower risk of developing allergies than children in small families

Germs While Young = Exposure to germs during infancy

<u>Cause</u>		<u>Effect</u>
Germs While Young	⟶	Lower Allergy Risk

Although the argument proceeds in a predictable fashion (the premise presents a phenomenon; the conclusion attempts to explain it), this is a challenging question due to the convoluted causality underlying the researchers' hypothesis. In order to strengthen it, you first need to understand why exposure to germs during infancy is reasonable explanation for the comparatively low incidence of allergies among younger siblings in large families.

The logic is as follows: the more people we come in contact with, the more germs we are exposed to. Hence, children raised in large families are typically exposed to more germs by their siblings than children raised in small families. Likewise, younger siblings in large families are exposed to more germs during their infancy than their older siblings were (the elders grew up in a family whose size was smaller). It turns out that the younger siblings in large families—the ones with the greatest exposure to germs during infancy—also have the fewest allergies. On the basis of this correlation, the researchers concluded that there is a causal relationship between exposure to germs during infancy and the likelihood of developing allergies.

Correlations between two variables do not automatically imply that one causes the other, as they may be coincidental effects of another cause. For instance, what if younger siblings in large families tend to eat less allergenic foods than their older siblings? This would explain why they have fewer allergies. Also, what if small families were more common in industrialized countries, where environmental pollutants play a greater role in the development of allergies than in less industrialized countries?

To strengthen the argument, look for answers that either eliminate such alternate causes, or show an analogous case in which the cause occurs (exposure to germs), and the effect also occurs (lower allergy risk). You can also support the cause and effect relationship by showing that when the cause does not occur, the effect does not occur.

Answer choice (A): This answer choice may seem attractive, because it provides further evidence of the negative association between family size and the incidence of developing allergies. However, we have no proof that the increased incidence of allergies in countries where the average number of children per family has decreased affected the younger siblings in those families. If it did not, the increased incidence of allergies may have been caused by something other than the decreased exposure to germs.

Furthermore, we need to take into account the incidence of allergies in countries where the average number of children per family *did not* decrease. If children in such countries also had an increased risk of developing allergies, then clearly something other than family size (and germ exposure) must have elevated the risk in both types of countries. Since this answer choice does not present a clear comparison, it is impossible to evaluate its effect on the conclusion of the argument.

Answer choice (B): This Opposite answer presents an alternate cause for the increased incidence of allergies. If children in small families eat more kinds of very allergenic foods than children in large families do, this would explain why the likelihood of developing allergies varies by family size.

Answer choice (C): This answer choice does not address the causal relationship between family size and the incidence of allergies. The question stem does not ask you to justify exposure of children to germs in order to prevent allergy.

Answer choice (D): This Opposite answer suggests that an alternate cause may affect the incidence of allergies: if children whose parents have allergies have an above-average likelihood of developing allergies themselves, then susceptibility to allergies would be hereditary. In that case, the chance of developing allergies would be determined at birth. This is clearly at odds with the premise that younger siblings in large families have fewer allergies than older siblings, and weakens the conclusion that an environmental factor (such as exposure to germs) makes people less likely to develop allergies.

Answer choice (E): This is the correct answer choice. If children from small families who entered day care before age one were less likely to develop allergies than children from small families who entered day care later, this provides additional evidence to support the hypothesis that exposure to other children (and therefore germs) leads to a decreased incidence of allergies. Note that this answer choice correctly compares the incidence of allergies in children from the same family size, which helps eliminate any potential biases inherent in the original study. Because early germ exposure via day care cohorts (as opposed to older siblings) results in the same decreased incidences of allergies, this answer choice presents an analogous case in which the cause occurs, and the effect occurs.

Question #23: Assumption. The correct answer choice is (D)

The stimulus contains the following structure:

Premise:	Film preservation requires transferring old movies from their original, deteriorating nitrate film to stable acetate film, which is a time-consuming and expensive process.
Sub. Concl.:	There is no way to transfer all currently deteriorating nitrate films to acetate before they disintegrate.
Conclusion:	Some films from the earliest years of Hollywood will not be preserved.

Take a closer look at the conclusion: "some films *from the earliest years of Hollywood* will not be preserved." All we know from the premises is that some deteriorating nitrate films will not be preserved: that alone does not mean that some films *from the earliest years of Hollywood* will not be preserved. What if all of them have already been transferred to acetate? And even if they have not, there is no reason to suspect that these films *in particular* will be the ones that never get transferred to acetate.

Because this is an assumption question, the answer you select must contain a statement upon which the argument depends, i.e. a statement that is *necessary* for the conclusion to be true. Typically, if you see a new or "rogue" element in the conclusion, look for a Supporter assumption answer that links the new element back to the premises. Since "films from the earliest years of Hollywood" did not appear anywhere else in the argument, the Supporter assumption must state that at least some films from the earliest years of Hollywood still exist in their original material (and are therefore deteriorating). This prephrase reveals answer choice (D) to be correct.

Answer choice (A): This answer choice may seem attractive, because it supports the idea that some currently deteriorating nitrate films will never be preserved. To double-check if this is an assumption, apply the Assumption Negation Technique—logically negate the answer and ask yourself if the following statement would undermine the argument:

> A new technology for transferring old movies from nitrate film to acetate film will be developed at some point in the future.

Even if a new technology for transferring old movies to acetate is invented in the future, it is still possible that some films from the earliest years of Hollywood are irrevocably lost. Recall the author's assertion that "there is no way to transfer all currently deteriorating nitrate films to acetate before they disintegrate." Clearly, unless the new technology is developed and implemented in the immediate future, there is a significant risk that the films currently deteriorating will have disintegrated by the time the new technology becomes viable.

Since the logical opposite of answer choice (A) does not weaken the conclusion, this is not an assumption upon which the argument depends.

Savvy test takers would eliminate answer choice (A) immediately, because it does not make any mention of the rogue element in the conclusion ("films from the earliest years of Hollywood"). Given that Supporters connect new elements, one would suspect that the correct answer would include this element.

Answer choice (B): The author never discussed the cost of film preservation, and no assumption was made regarding the relative cost of transferring films from nitrate to acetate. Because an assumption is something the author believed when forming the argument, correct assumption answers cannot contain extraneous information. This answer choice can also be eliminated because it does not make any mention of the rogue element in the conclusion.

Answer choice (C): This answer choice may seem attractive because it strengthens the conclusion of the argument. Indeed, if only a few films from the earliest years of Hollywood have been transferred to acetate, it is even more likely that time will run out before we can transfer the rest. However, just because a statement supports the conclusion does not mean it is ***necessary*** for the conclusion to be true. Apply the Assumption Negation Technique—drop the negative term ("not many") and ask yourself, "What would the author say to this negation?"

> Many films from the earliest years of Hollywood have already been transferred to acetate.

The author would reply that "many" does not mean "all," and that a sufficiently high number of non-transferred films can still disintegrate before they are preserved. Since the logical opposite of answer choice (C) does not weaken the conclusion, this is not an assumption upon which the argument depends.

Answer choice (D): This is the correct answer choice, as it is consistent with our prephrase of the Supporter Assumption. Consider the author's conclusion that "some films from the earliest years of Hollywood will not be preserved." Clearly, her conclusion depends on the idea that at least some films from the earliest years of Hollywood have not yet been transferred from nitrate to acetate, and therefore exist solely in their original material.

If this answer is troubling you, use the Assumption Negation Technique and ask yourself if the following statement would undermine the argument:

> None of films from the earliest years of Hollywood currently exist solely in their original material.

This clearly shows that the author's concerns are unfounded, since no films from the earliest years of Hollywood would be in danger of disintegrating. Because the logical opposite of answer choice (D) attacks the argument, this must be the correct answer.

Remember—when an Assumption answer choice starts with a phrase such as "at least one" or "some," chances are high that the answer will be correct. Although you should not immediately assume that it is, use the proper negation ("none") to check it by using the Assumption Negation Technique.

Answer choice (E): The author makes no statement regarding the kind of films that are the most likely to disintegrate. Therefore, there is no way to determine if an assumption has been made associating the relative popularity of these films with their likelihood of being lost.

In general, avoid answers to Assumption questions containing phrases such as "most" and "least." An assumption can be considered a "minimalist" answer, and cannot contain exaggerations or elements that are extraneous to the argument.

Question #24: Main Point-FIB, CE. The correct answer choice is (C)

In a recent study of arthritis, researchers failed to find a correlation between arthritis pain and the weather conditions most commonly associated with such pain. What they found was that arthritis sufferers who were convinced of the existence of such a correlation gave widely varying accounts of the time delay between the occurrence of the weather condition and the increased intensity of the pain.

The question stem asks you to fill in the blank with an appropriate answer. While this is not one of the most common question types on the test, Fill in the Blanks almost always indicate the presence of a Main Point question. Note that the placement of the blank is at the very end of the stimulus, and the sentence it completes begins with the conclusion indicator "thus." Therefore, you should fill the blank with the answer choice that best represents the main point of the argument. To achieve this goal, look for contextual clues in the stimulus revealing the direction of the argument and the author's intent.

The first two sentences, when taken together, contain all the information required to fill in the blank at the end of the question. From the outset, the author rejects the existence of any correlation between the intensity of arthritis pain and the weather conditions commonly associated with increased pain. Immediately after, she describes inconsistencies in the accounts given by arthritis sufferers who believed in such a correlation. Clearly, the author feels that no causal link exists between weather conditions and arthritis pain, and that the arthritis sufferers are mistaken in their beliefs about such a correlation. The last sentence then prefaces the blank by saying, "thus, this study______." The most logical answer would be one suggesting that the arthritis sufferers' beliefs are unfounded.

Answer choice (A): Although this answer choice describes a plausible hypothesis given the varying accounts of the time delay between the occurrence of the weather condition and the increased intensity of the pain experienced by arthritis sufferers, it ignores the assertion made in the beginning of the stimulus—researchers found *no correlation* between pain intensity and weather conditions. Therefore, the weather need not affect arthritis sufferers at all, despite any beliefs to the contrary. Because this answer choice fails the Fact Test, it is incorrect.

Remember—Main Point questions are a subcategory of Must Be True questions and thus fall into the First Family of question types. The correct answer choice must be true according to the stimulus (and also summarize the author's point).

Answer choice (B): This answer choice suggests that arthritis sufferers' beliefs about the causes of the pain they feel may affect their assessment of the intensity of that pain:

Cause Effect

Beliefs about Causes of Pain ⟶ Arthritis Pain

However, just because the study rejects the notion that weather conditions affect arthritis pain does not mean that one's *beliefs* about the causes of arthritis pain affect the intensity of such pain. The study provides no comparison of the pain intensity or delays experienced by believers and non-believers—the information we have pertains only to the inconsistent accounts given by those who believe that weather affects their pain. Had the study revealed that those convinced of the existence of a correlation experienced pain differently than those who were not so convinced, this would have been a useful comparison to support the conclusion in answer choice (B).

Answer choice (C): This is the correct answer choice. Given the researcher's failure to find any correlation between weather conditions and arthritis pain, those still convinced of such a correlation must be mistaken in their beliefs.

Answer choice (D): Given that the study found no correlation between the intensity of arthritis pain and weather conditions, there is no proof that weather-induced arthritis pain actually exists. Therefore, it would be unreasonable to conclude that some people are more susceptible to such pain than are others.

Answer choice (E): Just because one study found no connection between weather and arthritis pain does not mean that scientific investigation of such a connection is *impossible*. This answer choice exaggerates the facts and makes a broader statement that is not supported by the stimulus.

Question #25: Parallel Reasoning, SN. The correct answer choice is (C)

The above-average difficulty level of this question is primarily due to the confusing approach taken in creating the five answer choices, rather than the stimulus itself. The stimulus contains an argument with a relatively simple structure, as described below. The answer choices, however, test your ability to compare and contrast the abstract relationships that underlie each argument. It does not help that all five of them deal with the same topic, which—though irrelevant to the structure of each argument—makes your task even more challenging.

It may be helpful to diagram the argument contained in the stimulus as if it contained conditional reasoning. However, keep in mind that the relationships in each premise are less than absolute, due to the use of such phrases as "typically" and "tend to." Nevertheless, since our primary objective is to understand the logical structure of the argument as clearly as possible, such a conditional approach would be justified, albeit with a caveat.

The first sentence indicates that cities with healthy economies typically have plenty of job openings:

HE = Healthy economies
JOB = Job openings

S N

HE ⟶ tend JOB

The first clause of the second sentence states that cities with high-technology businesses also tend to have healthy economies:

Hi-Tech = Cities with high-technology businesses

S N

Hi-Tech ⟶ tend HE

You may notice that the two premises, when combined, produce the following chain:

High-Tech ⟶ tend HE ⟶ tend JOB

On the basis of this information, the author concludes that those in search of jobs should move to a city with high-technology businesses. In other words, those in search of the necessary condition should seek an area where the sufficient condition occurs. Note that this is not a Mistaken Reversal; the author does not suggest that the necessary makes the sufficient condition occur, but rather that looking for the sufficient condition is a viable approach if you want find the necessary condition.

Our job is to parallel the reasoning contained in the stimulus. To do that, we must parallel the conclusion as well as the premises, making sure to "match" the language of both. First, we need to find an answer choice in which the conclusion that uses the language of a recommendation (words such as "should," "must," "ought to," etc.) and suggests that seeking a sufficient condition is an advisable avenue if one seeks the occurrence of the necessary condition. On the premise side, the correct answer choice will contain the two premises that can be combined, and whose wording makes make the conditional relationship between them less than absolute.

Because the argument is not flawed, the question stem does not indicate the presence of a logical flaw.

Answer choice (A): This answer choice can be diagrammed as follows:

Premise (1): Older antiques ⟶ Usually most valuable antiques

Premise (2): Antique dealers ⟶ Authenticate age

Conclusion: Buy most valuable antiques ⟶ Antique dealers

You should notice that there is no "link" between the first and the second premise in this answer choice. Indeed, just because antique dealers authenticate the age of the antiques they sell, that does not necessarily mean that they sell older antiques. Since the conclusion does not follow from the premises, this answer choice is incorrect.

Answer choice (B): This answer choice, when re-worded, has the following argument structure:

Premise (1): The most valuable antiques are those whose age has been authenticated.

Premise (2): Dealers who authenticate the age of the antiques they sell have plenty of antiques for sale.

Conclusion: Buyers of valuable antiques should purchase them from antique dealers.

The conclusion in this argument does not take the same form as that in the stimulus. Also, having "plenty" of antiques for sale does not automatically make them the most valuable. Do not get distracted by the repetition of the word "plenty," which also appears in the stimulus—this similarity is irrelevant to the logical structure of the argument. Lastly, just because an antique collector is searching for valuable antiques, that does not mean she is in search for the *most* valuable antiques.

Since either of these inconsistencies would be sufficient to eliminate this answer choice from consideration, no conditional diagramming is necessary to prove it wrong.

Answer choice (C): This is the correct answer choice. The argument has the following structure:

Premise (1): Age authenticated ——→ tend Valuable antiques

Premise (2): Antique dealers ——→ generally Age authenticated

Conclusion: Valuable antiques ——→ Antique dealers

As in the stimulus, the two premises can be combined to form the following chain:

Antique dealers ——→ generally Age authenticated ——→ tend Valuable antiques

On that basis, the author concludes that collectors seeking valuable antiques should be purchase their antiques from antique dealers. Since antique dealers do sell valuable antiques, the author's conclusion is reasonable.

Some students object that the wording in this answer choice is not identical to that in the stimulus. But, "generally" and "tend" have the same logical force, and thus there is no problem with the wording; synonymous words and phrases are acceptable because you attempting to parallel the structure, not the exact wording.

Answer choice (D): This answer choice fails to Double the Conclusion and can easily be ruled out. The conclusion in this answer choice does not contain a recommendation ("should"), but rather a statement of fact ("most antique collectors who want antiques that are valuable tend to purchase their antiques from antique dealers"), which is sufficiently different to make this answer incorrect.

Answer choice (E): Hopefully, you were able to eliminate this answer choice rather quickly. The first premise indicates that many antiques *increase* in value once they have had their ages authenticated by antique dealers; however, this information is irrelevant to the remainder of the argument and cannot be combined with the second premise. Because the second premise provides independent grounds for the conclusion of the argument, the pattern of reasoning contained in this answer choice deviates significantly from that in the stimulus.

Question #26: Resolve the ParadoxX, #%. The correct answer choice is (D)

The relative ease of this question underscores the importance of keeping a good pace throughout any Logical Reasoning section, even if this means initially skipping some of the more challenging or time-consuming questions. Remember: each question is worth one point, regardless of how difficult it is. Many students who took the December 2010 exam wasted valuable time on questions 16 and 18 in this section, which prevented them from finishing before the time was up. The point, of course, is not to automatically "skip" difficult questions, but to know "when to say when." If you end up spending too much time on a particular question, chances are that you either misunderstood a critical idea in the stimulus, or you did not obtain a clear prephrase of the correct answer. Your best course of action may be to leave that question for later as and move on. Remember—if you keep a good pace, you can always return to the questions you skipped. More often than not, a second look is a lot more productive than the first.

In this stimulus, the sociologist describes a study in which people older than 65 were more likely to be malnourished to be poor, whereas among those younger than 65, the opposite was true:

Older than 65:	% Malnourished > % Poor
Younger than 65:	% Poor > % Malnourished

To explain the discrepant results, look for critical differences between the two age groups. After all, since the stimulus contains a discrepancy where two items are said to be different, an answer choice implying that they are similar will not explain it. The stimulus is followed by a ResolveX question, which means that among the five answer choices, the four incorrect answer choices will provide a resolution to the paradox, and the one correct choice will not provide a resolution.

Answer choice (A): If doctors are less likely to correctly diagnose and treat malnutrition in their patients who are over 65 than in their younger patients, this would explain why there is a relatively high percentage of malnourished people over 65. Because this answer choice resolves the discrepancy between the two age groups, it is incorrect.

Answer choice (B): If people over 65 are more likely to take medications that increase their need for certain nutrients than are people 65 or younger, it is reasonable to expect that those over 65 have a higher chance of not receiving the nutrients they need. Since this would explain why a greater proportion of them are malnourished in comparison to the younger population, this answer choice is incorrect.

Answer choice (C): If people over 65 are more likely to suffer from loss of appetite due to medication than are people 65 or younger, those over 65 would have a higher risk of malnutrition compared to those 65 or younger. This answer choice explains the discrepancy in the proportion of malnourished vs. poor people in each age group, and is therefore incorrect.

Answer choice (D): This is the correct answer choice. If people 65 or younger are just as likely to be poor as are people over 65, this implies that the two groups are similar in at least one critical respect—their likelihood of falling below the government poverty standards. As mentioned earlier, since the findings of the study indicate that the two groups are different, an answer choice implying that they are similar will not explain the discrepancy, and is therefore correct.

Answer choice (E): If people 65 or younger are less likely to have medical conditions that interfere with their digestion than are people over 65, this would explain why those 65 or younger are less likely to become malnourished. Since this answer choice helps resolve the discrepant findings of the study cited by the sociologist, it is incorrect.

CHAPTER SEVEN: GLOSSARY

Introduction

This section contains a brief definition of the terms used in this book. The terms are given in alphabetical order. For more comprehensive explanations of each term or concept, refer to either the *Logic Games Bible*, the *Logical Reasoning Bible*, or the *Reading Comprehension Bible*.

Alphabetical Glossary

#%: See Numbers and Percentages.

Additional Premise: Additional premises are premises that may be central to the argument or they may be secondary. To determine the importance of the premise, examine the remainder of the argument.

Agree/Disagree Test™: This test is used to solve Point at Issue questions. The correct answer must produce responses where one speaker would say, "I agree, the statement is correct" and the other speaker would say, "I disagree, the statement is incorrect." If those two responses are not produced, then the answer is incorrect. The Agree/Disagree Test crystallizes the essence of Point at Issue questions by forcing you to concretely identify the elements that determine the correct answer.

AP: See Author's Perspective and Tone.

Appeal Fallacies: A common error of reasoning that attempts to "appeal" to various insubstantial viewpoints of the reader (emotion, popular opinion, tradition, authority, etc.). However the appeal is not valid, and concrete evidence is needed to support the argument.

Argument: A set of statements wherein one statement is claimed to follow from or be derived from the others. An argument requires a conclusion.

Argument Part Question: A subset of Method of Reasoning questions. In Argument Part questions, the question stem cites a specific portion of the stimulus and then asks you to identify the role the cited portion plays in the structure of the argument.

Assumption: An assumption is an unstated premise of the argument. Assumptions are an integral component of the argument that the author takes for granted and leaves unsaid.

Assumption Question: These questions ask you to identify an assumption of the author's argument. Question stem example:

"Which one of the following is an assumption required by the argument above?"

Assumption Negation Technique™: This technique requires you to logically negate the answer choice under consideration, which results in a negated answer choice that attacks the argument. If the negated answer does not attack the argument, then it is incorrect. The purpose of this technique is to take an Assumption question, which is generally difficult for most students, and turn it into a Weaken question, which is easier for most students. This technique can only be used on Assumption questions.

Author's Perspective and Tone (AP): These Reading Comprehension questions ask you to select the answer choice that best reflects the author's views, such as, "The author of the passage would most likely agree with which one of the following statements?" Tone questions ask you to identify the author's attitude toward the subject.

Balanced (see also Grouping, Linearity, Unbalanced, Defined, Undefined, etc.): In a Defined game, when the number of variables to be selected is equal to the overall number of available spaces.

Block (See also Linearity): In Linear games, blocks reflect the idea of a fixed spatial relationship between variables. Blocks represent variables that are next to one another, not next to one another, or separated by a fixed number of spaces. Basic blocks indicate adjacency.

C: In diagramming Logical Reasoning questions, "C" indicates Cause. Also see Cause.

Cannot Be True Questions: Ask you to identify the answer choice that cannot be true or is most weakened based on the information in the stimulus.
Question stem example:
"If the statements above are true, which one of the following CANNOT be true?"

Causal Reasoning: Asserts or denies that one thing causes another, or that one thing is caused by another. On the LSAT, cause and effect reasoning appears in many Logical Reasoning problems, often in the conclusion where the author mistakenly claims that one event causes another.

Cause (C): The event that makes another occur.

Cause and Effect (CE): When one event is said to make another occur. The cause is the event that makes the other occur; the effect is the event that follows from the cause. By definition, the cause must occur before the effect, and the cause is the "activator" or "ignitor" in the relationship. The effect always happens at some point in time after the cause.

CE: See Cause and Effect.

Circular Reasoning: A flaw where the author assumes as true what is supposed to be proved. The premise supports the conclusion, but the conclusion equally supports the premise, creating a "circular" situation where you can move from premise to conclusion, and then back again to the premise, and so on.

Circular Sequencing: Games that consist of a fixed number of variables assigned to spaces distributed around a circle (usually a table). Essentially these games are Linear games wrapped around a circular diagram.

Complex Argument: Arguments that contain more than one conclusion. In these instances, one of the conclusions is the main conclusion, and the other conclusions are subsidiary conclusions (also known as sub-conclusions). In basic terms, a complex argument makes an initial conclusion based on a premise. The author then uses that conclusion as the foundation (or premise) for another conclusion, thus building a chain with several levels.

Conclusion: A statement or judgment that follows from one or more reasons. Conclusions, as summary statements, are supposed to be drawn from and rest on the premises.

Conclusion/Premise Indicator Form: The test makers will sometimes arrange premise and conclusion indicators in a way that is designed to be confusing. One of their favorite forms places a conclusion indicator and premise indicator back-to-back, separated by a comma, as in the following examples:

"Therefore, since..."
"Thus, because..."
"Hence, due to..."

Conditional Reasoning: The broad name given to logical relationships composed of sufficient and necessary conditions. Any conditional statement consists of at least one sufficient condition and at least one necessary condition. In everyday use, conditional statements are often brought up using the "if...then" construction. Conditional reasoning can occur in any question type.

Contender: An answer choice that appears somewhat attractive, interesting, or even confusing. Basically, any answer choice that you cannot immediately identify as incorrect.

Contrapositive: Denies the necessary condition, thereby making it impossible for the sufficient condition to occur. Contrapositives can often yield important insights in Logic Games.

Counter-premise: A premise that actually contains an idea that is counter to the argument. Counter-premises, also called adversatives, bring up points of opposition or comparison.

Defender: In the Supporter/Defender Assumption Model™, the Defender assumptions contain statements that eliminate ideas or assertions that would undermine the conclusion. In this sense, they "defend" the argument by showing that a possible source of attack has been eliminated.

Defined: In these Logic Games, the exact number of variables to be selected is fixed in the rules.

Double Arrow: Indicates that the two terms must always occur together. The double arrow is typically introduced in any of the following three ways:

1. Use of the phrase "if and only if"
2. Use of the phrase "vice versa" (as in "If A attends then B attends, and vice versa")
3. By repeating and reversing the terms (as in "If A attends then B attends, and if B attends then A attends")

Double-not Arrow: Indicates that two terms cannot occur together. The double not-arrow only prohibits one scenario—one where the two terms occur together.

Dual Option: When only one of two variables can occupy a single slot. Represented with a slash, as in "A/B."

E: In diagramming, indicates Effect. See also Effect.

Effect: The event that follows from the cause.

Either/Or: For the purposes of the LSAT, the definition of "either/or" is "at least one of the two." Note that this definition implicitly allows for the possibility that both elements occur, and the existence of this possibility makes diagramming sentences containing the "either/or" term confusing. A careful examination of the definition of "either/or" reveals that a conditional relationship is at the heart of the construction: since at least one of the terms must occur, if one fails to occur then the other must occur.

Elemental Attack™: When attacking Parallel Reasoning questions, compare the big-picture elements of the argument: intent of the conclusion, force and use of the premises, the relationship of the premises and the conclusion, and the soundness of the argument. The four tests you can use to evaluate answers are Match the Method of Reasoning, Match the Conclusion, Match the Premises, and Match the Validity of the Argument.

Errors in the Use of Evidence: A common error of reasoning that involves the misuse of evidence in one of these ways:

1. Lack of evidence for a position is taken to prove that position is false.
2. Lack of evidence against a position is taken to prove that position is true.
3. Some evidence against a position is taken to prove that position is false.
4. Some evidence for a position is taken to prove that position is true.

Errors of Composition and Division: A common error of reasoning that involves judgments made about groups and parts of a group. An error of composition occurs when the author attributes a characteristic of part of the group to the group as a whole or to each member of the group. An error of division occurs when the author attributes a characteristic of the whole (or each member of the whole) to a part of the group.

Errors of Conditional Reasoning: A common error of reasoning that involves confusing the sufficient condition with the necessary condition. Note that the authors can either mistake a necessary condition for a sufficient condition, or mistake a sufficient condition for a necessary condition.

Evaluate the Argument Questions: With Evaluate the Argument questions you must decide which answer choice will allow you to determine the logical validity of the argument. Use the Variance Test™ to prove or disprove answers as needed.
Question stem example:
"The answer to which one of the following questions would contribute most to an evaluation of the argument?"

Except: When "except" is placed in a question it negates the logical quality of the answer choice you seek. Literally, it turns the intent of the question stem upside down.

Exceptional Case/Overgeneralization: A common error of reasoning that involves taking a small number of instances and treating those instances as if they support a broad, sweeping conclusion.

F: See also Function.

Fact Set: A collection of statements without a conclusion. Fact sets make a series of assertions without making a judgment.

Fact Test™: The correct answer to a Must Be True question (and other First Family questions) can always be proven by referring to the facts stated in the stimulus. An answer choice that cannot be substantiated by proof in the stimulus is incorrect.

False Analogy: A common error of reasoning that involves an author using an analogy that is too dissimilar to the original situation to be applicable.

False Dilemma: A common error of reasoning that involves assuming that only two courses of action are available when there may be others (for example, "You are either rich or impoverished"). Do not confuse a False Dilemma with a situation where the author legitimately establishes that only two possibilities exist. Phrases such as "either A or B will occur, but not both" can establish a limited set of possibilities, and certain real-world situations yield only two possibilities, such as "you are either dead or alive."

First Family: Consists of question types that use the stimulus to prove that one of the answer choices must be true. No information outside the sphere of the stimulus is allowed in the correct answer choice. Includes the following question types: Must Be True, Main Point, Point at Issue, Method of Reasoning, Flaw in the Reasoning, and Parallel Reasoning.

FL: See Formal Logic.

Flaw in the Reasoning Questions: Flaw in the Reasoning questions ask you to describe, in abstract terms, the error of reasoning committed by the author.
Question stem example:
"The reasoning in the argument is flawed because this argument"

Formal Logic (FL): A standard system of translating relationships into symbols and then making inferences from those symbolized relationships.

Fourth Family: Consists of question types that use the stimulus to prove that one of the answer choices cannot occur. No informationoutside the sphere of the stimulus is allowed in the answer choices. Includes the following question type: Cannot Be True.

Function (F): These Reading Comprehension questions ask why the author referred to a particular word, phrase, or idea. This is essentially an extended Method of Reasoning question, requiring you to go beyond simply identifying the argument structure, and asking you the reasons behind the author's use of words or ideas.

Game Scenario: In Logic Games, introduces sets of variables, people, places, things, or events involved in an easy to understand activity such as sitting in seats or singing songs.

General Lack of Relevant Evidence for the Conclusion: A common error of reasoning that involves authors misusing information to such a degree that they fail to provide any information to support their conclusion or they provide information that is irrelevant to their conclusion.

Global: These Logic Games questions ask about information derived only from the initial rules, such as "Who can finish first?" or "Which one of the following must be true?"

Grouping: These Logic Games require you to analyze the variables in terms of which ones can and cannot be together.

Horizontality: When a game is diagrammed in a horizontal line (or setup), the relationship between variables arranged horizontally indicates adjacency, while the relationship of variables arranged vertically indicates similarity. This is also true of horizontality in blocks.

Hurdle the Uncertainity™: In Logic Games, during the placement of variables, situations occur where even though you cannot determine the exact variables being selected, you can "leap" that uncertainty to determine that other variables that must be selected. This powerful technique can be used in many different games, and it attacks a concept frequently used by the test makers an appears in virtually every Grouping game.

Hypothetical: A possible solution to a question that you quickly create to gain insight into Logic Game answers. Hypotheticals can be the fastest way to solve a question, and sometimes they give you information that can be used to solve other problems.

Inference: In logic, an inference can be defined as something that must be true. If you are asked to identify an inference of the argument, you must find an item that must be true based on the information presented in the argument.

Internal Contradiction: A common error of reasoning (also known as a self-contradiction) that occurs when an author makes conflicting statements.

Justify Formula™: Premises + Answer choice = Conclusion

The Justify Formula is a useful tool for understanding how Justify the Conclusion questions work. If the answer choice is correct, the application of the Justify Formula will produce the given conclusion. If the answer choice is incorrect, the application of the Justify Formula will fail to produce the given conclusion.

Justify the Conclusion Questions: Justify the Conclusion questions ask you to supply a piece of information that, when added to the premises, proves the conclusion.

Question stem example:

"Which one of the following, if assumed, allows the conclusion above to be properly drawn?"

Least: When "least" appears in a question stem you should treat it exactly the same as "except." Note: this advice holds true only when this word appears in the question stem! If you see the word "least" elsewhere on the LSAT, consider it to have its usual meaning of "in the lowest or smallest degree."

Linearity: Involves the fixed positioning and ordering of variables. In every Linear game, one of the variable sets is chosen as the "base" and is diagrammed in a straight line, either horizontally or vertically, and the remaining variable sets are placed into slots above or next to the base.

Linkage: Linkage involves finding a variable that appears in at least two rules and then combining those two rules. Often that combination will produce an inference of value. Linkage is the easiest and most basic way to make inferences.

List Question: In Logic Games, list questions present a list of variables that can either fill a slot or possibly solve the game. The best technique for attacking List questions is to take a single rule and apply it to each of the five answer choices, one at a time. The first question in a game is often a List Question.

Local: These games questions occur when the question imposes a new condition in addition to the initial rules, such as "If Laura sits in the third chair, which one of the following must be true?" Local questions almost always require you to produce a "mini-setup" next to the question.

Loser: An answer choice which immediately strikes you as incorrect.

Main Point (MP): Main Point questions are a variant of Must Be True questions. As you might expect, a Main Point question asks you to find the primary conclusion made by the author.

Question stem example:

"The main point of the argument is that"

Mapping: These games either do not fix the physical relationships among the variables (Spatial Relations), involve a fixed point and all other variables are placed North, East, South, and West of that point (Directional), or the makers of the test supply a diagram intended to represent the relationship of the variables (Supplied Diagram). There are no numerical elements in a Mapping game.

Mechanistic Approach: This approach requires you to reduce the stimulus to its component parts (a process that occurs naturally as you identify premises and conclusions), and then identify which elements appear in the conclusion but not in the premises. In a nutshell, the rules for this approach condense to: link new elements in the premises and conclusion and ignore elements common to both. The mechanistic approach works for the vast majority of Justify the Conclusion questions.

Method of Reasoning: Method of Reasoning questions ask you to describe, in abstract terms, the way in which the author made his or her argument.
Question stem example:
"Which one of the following describes the technique of reasoning used above?"

Mistaken Cause and Effect: A common error of reasoning that occurs because arguments that draw causal conclusions are inherently flawed because there may be another explanation for the stated relationship. This can occur by assuming a causal relationship on the basis of the sequence of events or when only a correlation exists. This can also occur due to failure to consider an alternate cause for the effect, an alternate cause for both the cause and the effect, or that the events may be reversed.

Mistaken Negation™: Negates both sufficient and necessary conditions, creating a statement that does not have to be true.

Mistaken Reversal™: Switches the elements in the sufficient and necessary conditions, creating a statement that does not have to be true.

Most (in Question Stems): In order to maintain test integrity the test makers need to make sure their credited answer choice is as airtight and defensible as possible. Imagine what would occur if a question stem, let us say a Weaken question, did not include a "most" qualifier: any answer choice that weakened the argument, even if only very slightly, could then be argued to meet the criteria of the question stem. A situation like this would make constructing the test exceedingly difficult because any given problem might have multiple correct answer choices. To eliminate this predicament, the test makers insert "most" into the question stem, and then they can always claim there is one and only one correct answer choice.

Most (in Formal Logic): A majority, and possibly all.

MP: See Main Point.

Must Be True: Must Be True questions ask you to identify the answer choice that is best proven by the information in the stimulus.
Question stem examples:
"If the statements above are true, which one of the following must also be true?"
"Which one of the following can be properly inferred from the passage?"

N: See Necessary Condition.

Necessary Condition (N): An event or circumstance whose occurrence is required in order for a sufficient condition to occur.

Negation: Negating a statement consists of creating the logical opposite of the statement. The logical opposite is the statement that denies the truth of the original statement, and a logical opposite is different than the polar opposite.

New Information: Information not mentioned explicitly in the stimulus of a Logical Reasoning question.

Not All: At least one is not, possibly all are not. Functionally equivalent to "some are not."

Not Block: Indicate that variables cannot be next to one another. Not-blocks only come into play once one of the variables has been placed.

Not Law™: Physically notate where a variable cannot be placed. Not Laws are very useful since it is essential that you establish the events that cannot be true in a game.

Not Necessarily True: The logical opposite of "Must be true." When an answer choice is not proven by the information in the stimulus.

NP: See Numbers and Percentages.

Numbers and Percentages (NP or #%): Numerical situations normally hinge on three elements: an overall total, a number within that total, and a percentage within the total. LSAT problems will often give you one of the elements, but without at least two elements present, you cannot make a definitive judgment about what is occurring with another element. When you are given just percentage information, you cannot make a judgment about numbers. Likewise, when you are given just numerical information you cannot make a judgment about percentages.

Numbers and Percentages Errors: A common error of reasoning that is committed when an author improperly equates a percentage with a definite quantity, or when an author uses quantity information to make a judgment about the percentage represented by that quantity.

Numerical Distribution: Allocates one set of variables among another set of variables. Numerical Distributions occur in every game except Mapping games.

Opposite Answer: Provides an answer that is completely opposite of the stated facts of the stimulus. Opposite Answers are very attractive to students who are reading too quickly or carelessly and quite frequently appear in Strengthen and Weaken questions.

Overloaded: Description of an Unbalanced game in which there are extra candidates for the available spaces.

Parallel Reasoning (in Logical Reasoning): Parallel Reasoning questions ask you to identify the answer choice that contains reasoning most similar in structure to the reasoning presented in the stimulus.
Question stem example:
"Which one of the following arguments is most similar in its pattern of reasoning to the argument above?"

Parallel Reasoning (in Reading Comprehension): These questions are usually broader in scope, asking you to find the scenario most analogous to an action in the passage. There is less of a focus on identifying premises and conclusions than in the Logical Reasoning section.

Partially Defined: There is a minimum and/or maximum number of variables to be selected, but the exact number of variables selected in the game cannot be determined.

Passage Organization (PO): These Reading Comprehension questions ask you to describe a characteristic of the overall structure of the passage. For example, "The second paragraph serves primarily to...," or "Which one of the following best describes the organization of the passage." These questions are similar to the Method of Reasoning questions in the Logical Reasoning section, but are generally broader.

Pattern: A variation on Linear games where the rules equally govern the general action of all variables, as opposed to the specific variable governance found in standard Linear games.

PO: See Passage Organization.

Point at Issue Questions: Point at Issue questions require you to identify a point of contention between two speakers, and thus these questions appear almost exclusively with two-speaker stimuli. Question stem example:
"Larew and Mendota disagree about whether"

Polar Opposite: A statement that is the extreme opposite of another. "Hot" and "cold" are polar opposites.

Premise: A fact, proposition, or statement from which a conclusion is made. Literally, the premises give the reasons why the conclusion should be accepted.

Primary Objectives™: A cohesive strategy for attacking any Logical Reasoning question. By consistently applying the objectives, you give yourself the best opportunity to succeed on each question.

Principle (PR): A broad rule that specifies what actions or judgments are correct in certain situations. These are not a separate question type but are instead an "overlay" that appears in a variety of question types and the presence of the Principle indicator serves to broaden the scope of the question.

Question Stem: Follows the stimulus and poses a question directed at the stimulus. Make sure to read the question stem very carefully. Some stems direct you to focus on certain aspects of the stimulus and if you miss these clues you make the problem much more difficult.

Random: A variable in a Logic Game that does not appear in any of the rules. Because randoms are not referenced in a rule, they are typically weaker players in the game.

Repeat Form: Simply restates the elements of a conditional statement in the original order they appeared. This creates a valid argument.

Resolve the Paradox Questions: Every Resolve the Paradox stimulus contains a discrepancy or seeming contradiction. You must find the answer choice that best explains the situation. Question stem example:

> "Which one of the following, if true, would most effectively resolve the apparent paradox above?"

Reverse Answer: Occurs when an answer choice contains familiar elements from the stimulus, but rearranges those elements to create a new, unsupported statement.

Rules: In Logic Games, a set of statements that describe the relationships between the variables.

S: See Sufficient Condition

Scope: The range to which the premises and conclusion encompass certain ideas. An argument with a narrow scope is definite in its statements, whereas a wide scope argument is less definite and allows for a greater range of possibility.

Second Family: Consists of question types that take the answer choices as true and uses them to help the stimulus. Information outside the sphere of the stimulus is allowed in the correct answer choice. Includes the following question types: Assumption, Justify the Conclusion, Strengthen/Support, and Resolve the Paradox.

Sequencing Game: A game type where the rules do not fix the variables in exact positions but instead provide information about the relative order of the variables, as in "J was hired earlier than K."

Sequencing Rule: Establishes the relative ordering of variables. The key to differentiating a sequencing rule from a block rule is that block rules precisely fix the variables in relationship to each other (for example, one space ahead or two spaces in between) and sequencing rules do not.

Shell Game: An idea or concept is raised in the stimulus, and then a very similar idea appears in the answer choice, but the idea is changed just enough to be incorrect but still attractive. This trick is called the Shell Game because it abstractly resembles those street corner gambling games where a person hides a small object underneath one of three shells, and then scrambles them on a flat surface while a bettor tries to guess which shell the object is under.

SN: Abbreviation for Sufficient and Necessary Conditions. May be seen separately in diagramming as "S" and "N." See also Sufficient Condition and Necessary Condition.

Source Argument: A common error of reasoning that attacks the person (or source) instead of the argument they advance. Because the LSAT is concerned solely with argument forms, a speaker can never validly attack the character or motives of a person; instead, a speaker must always attack the argument advanced by a person.

Some: At least one, possibly all.

Some Are Not: At least one is not, possibly all are not. Functionally equivalent to "not all."

Specific Reference (SR): These Reading Comprehension questions provide you with a specific line reference or a reference to an easily found word or phrase within the passage. To attack the questions, refer to the line reference in the question and then begin reading about 5 lines above the reference.

Split-blocks: Indicates that there is a fixed number of spaces between two or more variables.

SR: See Specific Reference.

Stacks: In Logic Games, when two variable sets occur in the same position, one set of variables is diagrammed normally (identified as the base), while the other variable set is placed in slots above the initial slots, essentially "stacking" the variable sets and allowing for the appropriate relationship between variable sets.

Straw Man: A common error of reasoning that occurs when an author attempts to attack an opponent's position by ignoring the actual statements made by the opposing speaker and instead distorting and refashioning the argument, making it weaker in the process.

Stimulus: A short passage containing arguments taken from a variety of topics reflecting a broad range of academic disciplines (including letters to the editor, speeches, advertisements, newspaper articles and editorials, informal discussions and conversations, as well as articles in the humanities, the social sciences, and the natural sciences) that presents all of the necessary information to answer the subsequent question stem.

Strengthen/Support Questions: These questions ask you to select the answer choice that provides support for the author's argument or strengthens it in some way.
Question stem examples:

"Which one of the following, if true, most strengthens the argument?"
"Which one of the following, if true, most strongly supports the statement above?"

Sub-conclusion: A conclusion that is then used as a premise to support another conclusion. This is also known as a secondary or subsidiary conclusion.

Sufficient Condition (S): An event or circumstance whose occurrence indicates that a necessary condition must also occur. The sufficient condition does not make the necessary condition occur; it is simply an indicator.

Super-block: In Logic Games, when two or more block rules can be combined to produce a single diagram. Super-blocks tend to be quite powerful and often control the game.

Supporter: In the Supporter/Defender Assumption Model™, the Supporter Assumptions link together new or rogue elements in the stimulus or fill logical gaps in the argument.

Survey Errors: A common error of reasoning that occurs when a survey uses a biased sample, the survey questions are improperly constructed or the respondents to the survey give inaccurate responses. Surveys, when conducted properly, produce reliable results. However, surveys can be invalidated when any of these errors occur.

Templates: In Logic Games, when certain variables or blocks have a limited number of placement options, the best strategy is often to show the basic possibilities for each option. This powerful technique can sometimes quickly solve the game, and at the least it tends to reveal important information about the relationship between certain variables.

Third Family: Consists of question types that take the answer choices as true and uses them to hurt the stimulus. Information outside the sphere of the stimulus is allowed in the correct answer choice. Includes the following question type: Weaken.

Time Shift Errors: A common error of reasoning that involves assuming that conditions will remain constant over time, and that what was the case in the past will be the case in the present or future.

2-Value System: In Logic Games, a section where all variables must be used and each variable must be placed in exactly one of two groups. Powerful inferences can be drawn from the fact that when a variable is not in one group it must be in the other group (these inferences often involve the contrapositive).

Unbalanced: In a Defined game, when the number of variables to be selected is not equal to the overall number of available spaces. Unbalanced games are either Overloaded or Underfunded.

Uncertain Use of a Term or Concept: A common error of reasoning that occurs when the author uses a term or concept in different ways instead of using each term or concept in a constant, coherent fashion. This error is inherently confusing and undermines the integrity of the argument.

Undefined: When the number of variables to be selected for the game is not fixed, and is only limited by the total number of variables. Undefined games are generally the most difficult type of Grouping game.

Underfunded: Description of an Unbalanced game in which there are not enough candidates for the available spaces. This lack is almost always solved by reusing one or more of the candidates.

Variable Set: The set of people, places, things, or events that are involved in each game. The variables will be involved in an easy to understand activity such as sitting in seats or singing songs. It is very important to always write down and keep track of each variable set.

Variance Test™: Consists of supplying two polar opposite responses to the question posed in the answer choice and then analyzing how the varying responses affect the conclusion in the stimulus. If different responses produce different effects on the conclusion, then the answer choice is correct. If different responses do not produce different effects, then the answer choice is incorrect. The Variance Test can only be used with Evaluate the Argument questions.

Verticality: When a game is diagrammed in a vertical line (or setup), the relationship between the variables arranged vertically indicates adjacency, while the relationship of variables arranged horizontally indicates similarity. This is also true of verticality in blocks.

Weaken Questions: Weaken questions ask you to attack or undermine the author's argument.
Question stem example:
"Which one of the following, if true, most seriously weakens the argument?"

More Information

Additional PowerScore Resources

Because access to accurate and up-to-date information is critical, we have devoted a section of our website to *Deconstructed Series* students. This free online resource area offers supplements to the book material, answers questions posed by students, and provides updates as needed. There is also an official book evaluation form that we strongly encourage you to use. The exclusive *Deconstructed Series* online area can be accessed at:

www.powerscore.com/deconseries

If you would like to comment on the *Deconstructed Series*, or make suggestions for additional sections, please send us a message at lsat@powerscore.com. We thank you for purchasing this book, and we look forward to hearing from you!

CONTACTING POWERSCORE

POWERSCORE INTERNATIONAL HEADQUARTERS:

PowerScore Test Preparation
57 Hasell Street
Charleston, SC 29401

Toll-free information number: (800) 545-1750
Website: www.powerscore.com
Email: lsat@powerscore.com

POWERSCORE LSAT PUBLICATIONS INFORMATION:

For information on the *LSAT Logic Games Bible*, *LSAT Logic Games Bible Workbook*, *LSAT Logical Reasoning Bible*, *LSAT Reading Comprehension Bible*, or *LSATs Deconstructed Series*.

Website: www.powerscore.com/pubs.htm

POWERSCORE FULL-LENGTH LSAT COURSE INFORMATION:

Complete preparation for the LSAT.
Classes available nationwide.

Web: www.powerscore.com/lsat
Request Information: www.powerscore.com/contact.htm

POWERSCORE VIRTUAL LSAT COURSE INFORMATION:

45 hours of online, interactive, real-time preparation for the LSAT.
Classes available worldwide.

Web: www.powerscore.com/lsat/virtual
Request Information: www.powerscore.com/contact.htm

POWERSCORE WEEKEND LSAT COURSE INFORMATION:

Fast and effective LSAT preparation: 16 hour courses, 99th percentile instructors, and real LSAT questions.

Web: www.powerscore.com/lsat/weekend
Request Information: www.powerscore.com/contact.htm

PowerScore LSAT Tutoring Information:

One-on-one meetings with a PowerScore LSAT expert.

Web: www.powerscore.com/lsat/content_tutoring.cfm
Request Information: www.powerscore.com/contact.htm

PowerScore Law School Admissions Counseling Information:

Personalized application and admissions assistance.

Web: www.powerscore.com/lsat/content_admissions.cfm
Request Information: www.powerscore.com/contact.htm

SCANTRON EliteView™ EM-250133-12:654321 SIDE 1

INSTRUCTIONS FOR COMPLETING THE BIOGRAPHICAL AREA ARE ON THE BACK COVER OF YOUR TEST BOOKLET.

USE ONLY A NO. 2 OR HB PENCIL TO COMPLETE THIS ANSWER SHEET. DO NOT USE INK.

A

USE A NO. 2 OR HB PENCIL ONLY — Right Mark — Wrong Marks

1 LAST NAME | FIRST NAME | MI
(A B C D E F G H I J K L M N O P Q R S T U V W X Y Z in each column)

2 SOCIAL SECURITY/ SOCIAL INSURANCE NO.
(0 1 2 3 4 5 6 7 8 9 in each column)

3 LSAC ACCOUNT NUMBER
L (0 1 2 3 4 5 6 7 8 9 in each column)

4 DATE OF BIRTH

MONTH	DAY	YEAR
Jan Feb Mar Apr May June July Aug Sept Oct Nov Dec	0 1 2 3 / 0–9	0–9 / 0–9

5 RACIAL/ETHNIC DESCRIPTION
Mark one or more
- 1 Aboriginal/TSI Australian
- 2 Amer. Indian/Alaska Native
- 3 Asian
- 4 Black/African American
- 5 Canadian Aboriginal
- 6 Caucasian/White
- 7 Hispanic/Latino
- 8 Native Hawaiian/ Other Pacific Islander
- 9 Puerto Rican

6 GENDER
- Male
- Female

7 DOMINANT LANGUAGE
- English
- Other

8 ENGLISH FLUENCY
- Yes
- No

9 TEST BOOK SERIAL NO.

10 TEST FORM

11 TEST DATE
MONTH / DAY / YEAR

12 CENTER NUMBER
(0 1 2 3 4 5 6 7 8 9 in each column)

13 TEST FORM CODE
(0 1 2 3 4 5 6 7 8 9 in each column)

Law School Admission Test

Mark one and only one answer to each question. Be sure to fill in completely the space for your intended answer choice. If you erase, do so completely. Make no stray marks.

	SECTION 1	SECTION 2	SECTION 3	SECTION 4	SECTION 5
1	A B C D E	A B C D E	A B C D E	A B C D E	A B C D E
2	A B C D E	A B C D E	A B C D E	A B C D E	A B C D E
3	A B C D E	A B C D E	A B C D E	A B C D E	A B C D E
4	A B C D E	A B C D E	A B C D E	A B C D E	A B C D E
5	A B C D E	A B C D E	A B C D E	A B C D E	A B C D E
6	A B C D E	A B C D E	A B C D E	A B C D E	A B C D E
7	A B C D E	A B C D E	A B C D E	A B C D E	A B C D E
8	A B C D E	A B C D E	A B C D E	A B C D E	A B C D E
9	A B C D E	A B C D E	A B C D E	A B C D E	A B C D E
10	A B C D E	A B C D E	A B C D E	A B C D E	A B C D E
11	A B C D E	A B C D E	A B C D E	A B C D E	A B C D E
12	A B C D E	A B C D E	A B C D E	A B C D E	A B C D E
13	A B C D E	A B C D E	A B C D E	A B C D E	A B C D E
14	A B C D E	A B C D E	A B C D E	A B C D E	A B C D E
15	A B C D E	A B C D E	A B C D E	A B C D E	A B C D E
16	A B C D E	A B C D E	A B C D E	A B C D E	A B C D E
17	A B C D E	A B C D E	A B C D E	A B C D E	A B C D E
18	A B C D E	A B C D E	A B C D E	A B C D E	A B C D E
19	A B C D E	A B C D E	A B C D E	A B C D E	A B C D E
20	A B C D E	A B C D E	A B C D E	A B C D E	A B C D E
21	A B C D E	A B C D E	A B C D E	A B C D E	A B C D E
22	A B C D E	A B C D E	A B C D E	A B C D E	A B C D E
23	A B C D E	A B C D E	A B C D E	A B C D E	A B C D E
24	A B C D E	A B C D E	A B C D E	A B C D E	A B C D E
25	A B C D E	A B C D E	A B C D E	A B C D E	A B C D E
26	A B C D E	A B C D E	A B C D E	A B C D E	A B C D E
27	A B C D E	A B C D E	A B C D E	A B C D E	A B C D E
28	A B C D E	A B C D E	A B C D E	A B C D E	A B C D E
29	A B C D E	A B C D E	A B C D E	A B C D E	A B C D E
30	A B C D E	A B C D E	A B C D E	A B C D E	A B C D E

14 PLEASE PRINT ALL INFORMATION

LAST NAME FIRST

SOCIAL SECURITY/SOCIAL INSURANCE NO.

DATE OF BIRTH

MAILING ADDRESS

NOTE: If you have a new address, you must write LSAC at Box 2000-C, Newtown, PA 18940 or call 215.968.1001.

FOR LSAC USE ONLY

LR	LW	LCS

B

SCANTRON EliteView™ EM-250133-12:654321 SIDE 1

INSTRUCTIONS FOR COMPLETING THE BIOGRAPHICAL AREA ARE ON THE BACK COVER OF YOUR TEST BOOKLET.

USE ONLY A NO. 2 OR HB PENCIL TO COMPLETE THIS ANSWER SHEET. DO NOT USE INK.

A

USE A NO. 2 OR HB PENCIL ONLY

● Right Mark   Wrong Marks

1 LAST NAME | FIRST NAME | MI

(A–Z)

2 SOCIAL SECURITY/ SOCIAL INSURANCE NO.

(0–9)

3 LSAC ACCOUNT NUMBER

L (0–9)

4 DATE OF BIRTH

MONTH: Jan, Feb, Mar, Apr, May, June, July, Aug, Sept, Oct, Nov, Dec

DAY | YEAR (0–9)

5 RACIAL/ETHNIC DESCRIPTION

Mark one or more

- 1 Aboriginal/TSI Australian
- 2 Amer. Indian/Alaska Native
- 3 Asian
- 4 Black/African American
- 5 Canadian Aboriginal
- 6 Caucasian/White
- 7 Hispanic/Latino
- 8 Native Hawaiian/ Other Pacific Islander
- 9 Puerto Rican

6 GENDER

- Male
- Female

7 DOMINANT LANGUAGE

- English
- Other

8 ENGLISH FLUENCY

- Yes
- No

9 TEST BOOK SERIAL NO.

10 TEST FORM

11 TEST DATE

MONTH / DAY / YEAR

12 CENTER NUMBER

(0–9)

13 TEST FORM CODE

(0–9)

Law School Admission Test

Mark one and only one answer to each question. Be sure to fill in completely the space for your intended answer choice. If you erase, do so completely. Make no stray marks.

	SECTION 1	SECTION 2	SECTION 3	SECTION 4	SECTION 5
1	A B C D E	A B C D E	A B C D E	A B C D E	A B C D E
2	A B C D E	A B C D E	A B C D E	A B C D E	A B C D E
3	A B C D E	A B C D E	A B C D E	A B C D E	A B C D E
4	A B C D E	A B C D E	A B C D E	A B C D E	A B C D E
5	A B C D E	A B C D E	A B C D E	A B C D E	A B C D E
6	A B C D E	A B C D E	A B C D E	A B C D E	A B C D E
7	A B C D E	A B C D E	A B C D E	A B C D E	A B C D E
8	A B C D E	A B C D E	A B C D E	A B C D E	A B C D E
9	A B C D E	A B C D E	A B C D E	A B C D E	A B C D E
10	A B C D E	A B C D E	A B C D E	A B C D E	A B C D E
11	A B C D E	A B C D E	A B C D E	A B C D E	A B C D E
12	A B C D E	A B C D E	A B C D E	A B C D E	A B C D E
13	A B C D E	A B C D E	A B C D E	A B C D E	A B C D E
14	A B C D E	A B C D E	A B C D E	A B C D E	A B C D E
15	A B C D E	A B C D E	A B C D E	A B C D E	A B C D E
16	A B C D E	A B C D E	A B C D E	A B C D E	A B C D E
17	A B C D E	A B C D E	A B C D E	A B C D E	A B C D E
18	A B C D E	A B C D E	A B C D E	A B C D E	A B C D E
19	A B C D E	A B C D E	A B C D E	A B C D E	A B C D E
20	A B C D E	A B C D E	A B C D E	A B C D E	A B C D E
21	A B C D E	A B C D E	A B C D E	A B C D E	A B C D E
22	A B C D E	A B C D E	A B C D E	A B C D E	A B C D E
23	A B C D E	A B C D E	A B C D E	A B C D E	A B C D E
24	A B C D E	A B C D E	A B C D E	A B C D E	A B C D E
25	A B C D E	A B C D E	A B C D E	A B C D E	A B C D E
26	A B C D E	A B C D E	A B C D E	A B C D E	A B C D E
27	A B C D E	A B C D E	A B C D E	A B C D E	A B C D E
28	A B C D E	A B C D E	A B C D E	A B C D E	A B C D E
29	A B C D E	A B C D E	A B C D E	A B C D E	A B C D E
30	A B C D E	A B C D E	A B C D E	A B C D E	A B C D E

14 PLEASE PRINT ALL INFORMATION

LAST NAME FIRST

SOCIAL SECURITY/SOCIAL INSURANCE NO.

DATE OF BIRTH

MAILING ADDRESS

NOTE: If you have a new address, you must write LSAC at Box 2000-C, Newtown, PA 18940 or call 215.968.1001.

FOR LSAC USE ONLY

LR	LW	LCS

● B

SCANTRON EliteView™ EM-250133-12:654321 SIDE 1

INSTRUCTIONS FOR COMPLETING THE BIOGRAPHICAL AREA ARE ON THE BACK COVER OF YOUR TEST BOOKLET.

USE ONLY A NO. 2 OR HB PENCIL TO COMPLETE THIS ANSWER SHEET. DO NOT USE INK.

A

USE A NO. 2 OR HB PENCIL ONLY — Right Mark — Wrong Marks

1 LAST NAME | FIRST NAME | MI

(A–Z bubbles for each letter)

2 SOCIAL SECURITY/ SOCIAL INSURANCE NO.

(0–9 bubbles)

3 LSAC ACCOUNT NUMBER

L (0–9 bubbles)

4 DATE OF BIRTH

MONTH	DAY	YEAR
Jan		
Feb		
Mar	0 0	0 0
Apr	1 1	1 1
May	2 2	2 2
June	3 3	3 3
July	4	4 4
Aug	5	5 5
Sept	6	6 6
Oct	7	7 7
Nov	8	8 8
Dec	9	9 9

5 RACIAL/ETHNIC DESCRIPTION

Mark one or more

1 Aboriginal/TSI Australian
2 Amer. Indian/Alaska Native
3 Asian
4 Black/African American
5 Canadian Aboriginal
6 Caucasian/White
7 Hispanic/Latino
8 Native Hawaiian/ Other Pacific Islander
9 Puerto Rican

6 GENDER

Male
Female

7 DOMINANT LANGUAGE

English
Other

8 ENGLISH FLUENCY

Yes No

9 TEST BOOK SERIAL NO.

10 TEST FORM

11 TEST DATE

MONTH / DAY / YEAR

12 CENTER NUMBER

(0–9 bubbles)

13 TEST FORM CODE

(0–9 bubbles)

Law School Admission Test

Mark one and only one answer to each question. Be sure to fill in completely the space for your intended answer choice. If you erase, do so completely. Make no stray marks.

SECTION 1 | SECTION 2 | SECTION 3 | SECTION 4 | SECTION 5

Questions 1–30 in each section, answer choices A B C D E.

14 PLEASE PRINT ALL INFORMATION

LAST NAME FIRST

SOCIAL SECURITY/SOCIAL INSURANCE NO.

DATE OF BIRTH

MAILING ADDRESS

NOTE: If you have a new address, you must write LSAC at Box 2000-C, Newtown, PA 18940 or call 215.968.1001.

FOR LSAC USE ONLY

LR	LW	LCS

B